THE GENERAL

'If you try to harm me, I'll say, "Can he get me?"
And you can't. I'm not afraid. There's nothing that
you can do to get me. I'll go down the lowest. I'll go
down so low that the only way left is back up. The
only thing is, I can't bow down to you. I'd rather be
dead, so I'll make fun of you. If you annoy me, I'll
make fun of you. I'll react but I won't attack. And I'll
keep on smiling.'

MARTIN CAHILL, INTERVIEW
IN GQ MAGAZINE, 1991

'Without this book all that might have been left would have
been the folk memory of a Robin Hood figure and we might
have forgotten the terror and misery this man brought to
those who were in his way. Paul Williams' book reminds
us of why we should say 'Good Riddance'.
THE IRISH TIMES

'a riveting good read'
IRISH INDEPENDENT

'a terrifically readable account ... in the very best tradition
of investigative journalism ... a book which reads like a
thriller ... our democracy needs more journalism like this'
THE SUNDAY TRIBUNE

THE AUTHOR

Paul Williams is crime correspondent with the *Sunday World*. A qualified criminologist, he is acknowledged as an authority on the Irish criminal underworld and broke many of the news stories on the General.

THE GENERAL

GODFATHER
OF CRIME

PAUL WILLIAMS

THE O'BRIEN PRESS
DUBLIN
IRISH AMERICAN BOOK COMPANY (IABC)
BOULDER, COLORADO

This revised edition published May 1998. First published May 1995
by The O'Brien Press Ltd.,
20 Victoria Road, Rathgar, Dublin 6, Ireland.
Tel. +353 1 4923333; Fax. +353 1 4922777
email: books@obrien.ie
website: http://www.obrien.ie
Reprinted May 1995, June 1995, August 1995, November 1995,
March 1996, November 1996, October 1997.

Published in the USA by the
Irish American Book Company (IABC)
6309 Monarch Park Place, Suite 101,
Niwot, Colorado 80503
Office: Tel. 303-652-2685; Fax. 303-652-2689
Orders: Tel. 800-452-7115; Fax. 800-401-9705

ISBN 0-86278-433-6

British Library Cataloguing-in-publication Data
A catalogue record for this book is available from the British Library

9 10
98 99 00 01 02 03 04

Typesetting, layout, design: The O'Brien Press Ltd
Cover Design: Designit
Cover photographs: Pat Redmond © Merlin Films
Cover separations: For Design Ltd
Printed by: Guernsey Press Co Ltd

Acknowledgements

This story could not have been told without the help of a great many people, from all walks of life, who generously endured long, exhausting hours of interviews. The kind advice, support and encouragement of many others also gave me the impetus to complete this difficult book.

I would like to thank the large number of Garda of all ranks who generously gave me their time and information. The members of the Dublin underworld were equally generous and gave the other side of the extraordinary man they called 'the General'. To both groups I would like to express my deepest gratitude. For professional and other reasons they wish to remain anonymous. I respect that.

I would also like to thank journalist Padraig Yeates of the *Irish Times* and co-author of the book *Smack,* for his invaluable assistance and first-hand knowledge of the man himself. Thanks also to Brendan O'Brien of RTE and Neil McCormick of *GQ* magazine in London; retired detectives Ned Ryan and Frank Madden; journalists Stephen Rae, *Evening Herald*, Jim Cusack, *Irish Times*, Feargal Keane, RTE, Tom McPhail and Diarmuid McDermott of the Ireland International News-Feature Agency; the library and photographic staff of the *Irish Times, Irish Independent, Sunday Tribune, Star, Sunday World* and *Irish Press*.

My gratitude is also due to my editor at the *Sunday World*, Colm MacGinty, for giving me the space and the time to complete this project. My special thanks also goes to barrister Hugh Mohan.

Thanks to my parents, Bernard and Patricia, for putting up with me for the first time since Leaving Cert; my close friend and confidant Gay Prior; computer genius Sharon Donnelly.

Most importantly of all, my heartfelt gratitude goes to my partner Anne Sweeney, the woman who sacrificed so much so that I could fulfill my obsession, and to Jake and Irena for their love.

Paul Williams, April 1998

Contents

Dedicated to my friend

The Sheriff

Prologue

'Tango One is down ... Tango One is down.' The message crackled frantically across the Garda radio network. 'Control, can you repeat that last message?' asked a disbelieving voice over the wailing of a squad car siren. 'The Number One man is down. Get everyone down here ... All other alarm calls to be put on hold. Priority for Tango One.' It was 3.20 on the afternoon of 18 August, 1994, and Ireland's most notorious gangster, Martin Cahill, the General, had just been shot dead.

Less than six minutes earlier the forty-five year-old gangster – code-named Tango One by the Gardaí he had eluded during two decades of organised and brutal crime – had become the last victim of the Provisional IRA. Soon the IRA would announce their historic ceasefire, but before they set out on the road to peace there had been some unfinished business to be taken care of. And it wasn't an outstanding debt which an enemy – some British agent or Loyalist killer – had incurred during the Long War. The business involved an enigmatic Dublin criminal of little consequence to events in the North. The IRA had bestowed upon the General the dubious honour of being its last victim. In death, as in life, Martin Cahill had made his mark on history.

The assassin had waited beside the Stop sign at the junction of Oxford Road and Charleston Road in the Dublin suburb of Ranelagh for most of that sun-drenched Thursday afternoon. The people out soaking up the rare spell of sunshine on the steps of the Georgian houses along Charleston Road took no notice of the hitman as he watched for his victim. Dressed as a Corporation worker, he pretended to conduct a traffic census with a clipboard in his hand. His accomplice was on a motorcycle, posing as a courier. He drove up and down Oxford Road for most of the afternoon, stalking Cahill. At regular intervals he turned into Swan Grove, the small cluster of Corporation houses where Cahill lived by night.

At 3.10 pm Martin Cahill finally emerged into the sunlight. He had a busy afternoon planned. First he had to leave a videotape back to the store – a Robert De Niro movie called *Bronx Tale* about a New York father's attempts to keep his kid out of the clutches of the local mobsters. Then he was due to meet his associates to discuss plans for another major crime and a possible shooting to sort out an ongoing problem with a former paramilitary. Tango One, a master of counter-surveillance, may have noticed the 'courier' consulting a map at the end of the *cul de sac* when he climbed into his black Renault 5. He probably assumed it was just another Garda stake-out. There had been a team watching his house earlier that day and it wasn't unusual to see replacements arriving by motorbike. After all the police had been watching Martin Cahill for the past twenty years, waiting for him to step out of line. No doubt he would have felt lonely without his Garda watchers around to play his favourite game of cat and mouse. He probably chuckled to himself at the thought of yet another ambitious cop hoping to make his name by nabbing the big bad General. A lot of grey-haired detectives had once shared the same aspiration. Anyway he would lose them on the way to his conference. Before Cahill turned the ignition key the 'courier' had vanished.

Less than five hundred yards away the hitman braced himself for the kill as his accomplice on the motorbike raced down Oxford Road, turned onto Charleston Road and stopped. That was the signal the hitman had waited for so patiently – the target was on his way. The modest car drove at no more than fifteen miles per hour as it cruised the short distance between Swan Grove and the Stop sign. As the General slowed down to stop at the junction the hitman dropped the clipboard and stepped over to the driver's door of the car. He reached into his jacket and produced a 'Dirty Harry' .357 silver-plated Magnum revolver – one of the deadliest and most powerful handguns in the world.

For a split second Cahill stared into his killer's eyes. Then the window exploded into a thousand tiny shards as the lethal weapon was fired once at point-blank range. The large bullet ripped through Cahill's shoulder and head, smashing bone and tearing tissue. The force of the blast pushed the General to one side. His car chugged across Charleston Road as if he had it in gear but was unable to put his foot on the accelerator. The hitman ran alongside and pumped another three shots into his victim. The car collided with the railings at the gateway to No 45, beneath a large horse chestnut tree.

As Cahill gasped his last breath, the gunman calmly reached in and pumped another round into his head. The General slumped lifeless to the left, still harnessed in the safety belt, his head touching the passenger's seat. His eyes and mouth were closed; his hands hung limply in his lap. Blood began to flow in a crimson stream from a hole the size of a golf ball in the left side of his neck. A string of dark blood flowed from his nose onto his shirt and denim jacket. The few strands of hair he once combed across his head to hide his baldness were matted and dangling over his drooped shoulder.

The cold-blooded killer was in no panic to get away. He put his head through the smashed driver's window to make sure that Ireland's most wanted man was terminated. Having satisfied himself that his mission was accomplished, the hitman – according to eye witnesses – began to grin. He was still grinning as he jumped on the back of the waiting motorcycle and vanished into the city traffic.

CHAPTER I

Birth of a General

Martin Cahill was never destined to die in his sleep. It would not have been a fitting end to a man who was the indisputable godfather of the Irish criminal underworld. He lived by the gun and died by it – despatched in the cold-blooded fashion of the gangland he once dominated. Cahill lived on a knife-edge for most of his criminal career. On that fateful afternoon in August he finally succumbed to what he knew was the inevitable.

Martin Cahill, Tango One, the General, Public Enemy Number One, did not conform to the psychological profile of a criminal mind. That was the way the underworld's hooded bogeyman wanted it. He was a man of many contradictions – from devoted father, loyal friend, prolific lover, absurd joker, to hated outlaw, feared gangster, sadistic fiend, meticulous planner. He was obsessive, conniving and extremely clever; sometimes cruel, sometimes compassionate; secretive with a malicious streak. The General was a complex character.

In appearance Martin Cahill looked anything but a crime boss. Short, rotund and balding, in well-worn jeans and stained tee-shirt, he could be mistaken for a down-at-heel handbag snatcher. He was no Ronnie Kray. He lived a frugal life between crimes and he did not drink, smoke or take drugs. His passions were pigeons, motorbikes, cakes and curries. The only less orthodox passions in his life were his love affairs with his wife and her sister. Outwardly Cahill seemed gentle, soft-spoken with a flat Dublin brogue. But behind the ordinary appearance lurked a colourful crook.

It was his crimes that had panache and style. From the slums of Dublin the General worked his way up from a small-time burglar to a major-league criminal, earning himself a reputation equivalent in stature to that of a high-profile politician or TV star. He came to epitomise the ultimate anti-hero, the one who satisfied the public's ambivalent, morbid fascination with the underworld. More than any other criminal icon, Cahill had a profound effect on the national psyche. His willingness to show off his Mickey Mouse underwear while hiding his face behind sinister balaclavas made him the subject of intense curiosity.

The day before his funeral, the *Sunday World* ran the first, full-colour picture of the grinning General. There he was, beaming out from the front page in an ill-fitting old leather jacket and tee-shirt. With strands of hair scattered across his bald pate, he stood proudly beside a little girl in a First Communion dress, outside the church where his Requiem Mass would be held. The newspaper sold out within hours. Everyone wanted to see what the man in the mask looked like.

The story of the life and crimes of Martin Cahill is an extraordinary one. In 1969, the year he turned twenty, Ireland was still a country where indictable crime was extremely rare and a much smaller police force boasted an almost hundred percent detection rate. But Martin Cahill and his contemporaries were about to change all that. He was one of the prime movers in the new generation of hoodlum that emerged from the confusion and panic accompanying the outbreak of violence in Northern Ireland. The General was the brains behind one of the country's most ruthless and successful armed crime gangs. Over two decades Cahill organised the theft of art, jewels and cash worth well in excess of £40 million in the biggest and most audacious robberies in Irish history. And he preserved his position of untouchable gang boss with a string of brutal crimes against his enemies, bombing, torturing or shooting those who irritated or challenged him. He was egalitarian in his choice of victim; they were from both sides of the fine crime-line. The name of the General was synonymous with violence, fear and intimidation.

Unlike most criminals who tend to avoid, as much as possible, conflict with the authorities, Martin Cahill launched his own revolt against the state. He waged an unrelenting war of wits against the Gardaí he hated with a venom – a feeling reciprocated by the men and women in blue. Getting one over on the police was sometimes the sole motivation for his more mischievous 'strokes'. But his contempt for the cops contained a contradiction. In a strange way he actually had a grudging respect for them.

He turned down requests from other Dublin hoods to take part in lucrative robberies in England in association with gangs in London and Manchester. He believed the English police were much more likely than the Irish to doctor the evidence and stitch him up. He often told his fellow gangsters that there were two things which made the Irish cop more honest than others. One, he said, was their Catholic rural background (the Garda force is largely made up of country people) and a deep-rooted sense of self-righteousness which would not allow them to tinker with the evidence. The other was their cut-throat rivalry, in which the least bit of dirt thrown by a disgruntled underling could jeopardise an officer's promotion.

But the well-hidden respect went no further than Cahill not leaving the country to do jobs. At every opportunity he tried to exploit weaknesses in the police force and make them look stupid. He even equipped his extensive arsenal by robbing the depot where the Gardaí stored confiscated illegal weapons. When the police got too close for comfort he bombed their top forensic expert and on another occasion stole the most sensitive criminal files in the land. He set fire to one of Dublin's law courts when the Gardaí tried to prosecute him on the last serious charge he would ever be tried on. And whenever the General was taken in for questioning there was an outbreak of tyre-slashing in middle-class neighbourhoods to embarrass the police. Cahill even dug holes in their prized golf club at Stackstown in Co Dublin and then made jokes about the act to their faces.

Cahill sometimes left clues at the scene of well-planned jobs, just to antagonise the investigating detectives who knew him best. He covered his tracks so well there was little hope of catching him. Cahill described it as a 'game' or 'grudge match' in which he was an adroit player. But it was a dangerous game with only one rule: don't get caught. The stakes were high, so high that he couldn't afford to lose. For if he lost the game, the result was either a prison cell or the morgue.

It all began on 23 May, 1949, when Agnes and Patrick Cahill had their second child, Martin Joseph. Patrick, a labourer who later became a lighthouse keeper, married Agnes Sheehan, a small, quiet-spoken woman, shortly after the end of World War Two. They set up their home in the heart of Dublin's inner-city slums at No 6, Grenville Street, on the northside of the river Liffey.

The post-war years in Ireland were dark days of poverty and deprivation for those who found themselves trapped in the ghettos. In fact from the turn of the century Dublin was blighted with some of the worst slum conditions in Europe. A chronic lack of education, combined with the Catholic Church's denunciation of birth control as the Devil's work, resulted in large families overcrowding the already insanitary, dilapidated tenements. The Grenville Street the Cahills moved into had changed little since 1898 when a newspaper report described it as 'Hell Street' where 'drunken brawls, stone throwing and filthy practices' were its main characteristics. The report reflected the attitude of the society which, more than fifty years later, would alienate people like the General. From the moment of his birth Martin Cahill was on the wrong side of the tracks.

Patrick Cahill's meagre wages as a lighthouse keeper could not support his growing family. He was also fond of drink, which he indulged in at the expense of his wife and children. Often there wasn't enough food to put on the table. Patrick Cahill's drinking habits sickened young Martin who never drank in his life. He would later recall, in a bitter tone, that his father had little to show for a life as an honest man. Agnes Cahill was pregnant a total of eighteen times. She miscarried on six occasions and one toddler was killed when she was hit by an ice cream van.

In 1960 the Cahill family moved to No 210, Captain's Road in Crumlin, one of thousands of newly-built Corporation houses. The area formed part of the Irish government's ambitious programme to clear the slums of inner-city Dublin, giving people decent living conditions in the suburbs. But, while well-intentioned, the overall effect was a breakdown in social cohesion with the dispersal of whole neighbourhoods. The new estates were dreary and impersonal with no sense of community. Poverty followed the former slum dwellers. By the time he was eight, Martin and his older brother, John, who was ten, were robbing food to supplement the family's income. Martin was often sent to the local convent with his go-kart to collect a pot of stew from the nuns to feed the family. The lack of food was to have a profound effect on Cahill. One of the hallmarks of his burglaries in later life was that, apart from robbing cash and valuables, he always stole meat and other food from the fridge. It was not unusual for him to make off with £50,000 worth of valuables and a few pounds of steak.

The young Cahills were sent to school in nearby Kimmage. At first Martin liked school but his natural bent for rebelling against authority soon put an end to that. One day after school he was playing around a dump where old school books were burned along with other rubbish. A nun demanded to know what he was doing and he told her it was none of her business. A few days later the nun took Martin, kicking and screaming, out of his class and put him in her own where she exacted revenge for his earlier recalcitrance. The nun, Cahill recalled, held him up as an object of ridicule in the class. She warned the other students that they could turn out to be like Martin Cahill, as if the child before them was some kind of imbecile.

He felt humiliated and began developing his own method for dealing with authority. He decided not to learn to spite the teacher. He began mitching from school and was brought before the juvenile courts dozens of times under the School Attendance Acts. These were also his first encounters with the police who would play such a major role in his life. The antiquated criminal justice system was to take over the education of young Martin. He once remarked: 'Reform school was my primary school, St Patrick's Institution my secondary school and Mountjoy my university – they taught me everything I know.'

One summer he and his friends were out playing in the GAA pitch at the back of his home in Crumlin. The grass had been cut and baled. Cahill and his pals cut up the bales, remade them into haystacks and began jumping onto them from a wall. The police arrived and Martin was arrested and charged. The youth was brought before the courts and fined five shillings – a fortune for a family that was already finding it difficult to live.

Meanwhile some of the Cahill brothers were becoming experienced burglars and major thorns in the sides of the police. On 15 September, 1961, at the age of twelve, Martin had his first criminal conviction recorded against him. It was for larceny. He got the Probation of Offenders Act – a caution. Two years later he was back before the Metropolitan Children's Court where he was again convicted of larceny. This time he was fined one pound. Two months later he was up again, this time for two counts of larceny and house-breaking. He received one year which was suspended. On 20 September, 1963, Cahill was given one month's detention in Marlboro House in Glasnevin on two charges for burglary. He was locked up in a small room for most of the day.

Martin's parents decided to help their son get a decent career which might keep him out of trouble. Before the Troubles in the North, scores of unemployed young Dublin men went off to join the British armed forces. Martin's father heard that the Royal Navy was recruiting in Belfast. In 1964, at the age of fifteen, Martin travelled to Belfast on the train for an interview. Before the interview, applicants were handed a leaflet listing in alphabetical order the trades and specialised areas of training in the Navy. Each applicant was invited to pick out a trade to which he felt suited. Martin chose the position of bugler. Unfortunately, due to his difficulties in school, he misread the word as 'burglar'. He reckoned that breaking into houses for the Royal Navy and being paid for it was a grand job. The officers sitting on the interview board in their well-pressed uniforms looked stunned when they asked the young Dublin chap to explain why he had picked this particular trade. He didn't get the job and took the train back to Dublin where he continued his chosen profession.

Cahill, like most of the lads he grew up with, did not see the error of his ways. A year later, at the age of sixteen, he was arrested by a young detective called Dick Murphy. While in custody Cahill, after been given cakes and fizzy drinks, confessed to two burglaries and made a statement. He was convicted in the children's court and got two years in industrial school in Daingean, Co Offaly. The experience would have a major effect on the rest of his life. He and Murphy developed an intense dislike for each other and remained sworn enemies until the latter's death. It was the last time that Cahill would ever confess to a crime.

The industrial schools were established under the 1908 Children's Act and were intended to feed and teach young offenders. In fact, the existence of these ten schools around the country was a monumental indictment of the successive governments who relinquished their responsibilities to the well-meaning, although unqualified, religious orders. The schools were tough institutions, used as dumping grounds for the country's orphaned and illegitimate children. In some cases the boys were regularly rounded up in what were called 'hobbles', the aim of which was to hunt out boys suspected of being homosexual. Often the boys didn't even understand what the brothers were looking for. Before bedtime the youngsters would be lined up in their night-shirts, ordered to bend over and beaten across their bare bottoms with a two-foot piece of leather strap, appropriately named the 'impurity strap'. Former inmates have always claimed that so-called 'nancy boys', the ones suspected of being sexually abused by some brothers, were often excused such punishments. Martin Cahill was never a victim of a 'hobble', but he was certainly no 'nancy boy' either.

The Oblate order which ran Daingean pursued the reformation of its young charges with a crusading zeal – and an iron fist. But Martin Cahill was their match. He was quiet, cautious and shrewd, sizing up every situation as it arose and making the most of a bad lot. Compared with the other hot-headed boys around him he came across as mature. Those who taught him recall that Cahill was a strong silent character with a 'hardness in his face'. It was a demeanour that would be evident in his criminal career.

If he saw a piece of paper on the ground Cahill would pick it up rather than suffer the indignity of being ordered to do so. He never made eye contact with his captors because to do so would mean acknowledging their presence and their authority. Once, as he walked along a corridor, a brother pounced on him and, as Cahill said later, 'burst his jaw with a punch'. The frustrated brother knew no other way of communicating with a withdrawn sixteen-year-old. Cahill claimed that was the only occasion on which he suffered corporal punishment.

One kindly priest who tried to break through the protective barrier around young Martin was gently rebuffed. The priest recalled how, whenever he tried to help Cahill, he was viewed with suspicion. Martin's younger brother Eddie, who was thirteen and also doing time for house-breaking, had his own way of dealing with the brothers and later the prison authorities. If he was told to do something he would tell the brother or prison warder to shove off and do it himself.

Martin Cahill was put working on the bog which provided the large school with its turf harvest. Other boys were allocated to the farm, the metal workshop or the carpenters' shop. Despite his non-confrontational stance, Cahill did not receive a single day's remission on his two-year sentence. When he was leaving in 1967 he asked why. The brothers told him that it was because he would not open up and talk to them. After he left Daingean Cahill recalled bitterly: 'If anyone corrupted me it was those mad monks down in the bog.'

The year that Martin Cahill was released from Daingean a special Dáil committee was set up to investigate the system of custodial care. The Kennedy Commission in its report two years later condemned the industrial school system as 'evolving in a haphazard and amateurish way' and said that it 'has not altered radically down through the years'. The Commission found that the children sent to Daingean were 'educationally sub-normal', although it exonerated the Oblate Fathers, many of whom had dedicated their lives to the place. Martin Cahill could barely read or write.

While Martin had been away the rest of the Cahill family had been experiencing hard times. They had fallen hopelessly into rent arrears on the house on Captain's Road and they were dumped in a dilapidated tenement in Rathmines, called Hollyfield Buildings. A year after he left Daingean, Martin planned to get married to Frances Lawless, the girl next door in his new Rathmines home.

Despite his feelings about Daingean and his antipathy to authority, Cahill was fond of some of the brothers at the school. In a rare letter, written just two weeks before his marriage, Cahill was uncharacteristically open and, for probably the only time in his life, talked about going straight. The letter, printed here as Cahill wrote it, read:

Dear Brother,

Sorry for not writing sooner, I just wanted to let you know how Im getting on, for a start it took me long enuf to get a job but I got one, my flat wages are £11. Some weeks I earn £16 to £17 a week but its hard work, and its okay.

I am geting over weight and pale, all I need up here is clean fresh bog air, and bog work to get my weight down. Anyway the money I got on the bog I put it into prise bonds and I still have it, and with a bit of luck, I might win a £100 this week I have a great chance, well who knows.

I kept out of trouble so far, please god I stay like that, you know I did [not] for get what you done for me, you made me feel as do I was free, in other words needed, I just want to let you know how greatful I am you made my time fly in.

I have met some of the lads some of them seem to be doing well, but I cant tell, I don't pal with any lads. You know I don't mix much, out straight I dont trust them, I tink that I get better along on my own so far, Im not stuck up or any thing like that. Im going with a girl a very nice girl and I am very happy the way I am. I met Frances two years ago and I lover her very much and we are getting married on 16th March next week.

I know it is very soon and you might tink that I should weight, but I tot very seriously about it, and its the only thing we want. I know there will be hard times and easy times, but please god that we will be happy and I will go about it the way you would want me to go about it, thats what I want to tell you.

I hope yurself is okay, some of the lads there need a good bashing and dont give into them bercause you dont hear them talking, as you say you have to be cruel to be kind, and let some of the loud mouths beat you in a cople of games of handball on till it goes to there heads and then beat them and take them down a peg or to, when they need it.

I will close now, sorry about my writing, wright soon. I want you to know that we are saving money since I came out as well as my bonds.

(Its not much but you know what to do).

I remaine,

sincerey yours,

Martin Cahill

Within a short time Martin Cahill had given up all aspirations to a life of honest work – he had worked briefly making boxes for Smurfit's and cloth sacks for Goodbody's. But soon he was on the road to being a big-time criminal. Two years later he would be in prison. The General was about to be born.

CHAPTER 2

The Anthill

Hollyfield Buildings in Rathmines was a semi-derelict complex of flats. It was the last step before homelessness for some of the Corporation's tenants who either could not pay their rents in other places or were deemed to be trouble-makers. Conditions were appalling. One former resident recalled: 'It was the worst, poorest, smelliest, rat-ridden scum-pit in Dublin.' A policeman who regularly had reason to visit Hollyfield gave the same verdict: 'You wouldn't put a dog into the place ... It was a hovel, a filthy dump.' To Martin Cahill, however, Hollyfield was both home and kingdom. There was nowhere else he would rather be.

Hollyfield Buildings was situated on Upper Rathmines Road in upmarket Dublin 6. The dwellings consisted of 120 one- and two-bedroom flats, built in two-storey blocks in 1911, and resembling a military barracks. By the time the Cahills moved into Nos 9 and 10 the place was in a state of chronic neglect. Accustomed to squalor and overcrowding they had little difficulty settling in.

Once, when Eddie Cahill ran away from Daingean, a priest came to Hollyfield looking for him. Rebellious by nature, Martin's younger brother incurred many beatings in the harsh industrial school. When the priest, who was known for his compassion to the youngsters, called into No 9 he was taken aback. He got a rare insight into the deprived background of one of his charges. In the middle of the room was a large table with all the family's food laid out. Mrs Cahill, who was surrounded by children, was courteous and chatty to the clergyman. She paid no heed to a contented toddler who sat on the table making a mess by putting its hands in the butter, then in the jam and the sugar, and licking its fingers. There were no presses or cupboards. In the corner was a large bed and nothing more. But to the Cahills

Hollyfield was home and they made the most of it. 'What [the authorities] never counted on was that we'd like it. Everyone knew everyone else and we all looked out for one another,' Cahill fondly recalled long after the place had been demolished.

The inhabitants were treated as social outcasts – ignored by an uninterested outside world. Out of this imposed isolation grew a clannish community and a lot of the families, like Martin Cahill's, married into each other. The people of Hollyfield were bound together by a sense of loyalty and an utter contempt for authority – the ingredients that moulded Martin Cahill's complex personality. He was happy in this strange underworld and had no desire to conform to the ways of the society beyond the walls that surrounded his domain. He often advised his people never to forget where they came from and to be proud of their roots.

Hollyfield was a breeding ground for outlaws. For most families crime was the principal source of income from which food and clothes were purchased for the children and porter bought in the few pubs that would serve the menfolk. By the end of the 1960s the Cahills and some of their neighbours were notorious. There was a constant stream of local boys being carted off to industrial schools or prison. By the time Martin came out of Daingean in 1967, he and his brothers, John, Eddie, Anthony, Michael and Paddy, had amassed a string of convictions.

The brothers became professional burglars and plagued the large houses in neighbouring districts. They were rarely seen out during the day. Cahill once compared Hollyfield at night to an anthill. 'If you were looking down into Hollyfield from above at night you would see the ants moving out in all directions in search of the honey-pot.' When Cahill looked across the table at the Royal Navy interview board and told them he was a very good burglar he was not lying. In fact he was one of the busiest 'creepers' ever to emerge in the Dublin underworld. Even when he hit the big time and began pulling multi-million-pound jobs he would still go out burgling or 'mooching'.

In many ways Cahill was also a glorified Peeping Tom who liked rummaging around in people's personal effects and watching what couples got up to when they forgot to draw the bedroom curtains. He often returned from a night foray grinning from ear to ear to relate to his pals the goings-on in the bedrooms of the big houses around Rathgar and Terenure. Cahill's prurience almost cost him his life once when he decided to take a peek through the window of a down-town massage parlour. He shinned skilfully up a drainpipe to a second-floor window where he got a bird's eye view of a client being entertained by a 'masseuse'. Just before the climax of the show the rusted drainpipe crumpled under his weight. He was fortunate enough to tumble down onto a bundle of refuse sacks.

Cahill had an uncanny ability to fade into the background and sense danger. He could sit in a tree or lie under a bush watching his chosen house for hours before moving. He once advised an associate: 'If you think that you can see everyone but they can't see you, then you will be invisible.' Cahill was often compared to an alley cat who knew every short cut and back lane on the southside of the city. Within a square mile of Hollyfield Buildings he had four houses which he used as landmarks. After a night of creeping he knew he was safe when he saw one of his 'lighthouses'. Once inside the square-mile radius he would have no problem disappearing.

After a burglary Cahill invariably buried his loot. There was the story told about how he once went back to recover stuff he had hidden in a ditch in the Dublin suburb of Rathfarnham. The local detectives had got a whisper about where Cahill's stash was and they lay in hiding, waiting for him to return. Cahill appeared and began walking towards the loot. A few yards from his haul he suddenly stopped as if he sensed the presence of the police. He began hissing, 'Rats. I smell rats,' and walked briskly away. The cops could only watch in amazement. Cahill decided to forget about the stash.

Like a squirrel, he sometimes forgot where he buried stuff. According to his former associates there is still fifteen stone in weight of silver hidden somewhere in the Dublin mountains. Cahill couldn't remember where he buried it and spent months digging holes under bushes. On another occasion he buried jewellery on a site near Tallaght. When he eventually came back for it, the Council had begun building a dual carriageway on the spot. In a fit of rage Cahill robbed a digger and went to retrieve his loot. But, with the fields cleared, one end of a road looked the same as the other. He gave up in disgust.

At some time during the early eighties, when he was still living in Hollyfield, Cahill even burgled the Garda Technical Bureau at St John's Road in Kilmainham, where confiscated illegal firearms were stored. He took a large number of handguns, grenades and a few machine-guns. The burglary was not discovered until much later, in September 1983, when the Bureau was in the process of moving to more secure premises in the Phoenix Park. According to Cahill's associates he had paid a number of visits to the 'gun store'.

The police authorities have never officially revealed what was taken, although it is known that some of the weapons were recovered by detectives after crimes committed by Cahill's gang. In 1984 Cahill conjured up a bizarre plot to embarrass the police by attempting to plant some of the stolen guns in the homes of journalists Vincent Browne and Colm Toibín, both of whom were involved in *Magill* magazine. At the time the two journalists had impressive reputations for uncovering injustice and corruption in the upper echelons of society. In an interview with the *Irish Times* Cahill had openly accused the cops of trying to plant weapons on him. He reckoned that if guns were then found by the police in Browne's and Toibín's houses the media would believe that the two men had been set up by the cops in a bid to silence them. Cahill even went so far as to tip-off the cops anonymously. He thought that he would be believed and the police totally discredited. The absurd plan flopped and the guns were never planted. Cahill later had one of his associates hand over two of the weapons he stole to *Irish Independent* security correspondent Tom Brady. The associate claimed that the guns had been given to him by detectives who wanted him to plant them on Cahill.

In 1970 Cahill received a four-year sentence after he was found in possession of a haul of cigarettes which were part of a truckload stolen in Portlaoise and discovered in a lock-up garage in Rathmines. In jail he was a model prisoner and got on well with the warders. He decided that that was the only way to make his time bearable. When there was trouble on the landings he would go quietly into his cell and shut the door. He found making trouble inside pointless. Cahill told other hoods how he prepared himself psychologically for being locked up in a cell: 'When the screws lock the door at night, remember that they are not locking you in, you are locking them out.' Three years later he was released.

In those three years armed robberies had become widespread. In Dublin, robberies jumped from just five in 1969 to over 150 a year in the early seventies. The outbreak of the Northern troubles had seen a big increase in the availability of firearms. One of the city's most formidable armed robbery gangs were the Dunnes, another large family of tearaway brothers from Crumlin. The Dunnes and the Cahills had got to know each other during stints in industrial schools and prison.

Henry Dunne was considered the most cold-blooded and efficient of all the 'blaggers', street slang for armed robbers. He had a talent for planning jobs. It was Henry who first began hitting security vans carrying large amounts of cash. There was little point in robbing one bank, he reasoned, when you could get the cash from ten in the back of a Ford van. All you had to do was watch, wait and then pounce. Crime was becoming a much more organised affair. In Martin Cahill, Dunne found a willing and able partner. The Dunnes were about to introduce the house-breakers from Hollyfield Buildings to armed crime.

The two groups provided the nucleus for a potent gang of robbers. On the Dunne side were Henry, Larry, Shamie and Christy 'Bronco', the head of the family; on the Cahill side, Martin, Eddie, Anthony, Paddy and John. The Dunnes were flash criminals who loved splashing out in nightclubs around town. The Cahills, especially Martin, were quiet and not fond of socialising. Cahill preferred to stay in his flat with his wife, Frances, and went out only to burgle houses. The arrangement between the two groups was purely business.

The Dunne-Cahill partnership did not last. After about a year, it split up over a row about the proceeds of a jewellery robbery. Some of the Dunne brothers were to retire from armed crime and move full time into drugs. The General and his brothers decided to go out on their own.

On 18 November, 1974, a security van collecting cash from the Quinnsworth store in Rathfarnham was hit. During the heist a security man was beaten over the head. The robbers got away with over £92,000 – the equivalent of almost £2.5 million in today's money.

Within twenty-four hours, teams of detectives swooped in an early-morning raid on Hollyfield. They had warrants for the arrest of three residents – Martin and Eddie Cahill and their neighbour and future brother-in-law, Hughie Delaney. The man that arrested them was Detective Inspector Ned Ryan who had been appointed to the Rathmines district a year earlier. Ryan was determined to stamp out the crime epidemic emanating from Hollyfield Buildings. He and Martin Cahill had met during the investigation of another armed payroll robbery from a sign-making factory in Ranelagh and the two men had taken an instant dislike to each other. Ryan, a tough country cop, told Cahill that his days as an up-and-coming criminal were over and he would be 'reduced to robbing grannies' handbags'. He was the first policeman to identify Cahill's potential to be a major gangster. The two men would remain sworn enemies for over sixteen years.

What particularly irritated Ryan was Cahill's ability to pick out a spot on the wall and completely ignore his interrogators. Cahill called it 'blanking'. He would later develop a mantra which he would chant over and over whenever he was taken in for questioning. It often drove detectives to distraction. Cahill also found other ways of manipulating such situations to his own benefit. At night when he was put in a cell he told the guard on duty to turn off the light. The officer refused and left it on. Cahill got what he wanted by requesting the opposite and exploiting the cop's determination to make life uncomfortable for the prisoner.

On 21 November, 1974, the two Cahills and Hughie Delaney were charged with the Rathfarnham robbery. All three covered their faces before the judge during their remand hearing. Eventually the charges against Martin and Eddie Cahill were dropped due to lack of evidence.

Delaney, who made a verbal admission, was acquitted at his trial when his arrest was ruled to be illegal.

Meanwhile Hollyfield had become Martin Cahill's domain. With the money from the Rathfarnham job he bought an 1100cc Harley Davidson motorbike – bikes were to be one of his passions and one of the few outward signs of his stolen wealth. Cahill paid £4,000 for the imported bike. He also bought a large second-hand Mercedes. The flashy car and motorbike looked incongruous parked outside a run-down slum building, surrounded by ruptured sewer pipes and yelping mongrel dogs.

Cahill also erected a flagpole over his flat and hoisted a tricolour, during the worst days of the mid-seventies, in an expression of patriotic solidarity with the battling nationalist minority in the North. And to get his message across to the other residents of Rathmines he placed loud speakers around the roof of the block and played rebel songs at full blast in the small hours of the morning. Whenever the local cops came in to turn down the din from Cahill's loud speakers he went on a burgling spree in the immediate vicinity to let them know they had annoyed him. He also erected a sign claiming that Dick Murphy, one of his growing number of enemies in the police force, was the so-called 'Rathmines Rapist'. Cahill hated Murphy because he was the only cop who had ever got him to confess to a crime. The fact that the 'Rathmines Rapist' did not even exist did little to change the General's mind.

Cahill also spent some of his new-found wealth on a colour TV which was considered a luxury in most Irish homes at the time. Now the General was able to view the world with comfort from his own flat. The sight of a colour TV aerial mounted beside a flagpole added to the surreal atmosphere of Hollyfield Buildings. One night when a detective unit drove into the complex some of the local criminals dropped a large block down on the car-roof, narrowly missing the two officers inside. It was the last straw for the cops who were regularly attacked when they entered Martin Cahill's squalid kingdom. The next day three carloads of detectives arrived and went looking for the culprits. Flats of known offenders, including Cahill's, were turned over and searched. In the mêlée that followed, Cahill's colour TV landed in several pieces in the courtyard below his first-floor flat. The following week he went out and bought another one.

In nearby Rathmines Garda Station it was not just the detectives who were keeping tabs on the shenanigans in Hollyfield. Each new uniformed recruit was instructed to learn the name and identity of every inhabitant living in the slum. Then the recruit could stroll up an alleyway and casually speak to one of the hoods, calling him by his first name. The cop would engage the bemused man in light-hearted banter about his girlfriend and such matters. This approach was a psychological tool designed to unsettle and create divisions among the Cahills and their cohorts.

In 1978, while Martin Cahill was serving a four-year stretch in prison for receiving a stolen car, Dublin Corporation began making moves to demolish Hollyfield and settle the residents in better accommodation. From his prison cell Cahill began campaigning to prevent the uprooting of his community. A dozen families who refused to leave were served with eviction notices and Cahill instituted legal proceedings to appeal the eviction order against himself and his wife. When the eviction notices were up a large force of police and Corporation officials moved in to put the Hollyfield people out. Many of the residents did not want to leave their neighbours: the sense of community was more important than getting more than one room to live in. When it suited the authorities, the Corporation tenants had been dumped in the anthill. Now they were being thrown out.

The eviction party stacked the residents' furniture and belongings outside and then broke up the fittings inside the empty flats. Holes were smashed in the ceilings and walls to prevent squatting. The only flat untouched was Cahill's because his appeal was still pending before the courts. When he was released from prison in 1980 Martin Cahill was the sole tenant left in a Hollyfield that was disappearing quickly under the hammers of the demolition men. His neighbourhood now looked like a bomb site. His corner flat was in the only part of the building complex to be left standing. The rest was demolished.

Cahill knew it was only a matter of time before he would have to move out, but he decided to take on City Hall. He also got some fun out of the experience. The Electricity Supply Board (ESB) cut off his supply: he promptly reconnected it. It worked fine until a particularly heavy rainfall. Water seeped down onto the bare cable, making the flat live. Cahill discovered the problem when his mother-in-law leaned against the wall. The next day Cahill reconnected the cable and this time covered it with concrete. The Corporation offered Cahill a flat at No 17, Upper Kevin Street, next door to the offices of Sinn Féin and across the road from the local Garda station. He found it unsuitable and demanded a flat on Brighton Road in fashionable Foxrock. It was the area where he found the best pickings while out burgling and it would save him the walk at night.

Eventually, in 1981, Frances had had enough and moved out with their four children, the youngest of whom had been born towards the end of 1980. But Cahill stubbornly stayed on. His battle with City Hall became a farcical affair as officials pleaded with him to move to his new home. Cahill was having a ball with the civil servants. 'That's my wife's got the house, the bitch, she kicked me out! Youse can go and live with her. I'm stayin' here,' he told them. Meanwhile Frances Cahill was refusing to pay her rent in Kevin Street on the grounds that it was too high. The exasperated Corporation officials pointed out that in one of her application forms she had said her husband was a well-paid skilled worker. 'Well, that's what he told me he was. I didn't know he was unemployed. The bleedin' cheek of him, all these years he's been going out every morning and coming in at seven in the evening. How was I to know?'

At night Cahill went out to conduct his various criminal enterprises and to call on his wife, her sister and his growing family. Before work began in the mornings he slipped back to the flat. One morning, however, he was late back and found the flat had been demolished in his absence. To show the Corporation that they had not won the game, Cahill fashioned a shelter out of the rubble of the flat. When the rubble was removed he installed a caravan. The caravan was mysteriously burned down and Cahill erected a tent. Eventually even the then Lord Mayor of Dublin, Ben Briscoe, got involved. He pleaded with Cahill to back down quietly and allow the building of the new houses which were badly needed by other families who wanted to live in decent conditions. Cahill was also promised a transfer back to a Corporation house in Rathmines.

Happy with the outcome of his bout with the Corporation, Cahill packed up his tent and moved off the site. In less than a year he and his family were in Swan Grove, a new Corporation estate in Rathmines. Martin Cahill always talked with undisguised affection about Hollyfield Buildings and what it stood for. When he bought a luxury four-bedroom house in Cowper Downs, a private middle-class estate, in 1984, it was because it was close to Hollyfield. 'I know people who have had nervous breakdowns after being cut off from Hollyfield and their friends. I wanted to stay in the neighbourhood and here I am,' he explained years later.

CHAPTER 3

The Club

By the mid-1970s Martin Cahill and some of his brothers were becoming active thieves. Armed crime, once the preserve of the paramilitaries, had now been taken over by well-organised Dublin gangs. Robberies were no longer sporadic and unplanned. Since his first collaboration with the Dunnes, Cahill had shown a natural aptitude for planning and executing a 'job'. The Cahills were, thanks to Martin, one of the first truly organised crime gangs. They were stealing a fortune.

Unlike their shy, oddball brother, the rest of the Cahill lads needed something more than the adrenalin rush of a well-planned heist. Much to Martin's annoyance, his brothers, whose world had once extended not far beyond the walls around Hollyfield Buildings, began leaving the nest to explore the 'real' world. When Eddie, Anthony and Michael started going into town for fun, Martin stayed at home, preferring the security of the grimy tenements which were his domain. His only forays were strictly 'business'.

The pool hall had become the in-place of the buzzing seventies. In the evenings some of Cahill's brothers hung out in a spot on South William Street where they played pool and chatted up the giggling girls who drank Coke and watched them strutting around the tables. At that stage the brothers rarely drank. Some of them smoked hash, which was still relatively scarce in Dublin. Their main source of fun was the opposite sex. With their wild eyes and long flowing hair, Anthony and Eddie were particularly popular with women.

Most of the hoodlums were in their late teens or early twenties and enjoyed accepting the advances of middle-class teenage girls. When the Cahill boys came home after a night on the town Martin would be waiting to hear stories of their conquests. The idea of the lads having sex with some snooty surburban Miss up against a wall at the back of a pool hall was a source of great amusement to the prurient General. Though he had an unconventional love-life, Cahill was not a womaniser in the accepted sense. But he still insisted on hearing every lurid detail of his brothers' encounters.

With the cash from the robberies piling up, the Cahill gang began to look around for some kind of business through which to launder it. Eddie and Anthony decided that a pool hall was the perfect front. They gave the job of running the place to an associate, Seán Fitzgerald, an accomplished fraudster. 'Fitzer' was a gentleman crook who had no interest in violence or armed robbery. Smooth talk and charm were the tools of Fitzer's trade. He had robbed banks all over the country armed with nothing more than a smile and a few dud cheques.

Fitzer eventually found a disused warehouse at Raleigh Square in the heart of Crumlin and took out a lease. It was the perfect location for the gang to hang out, as it was situated in the area where most southside gangsters lived. It was also in the middle of a warren of lanes and walkways which could provide speedy escape routes from the police. As the Cahills' front man, Fitzer converted the warehouse and bought over a dozen pool tables for cash. In the back of the building an office was constructed which the boys later equipped with a bed. Inside the front door a porch was erected so that, when the police came in to look around, the lack of natural light made it practically impossible to see some of the shadier customers lurking in the shadows.

At first Martin had reservations about the club but he eventually agreed to invest in the project. It was not long before he discovered that the pool hall had distinct advantages. Some months earlier the gang had robbed a security van carrying cash collected from the coin meters of the Dublin Gas Company. They struggled away with £10,000 in tenpenny pieces – 100,000 coins – which they buried in the Dublin mountains. The haul would have been difficult to change into notes had it not been for the club. But now the small change could be easily hidden in the bank lodgements of a thriving pool hall that dealt exclusively in coins. When Cahill dug up his buried treasure, the silver had turned black from the damp earth. The gang spent a night literally laundering the stolen cash. The coins were washed in buckets and then spread out on the pool tables and rubbed with blankets to restore their shine.

The pool hall was one of the first on the southside of the city and began doing a brisk business. For criminals living in the sprawling suburb of Crumlin it was an ideal meeting place. They would sit back in the shadows, away from the pool tables, planning robberies and sharing information. Inevitably the place also became the focus of police interest. Detectives would sit outside, watching the club's shifty-looking patrons. They regularly raided the place but found nothing.

The club became the place to parade success for some local bad boys who had done well out of crime. Outside, Eddie Cahill parked his Granada GXL alongside Fitzer's Jaguar XJ6. Martin Cahill regularly drove up on his Harley Davidson and gave the local kids spins around the square. Young thugs came to play pool and watch their underworld heroes sit around and plan jobs while the cops sat outside.

The club also attracted large numbers of starry-eyed young women who fantasised about the long-haired thugs. And, in the words of one cop who kept an eye on the place, it became a 'den of iniquity'. Dozens of young women had their first sexual experiences in the bed in the club's grotty office. Sometimes, according to former gang members, when the bed was 'full up' the pool tables were used for games they had not been designed for. There were even claims that some of the more enthusiastic groupies had sex with more than one gang member at a time. The gangsters enjoyed their new-found status as sex symbols. But the General himself did not participate in the debauchery.

One night things got out of hand at the club. A young woman had gone to the office to have sex with a member of the gang. Instead of making love he became extremely violent and sexually assaulted her with a pool cue. The other men heard her scream for help and raced up to see what was wrong. The girl had been injured in the brutal onslaught. Her clothes were ripped and torn off her back, she was hysterical and sobbing uncontrollably. They didn't know what to do – if the cops got wind of this it could be curtains for the lot of them. Then the General happened to walk in.

One of the few rules Martin Cahill lived by was that women should always be respected. Despite his prurient nature he disapproved of such outrageous behaviour. Had the man responsible for the assault not been a close associate, the General might have taken him up to the Dublin mountains and shot him. Instead Cahill ordered him out of the place and comforted the terrified girl. He spent the rest of the night pacifying her. At one stage he even went out and brought her back cream cakes. Whatever Cahill's motive – to comfort the girl, or dissuade her from going to the police – the tactic was successful. The young victim did not make a complaint to the police and later recovered from her ordeal. However the Gardaí did get to hear about the assault and made exhaustive enquiries, but the girl never came forward.

Years later, in September 1994, two weeks after Cahill's assassination, a former member of the Cahill gang, who had hung out at the pool club, at first did not recognise the attractive housewife who came up to him on the street. She knew him and when she said her maiden name, he remembered the young girl who had been sexually assaulted seventeen years earlier. Now in her mid-thirties she had not forgotten the ordeal. She told the former criminal that she could not believe that the 'kind man' who comforted her after the attack was the monstrous gangster being written about in the newspapers. She said she would never forget Cahill for what he did that night. The housewife smiled and walked away.

Word of the incident also filtered through to the local community and business at the pool hall began to drop. The groupies soon disappeared too. The gangster with the evil streak had scared them off. The glamour of the club faded. Less than two years after the attack the criminal was arrested during a payroll robbery. He later died in prison. Afterwards, members of the gang recalled how Seán Fitzgerald, sickened by the attack, decided to quit and go back to fraud.

Around the time the club opened there was a noticeable increase in the number of armed robberies in the area carried out by a gang using high-powered motorbikes. The Cahills and their henchmen were using the club as a base for a series of daylight heists, often doing one in the morning and another in the afternoon. Reports of the robberies carried out by the Cahill gang noted how they invariably vanished into the back lanes and walkways of the Crumlin area. There were other factors working in the General's favour. At the time the Garda vehicles were easily out-paced. They had an old fleet of squad cars and the few motorbikes they had were no match for those being used by the gang.

One morning in 1976 Cahill decided to prove just how easy it was to outrun the Gardaí when the gang hit Werburgh Street employment exchange and made off with £100,000 in cash right under the noses of the police. At the time the headquarters of the Dublin Metropolitan Area (DMA) and the Special Branch were in nearby Dublin Castle. Overlooking the back of the employment exchange on Ship Street were the offices of the Central Detective Unit (CDU). Armed detective units passed by the door of the exchange every five minutes on their way to CDU and Dublin Castle.

Cahill and his team drove up to the front door and ran inside brandishing handguns and sawn-off shotguns. They knew exactly where to go, as this was where they collected their unemployment assistance every week. During the two-minute raid one of the gang, Harry Melia, a close associate of Eddie Cahill, forgot about the main purpose of the job. Instead he ran around the building beating the uniformed cop who stood at the front door with a baseball bat. He later claimed that the officer had 'annoyed' him on the days that he went to collect his dole! The gang got away as detectives raced down the stairs from the CDU offices across the street.

One of Cahill's favourite bank branches was the Allied Irish Bank on the corner of Richmond Street, ten yards from the Garda Social Club on Harrington Street. The gang hit the branch several times. One morning on his way to a remand hearing in court Cahill robbed the branch at exactly 10.55 am. An accomplice was waiting to take the money and Cahill was dropped at the court for his appointment eight minutes later, with a cast-iron alibi.

Payroll robberies were perhaps the easiest targets of the new armed gangs that emerged in the 1970s. Factories and businesses were hit so often that after a time practically every firm in the country began paying staff by cheque. Martin Cahill began looking at the huge Semperit tyre factory in Ballyfermot. There was a large staff and the payroll would be substantial. For two months he planned the job.

In the early hours of the morning of 12 May, 1977, five armed and masked men burst into the home of Bernard and Elizabeth O'Neill near the tyre plant. They were held with their children until 10.50 am when four members of the gang, including the General himself, went to the plant's perimeter fence. With split-second timing the gang struck just as the payroll was being handed from the security van into the wages office. Cahill's men grabbed the bags, containing over £53,000 in cash. They fired a number of shots in the air and, in their getaway, a security guard was shot in the leg. The robbers got away on motorbikes.

Shortly after the heist Detective Inspector Ned Ryan got word that the General was behind the job. The 'Buffalo' – as Ned Ryan was known among his own men – was posted to the Central Detective Unit (CDU) in 1975. He had set up a squad of detectives, eventually referred to as the 'Flying Squad', to take on the big crime gangs. When the Cahills moved into the pool hall Ryan sent his squad to watch the place. In the weeks after the Semperit heist he had Cahill placed under close overt surveillance.

Cops spent long hours playing pool to irritate Cahill and his cronies. Surveillance was to become an occupational hassle during his criminal career and he soon devised tricks for slipping the net. One evening the General drove his Mercedes all over the wilds of Co Wicklow with his Garda tail close behind. Just before his car ran out of petrol on a lonely mountain road, Cahill pulled up and opened the boot. He took out a five gallon drum of petrol and filled up his tank. He smiled and waved to the cops who were sitting in their car a short distance away. Within a few miles they had run out of petrol and their target got away.

Shortly after that incident, about a month after the Semperit robbery, Cahill again slipped his Garda tail at Hollyfield. This time they caught up with him at Killiney Hill. The cops who found him reckoned that he was going to retrieve the buried money. They called their boss. As Cahill was coming back down the hill he met Ned Ryan and three of his men coming up towards him. Dusk was falling and Ryan carried a walking stick which Cahill thought was a gun. The cop smiled at his old enemy and told him: 'Now, Martin, you and I are going for a chat up that hill and when we come back down you'll have given back the Semperit money. It looks like this is the show-down.'

Cahill ran back up the hill. The cops followed. At the top they tried to catch him. They had never seen him so scared. Cahill jumped off a steep cliff at the side of the hill into the darkness below. Ryan's men were left standing at the top with Cahill's jacket in their hands. As he disappeared they could hear the strands in a barbed wire fence snap with the weight of the fleeing man. They thought he was dead and began searching for a body.

Amazingly, Cahill survived his jump. He spent the night hiding in a garden with a fractured shoulder, cuts and bruises. The next morning he called his solicitor and made a complaint against Ned Ryan and his men. He claimed that they had 'court-martialled' him. A subsequent internal Garda investigation found that there was no substance to the General's claims.

Cahill eventually got back to Hollyfield after being treated by a doctor. The next evening a detective from the Flying Squad called to the door of Cahill's flat and handed Frances his jacket and the keys to his Merc. He asked Frances if Martin was all right. She shut the door in his face. But Cahill's luck wasn't to hold out for long.

A few months after the Semperit job, he was arrested along with his brother Eddie while picking up a car they had stolen for another armed robbery. They had hidden the car in a lock-up garage in Terenure the previous day. When Martin Cahill sat in behind the wheel detectives appeared. On 24 November, 1977, Cahill got four years for receiving a stolen car. It would be his last major stretch behind bars. By the time he was released the criminal underworld would have undergone dramatic change – and so too would Cahill.

The pool hall eventually died a death following the sex attack on the young girl. It probably would have closed anyway – over the next two years Eddie, Anthony and John Cahill would also be arrested and jailed for serious crimes. Anthony and John got ten years each on 2 February, 1979, for a payroll robbery at Smurfit's in Clonskeagh. As they were making their getaway, John was hit in the chest in a shoot-out with the Gardaí. They caught up with him as he was trying to dig the bullet out with his fingers. Anthony later died in the Curragh military prison from a drugs overdose.

CHAPTER 4

Donovan Assassination Bid

Shortly after eight o'clock on the morning of 6 January, 1982, Dr James Donovan left his home at Belgard Heights, a private estate on the outskirts of Tallaght, and set out for Garda headquarters in the Phoenix Park where he worked as the head of the forensic science laboratory. Just before 8.30 am, as Donovan was turning onto the dual carriageway at Newland's Cross, an explosion ripped his car apart. The device detonated beneath the engine, throwing the vehicle into the air and seriously injuring the civil servant inside. The victim of the attack had incurred the wrath of organised crime in the person of one Martin Cahill.

The ferocity of the assassination attempt shocked the country. Never before had a state employee, who was not involved in the security forces, been so brutally attacked. In the initial investigation the attack seemed to be the work of the INLA or IRA except to the handful of policemen who knew the capabilities of criminals like Cahill. It was an extraordinary development in Irish crime. A criminal was now resorting to terrorism in his efforts to evade the law.

Dr Donovan began working as the state's forensic scientist in the mid-1970s. A civil servant employed by the Department of Justice and attached to the Gardaí, he is the police force's most important technical expert. What he finds under the lens of his microscope can, for the serious criminal, mean the difference between a stretch behind bars and freedom to conduct business as usual. Donovan's evidence has been crucial in convicting several leading criminals and subversives, including members of the Cahill family.

In fact, the first prosecution case in which Dr Donovan gave evidence was against Martin Cahill's younger brother, Anthony. He was accused of the murder of a student in Rathmines in March 1975 and Donovan's testimony was crucial to the state's case. The victim, John Copeland, had arrived home to find a burglar in his flat. During a scuffle Copeland was stabbed in the chest with a kitchen knife.

Anthony and his brother Michael or 'Styky' had burgled the flat earlier in the night. They were leaving the scene on a scooter when Anthony discovered that they had forgotten a torch. He returned to the house to retrieve it. Copeland then arrived home from a rugby training session. When the Cahills were taken in for questioning, Michael made a statement implicating Anthony. Martin was extremely annoyed with Styky for breaking the family code of silence and he was severely reprimanded. Forensic evidence given by Donovan linked Anthony Cahill's clothes to Copeland's flat. During two subsequent trials Anthony admitted the burglary but denied the murder. Eventually he was convicted of burglary but not of the murder.

In 1978 Eddie Cahill and his pal, Harry Melia, attacked and attempted to rob Ambrose Sheridan, the manager of The Belgard Inn, a pub in Tallaght. The victim and his wife were badly beaten with iron bars and kidnapped from their home. A jacket Eddie Cahill had thrown away after the attack provided the forensic key which resulted in his being charged in relation to the offence. When Dr Donovan's name appeared in the book of evidence in the case it showed that he was vital to Eddie's conviction – and Martin began taking an interest in the scientist. Later the General would take an even more personal interest in the scientific sleuth.

On the morning of 29 January, 1981, two armed and masked men – one of them Martin Cahill – walked into the office of Quintin Flynn Ltd. in the Western Industrial Estate in Clondalkin. The company specialised in the sale and hire of computer games and secretary Josephine Burke was preparing a cash lodgement for the bank.

She looked up and saw a man with a motorbike helmet standing at the door of the office. He shouted at her to get down on the floor. The second man, also wearing a helmet, walked in behind the first and ripped out the telephone lines. He opened the drawers of Ms Burke's desk and demanded to know where the cash was. The money was on the floor beside the safe. The second man began scooping up the cash in his hands and putting it in a dark-coloured carrier bag. In all they took £5,724.47, of which almost £1,000 was in coins.

On the way out they spotted a number of employees and Martin Cahill pointed a gun at them shouting, 'Back off or I'll shoot'. The raiders then picked up the bag of money and headed to a motorbike, a Kawasaki 750, registration number 521 ZD, which was parked outside. The silver in the bag was so heavy that the two men had to carry it between them, struggling as they went along.

A short time later uniformed Gardaí Colm Bowden and Raymond Barnes were driving through Kenilworth Square in Rathmines when they spotted a black Kawasaki motorbike being driven slowly down Leicester Avenue. The Gardaí recognised Martin Cahill driving with a pillion passenger. When he saw the cops Cahill speeded up and the squad car followed.

The two officers had noticed that the registration on the motorbike was now PTI 741, a bike registered in the name of Martin's brother Paddy as a Honda, not a Kawasaki. As the chase continued through Harold's Cross, Cahill reached speeds in excess of eighty miles an hour. Both men were wearing full-faced black helmets. What was distinctive about the pillion-passenger was that even at high speeds he held his left arm into his chest as if trying to hang onto something.

The squad car lost sight of the motorbike but continued its search. Forty-five minutes later they received a radio call reporting that a bike matching the description of the Kawasaki had been located at the rear of Bushy Park in Terenure. The park was one of Cahill's favourite hiding spots and easy to access from Rathmines through a series of lanes and walkways.

Other detectives and uniformed officers had found the abandoned bike on a pathway beside the Dodder River just behind a convent school. As the officers began a search Martin Cahill and a man called Christy Dutton came walking around a corner in the direction of the bike, carrying two full-faced black safety helmets. The two men matched the descriptions of the raiders earlier that morning.

Christy Dutton, a forty-year-old professional criminal from Bally-fermot, had been a close friend of Martin Cahill's since childhood.

Both men worked together on robberies and Cahill had named his second son, Christopher, after Dutton. First in trouble with the law at the age of eleven, Dutton was given two weeks detention for house-breaking. Since then he had accumulated thirty convictions including burglary, robbery with violence, wounding with intent, possession of a firearm and a number of charges for assaulting police officers. He had served time in prisons in England and Ireland and was, at this time, awaiting trial for another assault. Almost two hours before the Clondalkin robbery Dutton had been in District Court 4, Chancery Street, where he was remanded on continuing bail. Cahill and Dutton were later seen leaving on a motorbike. Both men were arrested under the Offences Against The State Act and held for forty-eight hours for questioning.

Cahill and Dutton were taken to the Bridewell Garda Station in the city centre next door to the Courts. Officers from the Technical Bureau, which provides all expert knowledge in forensics, ballistics, finger-printing and so on required by police in the field, took the men's helmets, gloves and jackets which matched descriptions given by witnesses to the robbery. They also took possession of Dutton's shoes which had melted on the exhaust pipe of the motorbike. For the next two days Cahill repeated his mantra: 'I don't want to talk to youse men ... Leave me alone.'

On the following morning Detective Garda Felix McKenna, who was attached to the Central Detective Unit and knew Cahill of old, uncovered the money from the robbery in a ditch along the Dodder River. That afternoon Cahill had a visit from his mother Agnes. He sent word through her to an associate instructing him where to recover the two guns which he had hidden in the park. That night the guns were found by the associate and removed from the park.

Cahill and Dutton were charged with armed robbery and posses-sion of fire arms on 31 January, 1981. In all, Dr Donovan eventually examined fifty-eight pieces of evidence upon which the state's case would be largely based. He found evidence linking Cahill and Dutton to the spot where the stolen money was recovered and to the stolen motorbike.

Faced with a long stretch, Martin Cahill began working on how to prevent the case going ahead. Eddie was also facing a long stretch on the abduction charge in Tallaght of the couple from The Belgard pub and both cases depended on the evidence of the forensic scientist. Ironically the two brothers almost found themselves on other robbery charges eight months later in August 1981. The Cahills had tied up the occupants of a house during a burglary in Castleknock in Co Dublin and were making their escape on a motorbike when a Garda squad car spotted them and gave chase. Martin, who was driving, lost control at the junction between Sundrive Road and Crumlin Road. The brothers fell off and rolled across the road right outside the door of Sundrive Station where a number of smiling cops were waiting to assist them. Cahill managed to throw away the jewellery, some of which fell into a gutter. He suffered a chest injury and was hospitalised for a week. However, he was not charged with the burglary on the grounds of lack of evidence. Eddie was subsequently charged with receiving and was convicted.

On Friday 16 October, 1981, Martin Cahill was returned for trial from the District Court to the Circuit Criminal Court on the Clondalkin robbery charge. He smirked as he stood in the back of the courtroom to hear the news. That night Cahill broke into the office of John Tidd, the senior clerk at the District Court Buildings on Chancery Street. He found his own and three other trial files, placed them in the middle of the floor and set fire to the lot. The office was badly damaged in the blaze and the files were destroyed.

But Cahill's plan did not work. A new file was constructed and eventually placed in more fireproof offices in the Circuit Criminal Court. Martin wasn't dissuaded. A number of weeks later Cahill sent two of his associates to set fire to the main courts building to register his annoyance with the law which now had an opportunity to put him away for twelve years. He set fire to the chambers of the Central Criminal Court in the Four Courts causing extensive damage.

The cost of the blaze ran into tens of thousands of pounds and closed some of the highest courts in the land for over a month. Not since the Irish Civil War in 1922, when the Free State army fought street battles with the rebels who opposed the Treaty with Britain, had the building suffered such an attack. This time the attacker was an unknown rebel with a cause of a very different kind. Martin Cahill had declared his own private war against the state.

The arson attacks, Cahill now knew, would not prevent his trial and he began formulating a sinister plan – to kill the man he feared could put him behind bars, James Donovan. At first he contemplated an abduction or shooting but there was always the risk of being caught in the act. Then he looked to the IRA's campaign in the North for guidance – and opted to use a bomb to rid himself of his enemy. The paramilitaries, particularly the IRA, had begun using car bombs as a most effective terror weapon in the North and in Britain.

Cahill also reckoned that such an attack would be blamed on the Republican paramilitary groups. The IRA would be the most likely suspects. Donovan's evidence had put away Thomas McMahon for the blast which killed Lord Mountbatten in 1979. In fact, in many of his criminal conspiracies Cahill was not reluctant to smudge the trail by making the work look like that of the Provos.

In Dublin several renegade Republicans were involved in organised crime, taking part in robberies and supplying weapons. One of those men was former Provo Thomas McCarton who had joined the INLA. The thirty-four year-old from the Turf Lodge in Belfast had been living with his family at Cashel Avenue in Crumlin since completing a prison sentence in the late 1970s. In 1976 he was part of an INLA assassination squad dispatched to Dublin to murder Irish Republican Socialist Party leader Seamus Costello. McCarton never got to 'hit' his target. He was shot and wounded by a detective who was lying in wait for him and his comrades when they arrived at a safe house in the Dublin suburb of Clontarf. McCarton was subsequently jailed by the Special Criminal Court for possession of a firearm. On his release, McCarton became involved in crime along with members of the Cahill gang who also lived in Crumlin. Ironically, McCarton was eventually to be murdered himself when the INLA imploded in a bloody internecine feud in 1987.

Cahill asked McCarton to manufacture a car bomb to blow up the state forensic scientist. For his part, Christy Dutton, Cahill's co-accused, had no knowledge of the plan and Dutton would not have approved of such drastic action. Such an atrocity would only serve to increase Garda pressure.

Donovan was an easy target for Cahill. Despite the highly sensitive nature of his work, he received armed Garda protection only during major cases involving subversives.

The General made his first attempt to kill the scientist three weeks before Christmas 1981. He and an accomplice attached a petrol device beneath the engine of Donovan's car. The heat from the engine would detonate the bomb while the car was being driven at speed, engulfing it in flames and causing a serious crash. The device, used by the mafia and other organised crime outfits around the world, is designed to produce an effect like that of an accident. But on this occasion the device exploded prematurely, setting the engine on fire as Dr Donovan approached Newland's Cross. He was driving at twenty miles an hour and managed to control the car which veered onto the grass margin. Later it was thought that the sudden fireball had been caused by petrol leaking onto the manifold. Cahill and McCarton went back to the drawing-board.

Then, in the early hours of 6 January, 1982, Cahill and an associate from the north inner-city planted McCarton's homemade device, stuffed in a shaving foam container, underneath the car at the point where the exhaust pipe enters the engine.

Donovan had travelled only a mile and a half from his home when the heat of the engine detonated the device in rush-hour traffic. The power of the blast lifted the car off the road. It landed in a crumpled heap a few yards away. Astonishingly Donovan survived the blast which had clearly been meant to kill him instantly. He was rushed to St James's Hospital where surgeons spent several hours operating to save his left leg and foot. Dr Donovan lost half of the left foot.

The attack caused universal outrage. The finger of suspicion automatically pointed to the paramilitaries. The two organisations promptly made statements denying responsibility. Although they did not express any sympathy for what had happened to the scientist, they gave curt but convincing explanations. An IRA spokesperson declared: 'The IRA has more to lose by carrying out such an act because of the anti-Republican hysteria it would arouse.' The INLA's response was even shorter: 'It serves no useful purpose.'

When it began to emerge that organised crime had been responsible for the attack, there was deep anxiety that Irish gangs were now adopting the tactics of the Sicilian mafia. Crime had undergone dramatic transformations in the previous twelve years and it was feared that this blatant attack on the state was the beginning of a new, much more brutal, phase in criminal activity.

To senior Garda officers like Ned Ryan and Dick Murphy – Cahill's hated foes – it was a not unexpected departure. They had argued for several years that gangsters like Martin Cahill were being allowed to thrive while the government diverted resources to combating paramilitaries. On several occasions in the late seventies there had been requests from Dublin officers, including Ryan and Murphy, for some form of specialist serious crime squad with the manpower and financial resources to mount operations against major criminals. Instead, most armed detectives were deployed escorting security vans. At that time, the Garda Síochána as an organisation was cumbersome and slow to change with the times. There were constant internal rivalries and jealousies, a preoccupation with regulations and a deep-rooted suspicion of individualism and flair. Professional rivalries sometimes contributed to the failure to catch major-league criminals like Cahill.

The Force's paymasters, the government, were also responsible for the situation they were now facing. Their overriding concern was with the paramilitaries. The results were there for all to see. Drugs were taking hold at an alarming rate and causing a new crime crisis. The number of crime gangs involved in robbery now greatly outnumbered the Provo 'blag' teams who had dominated during the early seventies. Martin Cahill understood this situation probably more than most and he often exploited it in his efforts to frustrate the police while conducting 'business' and staying out of prison.

In the aftermath of the bomb a team of over sixty detectives from across the city planned one of the biggest swoops on criminal and subversive elements ever seen in Dublin. Each case that Dr Donovan had an interest in was studied closely. Over the following months, up to forty individuals were arrested and held for questioning. As detectives continued to sift through the mountain of evidence, Martin Cahill's name began to emerge. Criminal sources had also confirmed that Cahill had a reason to get at the forensic scientist. Ned Ryan and his men moved to arrest Cahill on 9 February, 1982. They dragged him kicking and screaming from his flat in Kevin Street and took him to Ballyfermot station for questioning.

It would later emerge that even the day before his arrest Cahill, far from feeling the need to keep his head down, had been involved in an armed hold-up at the Allied Irish Bank in Drumcondra, during which a security guard had been shot and injured.

While he was in custody detectives were treated to Cahill's by now well-known mantra. When it came to being photographed and finger-printed he kicked up a fuss. He screamed and roared as ten detectives lifted him forcibly off the ground and held his right hand to be printed. Cahill would later tell that he got several 'digs' in the ribs during the scuffle. One detective told him that he was going to be finger-printed even if his hand was 'accidentally' broken in the mêlée. He agreed to co-operate.

When they had finished finger-printing Cahill, the cops tried to take his 'mug shot' – a polaroid picture used for identification purposes. Determined that the cops would not get the better of him, Cahill began rubbing the finger-print ink into his face. They never got the picture. From then on Cahill began disguising his face from public view. Whenever the police raided his home over the next twelve years they would meet a grinning Al Jolson lookalike at the door. He also began wearing the balaclavas for which he was so well-known until the time of his death.

The investigation into the bomb attack on Dr Donovan continued for several months but never led to a single conviction. Cahill had left no tracks, forensic or otherwise, that could have connected him with the crime. He counted himself lucky to escape and confided his role in the atrocity only to a handful of trusted associates. Although he never suffered pangs of guilt after his nastier crimes, the bomb attack was something he never bragged about. In the handful of interviews he gave Cahill did make very oblique references to the incident by expressing his contempt for forensic scientists.

James Donovan courageously overcame his injury and returned to his duties. In October of the same year it was evidence from his laboratory that convicted Harry Melia and Eddie Cahill when the Belgard case was heard in the refurbished Central Criminal Court.

Because of all the delaying tactics, Martin Cahill and Christy Dutton did not stand trial for the Clondalkin armed robbery of 1981 until 29 May, 1984, before Judge Frank Martin. It was to be a dramatic case. Both men dressed in good suits although Cahill looked a little incongruous in a pinstripe about two sizes too big for him. The trial lasted for four days in Circuit Criminal Court number 15. Even at this late stage Cahill wasn't going down without a fight. During the first two days he brought down different members of his organisation to 'pick out' jury members with a view to intimidating them. He also instructed some of his people to tail the jurors home after the court was over each day.

The most poignant moment in the hearing came when Dr Donovan was called to give his evidence. It was the first case in which he had taken the stand since the bomb attack. There was silence in the courtroom as the expert hobbled past Cahill to take his seat on the stand. Cahill looked at a spot on the ceiling as his victim passed. Judge Martin stared intently at Cahill as the scientist got into his seat. Then he conveyed to Donovan the sympathies of the court for his appalling injuries and congratulated him on his recovery and decision to return to work.

The drama didn't end there. For one day of the trial Cahill fired his legal counsel and also fell out with his co-accused, Dutton. He began conducting his own defence which at times descended to farce. When he was cross-examining one Garda witness he asked the same question five times. Unlike the more capable practitioners, Cahill was unable to rephrase his questions to out-manoeuvre the witness. Judge

Martin advised him to move on to another question as there was little point in the Garda answering the same question over and over again. Realising that his courtroom technique was not going to win his freedom, Cahill re-appointed his legal counsel.

He tried another tactic. On the second day two men suddenly interrupted the trial and began hurling abuse at the accused man from the public gallery. 'Martin Cahill, ye'r only a dirt bird drug dealer who killed my sister,' one of them roared. The intention was clear – the outburst would result in the jury being discharged because the accusations could influence their final decision and the trial would be aborted. It was not the first time Cahill had pulled this one. Once, in the 1970s, while Cahill was standing trial for burglary, a man stood up in the public gallery and confessed to the judge that, in fact, he had committed the burglary, not Martin Cahill. The stunt eventually won Cahill an acquittal. This time it didn't work. 'Ye'r a murderin' bastard,' the hecklers continued as detectives scrambled to drag the saboteurs from the courtroom. Judge Martin, spotting the stunt a mile off, allowed the trial to proceed and sent the two men to prison for contempt.

Detective Inspector Dick Murphy and his team felt they had sufficient evidence to convict Cahill. But at the end of the prosecution's case, counsel for Cahill and Dutton made an application to the court. They claimed that the state had failed to prove a vital ingredient in the charge of armed robbery – that the company secretary, Josephine Burke, had been put in fear of her life during the heist.

On 1 June Judge Martin had to instruct the jury to acquit both men, having accepted the counsel's application. Cahill was jubilant. The Gardaí were in a state of shock. Their hated adversary had been caught with strong evidence. But Cahill's extraordinary luck had held and he walked out free.

Afterwards Cahill and his overjoyed contingent left and went to the Tilted Wig pub across the road to celebrate. Everyone drank while Cahill had coffee and sat grinning. Crestfallen, Detective Inspector Murphy was standing among his detectives still coming to terms with the outcome of the case as Cahill walked past, a free man. He turned in his ill-fitting suit and shouted: 'Hey, Murphy! Get up ya! See ya again.' Then he gave the group of detectives the two fingers and walked down the steps. It would be the last time that Martin Cahill ever faced a serious criminal charge.

CHAPTER 5

The Heist and the Crucifixion

The bomb attack on Dr James Donovan earned Martin Cahill a reputation among the Gardaí and the underworld as one of the country's most formidable and dangerous criminals. In early 1983, however, the General was still largely unknown to the Irish public. Martin Cahill was quite happy to remain anonymous. He was facing a trial for the armed robbery in Clondalkin in 1981 that, despite his brutal efforts to stop it, was still going ahead, bringing the likelihood of a long stretch in prison. In the meantime Cahill decided to make the most of his freedom and expand his criminal organisation.

His timing could not have been better. In the early eighties, the Gardaí were fighting a desperate battle against organised crime gangs like the Dunnes who were now heavily involved in drug racketeering. An army of addicts was causing an unprecedented crime wave as they robbed and mugged for money to buy 'gear', as heroin was known. But, as the new drug war raged, the General's gang were on their way to the big time – and notoriety. In January 1983 an associate brought Cahill information on a robbery which would catapult him into Irish criminal history. The job was O'Connor's jewellers in Dublin. The loot would be gold, gems and jewels worth over £2 million. It would be the biggest, most audacious robbery since the establishment of the Irish state. It would also be the catalyst that would take Dublin to the brink of all-out war between organised crime, the IRA and the Gardaí. There were dangerous times ahead for the eccentric joker.

The Thomas O'Connor and Sons jewellery manufacturing plant in Harold's Cross was an Aladdin's cave of precious gems and had been a source of intense interest to both criminal and subversive groups for years. The plant had been cased on a number of occasions with a view to liberating its multimillion pound contents. The IRA had abandoned plans for a robbery because they felt the high-tech security system, which was directly linked to the Garda Metropolitan Headquarters in Dublin Castle, made the place impregnable. In 1982, Henry Dunne, the man who helped introduce Martin Cahill to armed robbery, had also looked at O'Connor's and was believed to have drawn up plans to hit the place with a team dressed as Gardaí – the Dunnes' favoured *modus operandi* in other robberies. Events overtook Henry's plan when he was arrested following a shoot-out with detectives on his way to a job. He was given a ten-year sentence in February 1983.

Cahill and a few of his gang had made a half-hearted attempt to tunnel underneath the factory from beside the nearby greyhound track but only succeeded in alerting the Gardaí. Over a six-month period between 1982 and 1983 heavily-armed officers from the Serious Crime Squad staked out the premises, regularly locking themselves in the factory's main office and strong-room at night, waiting for the thieves to arrive. They never showed and Garda chiefs believed that they had given up the idea.

By-passing the elaborate security system at O'Connor's was not the only problem facing the ambitious thief. There was also the staff of over a hundred to be dealt with and, because of the plant's location, escape was almost impossible if the Gardaí were alerted at any stage during the raid. This time, however, Cahill's trusted lieutenant had someone on the inside who was willing to co-operate with the gang in return for a share of the loot. For several months the associate had quietly been taking delivery of small quantities of gold dust and uncut jewels from the inside man. The associate had once received a small matchbox full of gold filings from the floor of O'Connor's which he converted into £1,000. At first Cahill didn't show much enthusiasm for the 'stroke' but with the potential reward so high, he immediately began planning.

Over the next six months Cahill planned every aspect of the robbery which was to earn him his nickname 'the General'. The name came from General Douglas MacArthur, the US Army chief who gained fame for meticulous planning of a more legitimate nature almost forty years earlier. Planning was Cahill's *forte*. It was his greatest pleasure in life apart from getting one over on the Gardaí and eating rich cream cakes. Up to the time of his death he would have as many as ten robberies or kidnaps planned, the details of which were known only to him. He was paranoid about security before his crimes. As the plans progressed his associates were informed on a need-to-know-basis only. It was not unusual for Cahill to order his men to prepare for a particular robbery only for them to find that the target had been changed to another venue en route. It was Cahill's fail-safe method of ensuring that even the smallest amount of innocent talk would not jeopardise his liberty.

Cahill was handed photographs and detailed plans of the security system and the lay-out of O'Connors during a series of secret meetings in Ashton's pub in Clonskeagh between his associate and the inside man. Cahill kept his masterplan a closely-guarded secret. He did not trust the inside man who, he feared, was susceptible to pangs of conscience. After all he wasn't a proper criminal and Cahill didn't trust anyone who hadn't a proven track record. He even treated his associate with a degree of caution, despite the fact that they were involved in setting up the robbery together.

In June 1983 Cahill began putting his team together. He calculated that ten men were necessary in order to subdue the staff effectively and shift an estimated haul of over half a ton. But he had a problem – he could no longer look to his immediate family to make up the bulk of his team. Eddie was in the Curragh Military Prison while John was in Mountjoy. His brother Anthony had died in the Curragh in March of the same year and while Cahill never showed his grief – he felt that showing emotion was a sign of weakness – he confided to another gangster once that he wanted to dedicate O'Connor's to Anthony's memory. Brother-in-law Hughie Delaney had also been in prison since January, as had Harry Melia, another trusted family friend, jailed for the same robbery as Eddie.

For the robbery Cahill chose two of his relatives and seven long-established associates from Crumlin, Rathmines and Ballyfermot.

Some of them had taken part in earlier heists, including a £120,000 post office robbery in Mallow, Co Cork, in June 1982. The last man recruited to the gang was Thomas McCarton, the INLA man who had provided Cahill with the bomb used to blow up Dr James Donovan eighteen months before. Cahill had broken an old rule about not including paramilitaries in his organisation. As a professional criminal he looked down his nose at the IRA and other subversive groups. He considered them amateurs who were easily broken down by the police. McCarton, however, had proved himself a worthy member of the gang through his associations with Cahill's men.

Cahill timed the robbery to take place between the evening of Tuesday 26 July and the following morning. Normally there were a hundred staff working in O'Connor's but due to summer holidays that figure would be reduced to just twenty-five. The first task for the gang was to begin stealing the fleet of vehicles required for the robbery. Between 30 June and 26 July three Datsun Bluebird cars, a blue Hiace van and a gold Ford Granada were stolen across the south city. A sixth vehicle was bought from a Traveller. Cahill planned to use one of his own motorbikes, a Kawasaki 550, which was registered in someone else's name and fitted with false number plates.

On Sunday 24 July, Cahill's associate called to Michael Egan at his home in Crumlin, less than a mile from O'Connor's. Egan was a forty-eight year-old aluminium fitter from Co Offaly drawn to the company of major criminals who had little compunction about using him for their own ends. The associate told him that Cahill needed a favour and wanted to hide a van in the workshop at the rear of his house. There was a 'small stroke going down' and he must allow members of the gang to hide overnight in his garage and to open the doors at exactly nine o'clock on the morning of 27 July. Egan agreed to assist.

As the final preparations were being made Cahill began working on his alibi. For the two days before the robbery he made himself as publicly visible as possible. He staged a one-man picket outside both the Department of Justice and the Dáil, complaining that forensic evidence had been planted on him in a robbery case. The irony was not lost on the police who stood guard outside the two buildings and who knew Cahill had blown up their forensic scientist. As in most of his major crimes Cahill went to work with a strong alibi.

Martin discarded his placard on the evening of Tuesday 26 July and faded out of view. Just hours before the robbery there was an unexpected setback. At six o'clock Cahill sent a man to Thomas McCarton's home at Cashel Avenue in Crumlin to inform him that the gang were meeting for the job at nine o'clock but McCarton, who had been on standby, was not at home. Cahill was furious and accused the paramilitary renegade of losing his 'bottle'. 'Ya see,' he told his team, 'ya can't trust those fuckers. They've no bottle, no trainin'.' In his final briefing Cahill warned the assembled men that no unnecessary force was to be used during the heist. It was one of his idiosyncrasies. He would not tolerate violence against the victims of a robbery unless they 'had a go'. 'Fear is a calculated weapon but force is a sign of failure,' he would reflect philosophically. Paradoxically, Cahill had little difficulty torturing or shooting anyone whom he even suspected of crossing him.

Around nine o'clock the gang gathered in the Dropping Well pub in Milltown. To other unsuspecting drinkers they were nothing more than a scruffy-looking soccer team on their way from a game. Each one of the 'footballers' carried a sports bag and they laughed and joked about the 'match'. But the contents of the sports bags they kept close beside them were a lot more deadly than sweaty jerseys and muddy boots – each one contained either a revolver or an automatic pistol. There were also hand grenades, smoke bombs, balaclavas, gloves, walkie-talkie radios and coal sacks to put the loot in.

Cahill had supplied the weapons from one of his hidden arsenals and attached lanyards to each weapon so the gang members could carry them around their necks while filling the sacks. He ordered soft drinks and sat making small talk with his men. He was on a high. This was what he lived for.

Shortly before closing time the 'soccer team' finished their drinks and filed out of the pub and into a waiting blue Hiace van. The van drove the gang down to the side of the O'Connor's complex which consisted of a two-storey L-shaped factory building with a courtyard surrounded by a twelve-foot-high wall. Three members of the gang scaled the wall and forced their way into the plant's boiler-room which was not hooked up to the main security system. The rest of the gang dispersed to collect the stolen cars and await their cue to strike at exactly eight o'clock in the morning. Some of the gang hid with the van in Michael Egan's garage on Sundrive Road.

At 7.55 am the company's production manager, Robert Kinlan, arrived to open up the premises. He noticed nothing unusual and opened the front gates which automatically de-activated the alarm system linked to the Gardaí at the metropolitan headquarters in Dublin Castle. He parked his car and went into the factory to switch off the building alarm and open the doors for the staff who began to arrive. Cahill's men watched and waited. The general manager, Daniel Fitzgibbon, arrived at eight o'clock. He went into the main office where he was in the process of opening the strong-room when Bobby Kinlan returned. At the same time the gang struck. The van and one of the stolen cars were driven into the complex. Cahill took up a position at the gate on his motorbike where he covered the front entrance and controlled events inside by using a walkie-talkie.

Another gang member sat in a car along Harold's Cross Road watching the arrival of the employees. The men in the boiler-room burst out and grabbed the staff members as they walked to the entrance of the building, forcing them into the toilets where they were held at gun-point. All the main doors and exits of the building were covered by armed men within seconds. In the commotion one of the raiders who was nervous and agitated jumped a member of his own gang. He got a slap across the head from another robber to calm him down. In the main office more masked men forced Daniel Fitzgibbon to open the safe and show them where the diamonds were. He and Robert Kinlan were also ordered into the toilets.

Apart from the nervous raider the rest of the gang were cool and professional and reassured the staff that they would not be harmed as long as they co-operated. The staff would later tell arriving Gardaí that the raiders seemed to know their way around the factory. All twenty-five staff members were rounded up and accounted for within five minutes. The gang spent the next thirty-five minutes removing the entire contents of the strong-room including gold bars, gems, diamonds and thousands of gold rings in a finished and unfinished state. The haul weighed over half a ton and was valued at almost £2 million. The robbery would eventually force O'Connor's to close down with the loss of all one hundred jobs.

Cahill set off a smoke grenade to warn the captured staff not to raise the alarm as his gang piled into the stolen cars and van. Then he hopped onto his motorbike and brazenly led his convoy out into the rush-hour traffic. The convoy drove across Harold's Cross Road and onto Kimmage Road. As they turned onto the road beside the Park Inn pub a bag of diamonds and gems, worth almost £500,000, was thrown to an accomplice standing on the corner. The man then ran over to Mount Jerome cemetery where he had been instructed to bury the bag. One of the cars broke away from the convoy as part of the getaway plan. At the same time the blue Fiat car the gang had bought was being set alight two miles away at Cherryfield Road in Walkinstown. Cahill was leaving a decoy for the Gardaí who would think, in the initial confusion, that the car had been abandoned by the gang as they split off in different directions.

At exactly nine o'clock Michael Egan opened the door of his garage as the blue van swung into the laneway which runs along the rear of Sundrive Road just a few hundred yards from Sundrive Garda Station. He slammed the door shut again as the van reversed inside. Five masked men jumped out. One of them held a gun up to Egan's head and told him: 'If you want to live keep your mouth shut about this, and I mean what I say.' The rest of the gang dispersed leaving three men behind: Cahill, the associate who helped to plan the job and another criminal. Cahill and the third criminal kept their balaclavas on – the associate was the only one known to Egan.

The three robbers put on gloves and started sorting the huge haul. Egan brought them out tea with bread and jam. The two masked men ate their sticky sandwiches through the hole in their balaclavas, leaving jam matted in the woollen masks. They continued their work in silence. They had a radio scanner turned down low to eavesdrop on the police. Cahill chuckled as he strained to hear the frantic voices of officers in the squad cars chasing around the southside of the city in search of the O'Connor's robbers.

A short time later a much louder crackle from another police radio sounded from outside the garage door. Two detectives were checking all the lock-up garages in their search for the gang. The three reached for their guns, cocked them and prepared to open fire. Cahill peeped out to see a green Renault 18 car and two officers coming towards the garage. One of the detectives started banging on the door and tried to open it. The three gangsters braced themselves. Cahill's associate had placed sods of grass around the base of the door to give the impression that it had not been opened for a long time. But the two detectives seemed determined to look inside.

Suddenly their radio crackled with an urgent call to go to Terenure Station. The detectives considered the garage door for another second before jumping into their car and speeding out of the laneway. They would never know how near they came to being shot. Cahill was sweating. The three put down their weapons and went back to separating the gold and the gems scattered across the floor.

Later one of the criminals took a break and went into the nearby Crumlin Shopping Centre to clear his head after the excitement of the morning. As he walked in, a detective he knew came walking towards him with a big grin on his face. The criminal thought he was about to be arrested. 'We caught a big fish this morning,' the cop said, beaming. 'Who would that be then?' the criminal asked nervously, thinking that some of the gang had been caught. 'Shamie Dunne, that's who. What do you think of that?' The detective didn't wait for an answer but went off to share his good news with someone who might appreciate it more. Just a few hours earlier, while Cahill and his men were rifling through the strong-room in O'Connor's, under-cover detectives had burst into a luxury apartment in Milltown and caught Shamie Dunne cutting up thirty-two ounces of high-quality heroin on a glass table. It was the culmination of months of secret surveillance by a newly-organised Serious Crime Squad who would eventually turn their attentions to the activities of the General.

Cahill and his men spent the rest of the day and night in Egan's garage. When they finished around midnight they had divided the loot into fourteen sacks, each one weighing around three stone, to be divided equally among all those who were involved in the robbery, including the inside man and Egan. Martin Cahill was scrupulous about sharing every last penny from a robbery equally. The robbers moved the loot in two cars to a garden at the back of a house in Ballymount two miles away, where a sixteen-foot-long trench had been dug. The bags of loot were placed in the trench along with the guns and covered over with peat moss. Shrubs and heathers were then planted on the spot.

The three men returned to Egan's garage to collect the van. Egan was waiting at the door at 1.45 am. Cahill and one of the two others, still wearing balaclavas, got out and loaded a petrol can into the back of the van which was strewn with jewellery and some cash from the robbery. They said goodnight to Egan and drove to Poddle Park in Crumlin a mile away. They threw petrol bombs into the van to burn it. One of the bombs ignited prematurely as it was being thrown, melting the rubber glove onto the hand of the man throwing it. Cahill helped the injured man back to a waiting BMW and warned the associate behind the wheel to drive 'nice and slow' so as not to attract attention. They drove the injured man to his home in Tallaght where they dressed the wound. Two days later he was treated in hospital for the burns to his hand. The injuries were consistent with a plastic object melting on his hand. In the hospital, he claimed that he had received the injury when a chip pan caught fire. A subsequent search of his house by Gardaí found no evidence that there had ever been a fire of any kind. Within a few days of the O'Connor's robbery Gardaí received intelligence reports that Martin Cahill and his gang were responsible. One of the men heading the investigation was Detective Superintendent Ned Ryan, who had been moved to Crumlin on promotion in 1980. When he arrived to take up the post, Cahill was waiting outside the station with a group of protesters.

Despite his best efforts however, Ryan was not given permission to arrest Cahill. This refusal was to be a recurring headache for the detectives investigating serious crimes where Cahill was the major suspect. The reason was often given by some senior officers that there was no point hauling the General in, even if there were strong grounds for suspecting him. He would just pick a spot on the wall and repeat his mantra for the duration of his detention.

In the following days a total of nine individuals were arrested and questioned under the Offences Against The State Act. While one of the gang was being questioned in Terenure Station he noticed a team of officers in the yard outside with shovels and wearing workclothes. The accomplice who was given the bag of diamonds to bury in Mount Jerome cemetery had dropped some in his haste to conceal them. A major Garda search of the forty-seven acre site began when the diamonds were found. When he was released the gangster went to see Cahill at his new home in Kevin Street flats and told him the cops were searching the cemetery. 'We have to dig that stuff up in the cemetery before those fuckers rob them on us,' Cahill remarked.

On the night of 3 August, Cahill, the associate who helped set up the job and another gang member recovered the haversack of diamonds from its resting place in the cemetery. They climbed over the wall which runs along Clogher Road in Crumlin and left the stuff in a house. Cahill and his team got two cars. They went to the newly-planted shrubbery at the back of Ballymount Road and dug up their buried treasure and guns. Cahill was determined that no one was taking the jewels from him. 'We are stoppin' for no one. If anyone stops us we come out shootin',' he told his team. With all the gems collected the loot was buried near Brittas in Co Wicklow. Afterwards Cahill was concerned that the haul might be found when a gang member's car was spotted parked in the same area and reported to the police. The owner was taken in for questioning and the area searched but nothing was found.

Cahill's next concern was the disposal of the loot. Even if it was valued on the legitimate market at around £2 million it could only realise a fraction of that amount in the underworld. Les Beavis was one of the top fences in London's West End. A small, dapper cockney in his early fifties, Beavis had been introduced to members of Cahill's gang by Shamie Dunne who had extensive contacts in London and Manchester 'firms'. Beavis was one of the names on Scotland Yard's most wanted list. They had mounted a number of operations to catch him but he had outwitted them every time. He was no stranger to Dublin and he travelled over to examine the O'Connor's haul and make a bid.

A number of meetings took place at the Kilternan Sports Hotel outside the city. Beavis and his valuer examined the haversack of gems in a house in Tallaght once Cahill had decided that everything was above board. The fence's valuer spent a full day checking through the haul which contained 1,000 carats of diamonds, 3,000 carats each of sapphires, rubies and emeralds. Beavis offered Cahill and his associate £50,000 for the lot. They laughed and the horse trading continued until they eventually agreed a price of over £100,000, payable in cash sterling. The money was distributed equally among the members of the gang. Each one also had his own bag of gold which he could off-load as he wished. A number of them, including Cahill, sold theirs to Beavis for around £40,000 each. Other members of the O'Connor's team opted to swap their bags of loot for heroin and cannabis through contacts in Manchester's Quality Street Gang, which increased their 'investment' when sold to the army of addicts on the streets of Dublin.

Over the next six weeks Beavis had the gold and jewels smuggled to England on the Cork to Swansea ferry, hidden in the door panel of a car driven by a 'husband and wife'. In all he made six runs. Later Cahill bought a bag of gold from one of his men which Beavis also agreed to buy. Cahill asked one of the men on the periphery of his gang, who had connections in the garage business, to arrange transporting the stash to Beavis in London. In turn, the gang member asked a middle-class acquaintance with no criminal record to do the run to England in a car on legitimate business. Before the car was to be driven to the ferry the gang member took it away and loaded Cahill's loot into the door panel.

When the car arrived in London, the gang member who had

arranged the transport was waiting with one of Cahill's closest lieutenants to hand over the loot to Beavis. They opened the panel to discover that the gold had gone. Someone had robbed the robbers. The lieutenant was furious and caught a flight to Dublin that evening where he reported directly to Cahill. The gang member stayed on in London for a further two weeks without contacting Cahill with an explanation. His reluctance to face the music convinced Cahill that he was the guilty one. In Cahill's world stealing from a robber was the ultimate sin.

In a bizarre way Cahill was a very honest man. He was not greedy when it came to the share-out of loot and never conned a member of his gang out of a single penny of his share. And he insisted that the gesture be reciprocated. When the gang member returned he went to see Cahill and pleaded with him to believe that he had nothing to do with the disappearance of the gold. Cahill said nothing to him. The man wasn't sure whether he was off the hook or not. He found out two days later.

What happened next has become part of the folklore of Dublin gangland and struck fear into every criminal who might contemplate conning Martin Cahill in the future. During the research for this book individual members of Cahill's organisation verified the following story. Cahill and the lieutenant who had been present for the handover in London were waiting outside the suspect's house in Rathmines as he came home one night from the pub. They bundled him into a car and drove to a derelict house near the site of Hollyfield Buildings.

The two men dragged their victim upstairs where he was questioned about the whereabouts of the jewels. At first Cahill and the lieutenant gave the terrified gang member a few slaps. When he wasn't forthcoming with what Cahill considered to be the truth, the man was pinned to the floor. Cahill walked around him and kept repeating the same question. 'Tell me what you done with the stuff and who ya gave it to?' The man replied that he had done nothing. Cahill then stapled each of his fingers to the floor. With each finger he asked the same question. The gang member began to scream that he was not guilty of the 'crime' he was being accused of. But the General wasn't satisfied.

He produced a claw hammer and two six-inch nails. The accused man cried and begged for mercy, insisting that he had not stolen the jewels. But in the General's court there was no mercy. Cahill placed the point of the nail in the palm of the man's right hand and raised the hammer in the air. He asked the question again. When he got the same answer Cahill struck down hard on the nail with the hammer, driving it through the man's palm. He struck it a second time, punching the nail into the wooden floor. He moved to the left hand. Again Cahill asked the same question with the nail positioned in the man's palm and the hammer raised in the air. When he got the same answer, Cahill completed the crucifixion.

The ordeal lasted most of the night. Cahill later confided to associates that he wasn't proud of what he had done. He claimed disingenuously that he had been forced to 'nail' a problem down. Cahill was compelled by his own warped principles. No-one, the paramilitaries, other criminals, not even the state was going to beat him. Whether that meant having the audacity to blow up the state forensic scientist or nailing an underworld recalcitrant to the floor, in Martin Cahill's eyes it had to be done or else he lost the 'game'. 'People remember pain,' he said. 'A bullet through the head is too easy. You think of the pain before you do wrong again.'

Cahill and his lieutenant were satisfied that the accused was innocent when he still denied the 'crime' after his harrowing trial by ordeal. Cahill got a pinch bar and pulled the nails out of the victim's hands. The pain of having the nails taken out was even more excruciating than having them hammered in. Cahill suddenly changed his attitude. He gave the injured man a cloth for his bleeding hands. He put him in a car and drove him to the casualty department of the Meath Hospital. Outside Cahill opened the door and helped him out of the passenger seat. It was as if the last eight hours had never happened. He knew that the victim would be too scared to make a complaint to the police. As he limped to the door of the casualty department Cahill called him back and, in a soft-spoken voice, offered some fatherly advice. 'If I were you I would bring a compensation claim against the Corporation for malicious injury. You've got a great case.'

In fact, the haul had been stolen the night before it was due to be taken to England. The circumstances of the discovery were suitably absurd. Someone had found the loot in the door panel and then abandoned the car near a Travellers' camp. He hoped that the car would be taken apart and, when eventually found, the Travellers would be blamed. Within an hour a Garda squad car recovered the car and it was returned to the driver who took off as planned for England. Following the nailing incident an Afghan dog dug up £50,000 worth of jewels in the garden of a house in Terenure. The O'Connor's story was still far from over.

Within a week of the robbery a senior IRA figure sent a message to Cahill arranging a meeting. The meeting took place in a coffee shop in Crumlin Shopping Centre near Sundrive Garda Station. At the meeting were two senior figures from the Dublin command of the IRA. Cahill was accompanied by the associate with whom he had set up the robbery. One of the Provos congratulated Cahill on a 'job well done'. Cahill grinned and reminded the Provo that it was a pity his organisation had found it such a hard nut to crack.

The senior IRA man abandoned the plaudits and got down to business. He told the General that the IRA wanted half of the proceeds from the O'Connor's job. Cahill smiled and replied: 'If you want gold then go out and rob your own gold like we did.' The Provo became agitated at Cahill's attitude and told him that if he didn't comply with the demand there would be 'very serious consequences'. Cahill stood up from the table and moved his face down closer to the Provo's. 'You do your strokes and we'll do ours. Ye'r not gettin' a fuckin' penny.'

Cahill walked out with his associate. The meeting had lasted less than ten minutes. The General had left the Provo chiefs in no doubt that he was not afraid of them or any other paramilitary organisation. Cahill was cocky and confident. The Provos knew that Cahill was no pushover. For the next six months they would watch him and his gang very closely. When the opportunity was right they would make their move.

CHAPTER 6

Shadow of the Gunmen

Shortly after the O'Connor's heist, and the General's subsequent rebuff to the paramilitaries, there was strong speculation about how he had off-loaded the huge haul. The only way to realise the loot's full value was to barter it for drugs, a new and highly profitable development on the criminal scene. When Martin Cahill was released from Mountjoy Prison in February 1980 he had come back to a gangland which was undergoing an extraordinary transformation. In the few years he had been behind bars, Dublin criminals had discovered heroin and a multimillion pound industry. Dealers became wealthy men overnight by supplying a generation of miserable teenagers eager to escape the drudgery of no work and no opportunities in working-class Dublin. In the space of weeks, Dublin's inner-city ghettos were in the grip of a devastating heroin epidemic. Scores of kids as young as twelve were becoming addicts at the hands of unscrupulous pushers who gave heroin out free in the schoolyards.

Under the banner of the Concerned Parents Against Drugs (CPAD) residents of working-class areas began to take the fight to the drug dealers. Traditionally, they had turned a blind eye to the activities of the criminals living among them. Now, suspecting many of those criminals of involvement in drugs, the people were no longer too scared to speak out. In the background the Provos were poised to take action and caught in the middle were the Gardaí fighting in vain to keep the lid on an extremely volatile situation. In the wake of the O'Connor's robbery it was the heroin explosion which would give the IRA an opportunity to take on the General.

The Provos and the INLA held a meeting in which they shared intelligence on Cahill. At that meeting INLA member Thomas McCarton was particularly helpful. He was still sore at not getting a cut of the action after failing to turn up for the robbery. Other members of the gang who hadn't sold their shares to the London fence, Les Beavis, were already suspected of turning their loot into heroin.

The rumour machine began linking Cahill with drugs. The rumours were fuelled by his friendship with one of the most notorious heroin dealers in the city, Ma Baker. The peroxide blonde, middle-aged granny was paying kids to mitch from school to distribute her drugs. She was also accused of selling heroin to her own children. While Cahill's friendship with Ma Baker was damaging to him at a particularly sensitive time, out of loyalty he was prepared to protect her from anti-drug zealots. Despite the intense speculation there was little evidence that Cahill was ever involved in drug dealing. Relying on his instinct for survival, he had steered clear of the burgeoning narcotics trade and preferred sticking to ODC (Ordinary Decent Criminal) activities like armed robbery – investing his money in legitimate business. A number of factors made him reluctant to become a drug baron.

Cahill was a workaholic thief whose life revolved around planning and carrying out robberies. The more spectacular and embarrassing to the police and the state the better. And to pass the time in between high-profile robberies, he was out committing burglaries or, as he would say himself with a grin, 'moochin', just for fun. He was considered an oddball by other criminals because he shunned the life of the high-rolling gangster. Swilling champagne and womanising were not for him. Sitting back while an army of pushers did his dirty work and watching the cash mount up was not the sort of 'game' he liked.

His family had also been adversely affected by the new scourge. Anthony, who had been jailed for his part in the Smurfit's payroll robbery in 1978, died in prison in March 1983 from a heroin overdose. His brother and sister, Michael and Una Cahill, were heroin abusers. Una's husband, Hughie Delaney, was also an addict and later became a dealer. Delaney, once an integral part of the Cahill gang, was now in and out of prison on drug possession charges and Martin had distanced himself from him. Hughie was jailed for a year in January

1983. While he was inside, Una was busted and later got eight years for possession of heroin.

Delaney's drug dealing also contributed to the rumours about Cahill. Gardaí had suspected, as was later confirmed, that the General had put up £50,000 for Delaney to buy a shipment of heroin. Cahill later claimed that he had asked his brother-in-law to look after the money for him but Delaney had squandered it on drugs. The General distrusted junkies and refused to work with them. In an interview with the *Irish Times* in 1984 Cahill explained why: 'Never trust a drug fella ... they're like a helpless thing, not a human being at all.' He also revealed why he had not got involved in the rackets. 'I was asked to go into drugs when I came out of prison, but everyone was knackered. They would sit around all day talking about drugs and money, but they had no money. When I said: "Yeah, let's do a robbery," they'd start talking about robbing drug stores and I knew I was wasting me time. I hate drugs, they have ruined members of my family.'

The General said often that drugs were damaging to the criminal profession. He felt that the profits were not worth the complications or the social repercussions. His former partners in crime, the Dunnes, tried to entice him into the drug business. They had moved exclusively into drug dealing since 1980, utilising extensive underworld contacts in London and Manchester. With the two families working together, they told Martin, the Dunnes and the Cahills would be unbeatable, untouchable – and very rich. The profits from drug dealing were prodigious with a lot less risk than jumping across a bank counter with a sawn-off shotgun.

But the General disapproved of the flamboyant, swaggering style of the Dunnes and the ostentatious way they displayed their profits. By the time he pulled the O'Connor's job in 1983, the Dunne brothers – Shamie, Mickey, Larry and Boyo – were in the 'most wanted' category of criminal. Specialist undercover Garda units were set up to target the family and by 1985 practically every member was behind bars.

The Concerned Parents Against Drugs was a powerful new organisation born out of the despair of residents in the Corporation estates and flat complexes across the city which had been overrun by pushers and addicts. People were terrified to leave their homes after dark for fear of being mugged. Addicts injected themselves openly on stairwells, street corners and even in children's playgrounds. When individuals attempted to stop the pushers they were beaten up or threatened at gun-point.

Faced with the people power of the CPAD, however, the pushers could no longer threaten or intimidate with impunity. Some of the CPAD's organisers were members of Sinn Féin and there was speculation that the IRA had also infiltrated the organisation. The Concerned Parents began evicting suspected drug dealers and abusers from the flats. At night the men patrolled the complexes and set up road blocks to prevent the pushers and their junkies getting through. Life began to return to normal and the rekindled community spirit boosted the residents' morale. Soon the pushers and their customers were moving out of the inner city to adjoining residential areas.

The worst-hit area after the junkie exodus was Crumlin, which is also home to a large number of the Dublin underworld's serious criminals. In fact the majority of criminals in Martin Cahill's gang had at some stage lived in the neighbourhood. The Cahills had lived there as children before being evicted for rent arrears in 1965 and dumped in squalid Hollyfield Buildings. The Dunnes also came from the sprawling suburb, as did Ma Baker. In February 1984 the CPAD was organised in Crumlin and almost immediately found itself on a collision course with the criminal community. The CPAD's tactic was to identify the house where a drug pusher was operating and then march on it, demanding that the pusher get out or stop dealing. The tactic was highly controversial and faced allegations of heavy-handedness.

The Concerned Parents movement in Lower Crumlin had its first meeting on Thursday, 16 February, 1984, in the hall of the local Christian Brothers school. There had been rumours that drug pushers were offering heroin to the children in the schoolyard of Scoil Íosagáin. The local women decided to stand watch over the children coming to and from the schools. The men erected checkpoints and began patrolling the side roads of the worst-affected areas. On the evening of Sunday, 19 February, the Concerned Parents braved heavy rain and cold to march on the homes of suspected drug dealers.

During the march the group stopped outside the homes of local criminals suspected of being drug pushers. The criminals had blazing rows on their doorsteps with the marchers. What angered them most was the fact that they considered the march leader, John 'Whacker' Humphrey, to be one of their own. Humphrey was a former criminal and a founding member of the CPAD. The thirty-three year-old married man, who had recently moved to Crumlin, had earlier convictions for armed robbery, assault and malicious damage, but had not been in trouble with the law since 1981. 'Whacker' was now involved in more legitimate business with his family who had a flower stall at the gates to Mount Jerome Cemetery. The criminals also objected to the presence of the checkpoints which would make life difficult and inhibit their nocturnal activities.

Following the same march the CPAD protesters decided to head for the home of Thomas Gaffney, a petty criminal and close friend of Martin Cahill, who lived at Captain's Road in Crumlin. The thirty-four year-old was married with one child and had served time in Mountjoy along with Whacker Humphrey. Neither man had much affection for the other.

The local belief was that some of the Gaffneys were drug dealers. Three of the brothers were addicts – and Ma Baker was a close family friend. This suspicion in turn fuelled the rumours about the General's involvement in drugs. Gaffney had also been one of the men arrested for questioning in relation to the O'Connor's robbery and, although Gardaí had cleared him of suspicion, the Provos began taking a keen interest in him.

As the march neared Gaffney's house, Tommy confronted the Concerned Parents and warned them not to harass his family. He admitted that members of his family were addicts but denied that they were involved in dealing. Faced with Gaffney's determination not to allow them near his home the marchers dispersed. Later that same night Gaffney went drinking with his best friend, Martin Foley. They were joined by Seamus 'Shavo' Hogan from Rutland Grove in Crumlin. Both Hogan and Foley were members of the General's gang and were dangerous, hardened criminals with the records to prove it.

Hogan, one of the gangsters closest to Cahill, was in an agitated mood. His was one of the houses visited earlier in the night by the CPAD who had accused him of drug pushing. At closing time he expressed worry about passing through the pickets which by then had been placed on the main routes to his home. Foley and Gaffney agreed to travel with him as moral support and they headed off in two cars accompanied by their wives. Earlier they had contacted Cahill and informed him of the events unfolding in Crumlin. He advised them to seek Garda protection at Sundrive Station. Unfortunately, when the trio went to the station, no squad car was available to escort them.

At Rutland Avenue the cars were stopped by a picket. A row ensued when Foley refused to open his boot for one of the CPAD men with whom he had a previous disagreement. A squad car arrived as a fist-fight was breaking out between the two groups. Garda reinforcements were called and Gaffney, Hogan and Foley were taken into protective custody to allow things to cool down.

But things were going to get a lot hotter. The following morning Cahill went to Hogan's house for a meeting with a group of Crumlin criminals, where he listened to the accounts of the previous night's drama and other confrontations with the CPAD. He suggested that the ODCs – the criminals not involved in drugs – set up their own organisation to counter the CPAD. After some debate Cahill came up with the name, the Concerned Criminals Action Committee (CCAC). The concept was typical of the General's penchant for the absurd. A march was organised for three o'clock that afternoon.

Cahill ordered every criminal he knew in the southside to take part, although he didn't appear himself. Those who were reluctant to join in the protest kept their reservations to themselves – everyone had heard about how the General 'nailed' down problems of loyalty. The marchers began calling to the homes of Concerned Parents activists en route. Such was the heavy approach of the CCAC that most of those visited denied any involvement. They also called to the home of Whacker Humphrey and smashed some of his windows. The gangsters returned to Shavo Hogan's house to await further developments. The General was taking care of other business.

Later that evening the homes of Whacker Humphrey and Noel Sillery – the latter was a Sinn Féin member and chairman of the Dolphin House Concerned Parents committee – were wrecked by masked men. Then, shortly before midnight, two armed and masked men entered the St Theresa's Gardens flats complex and confronted two CPAD activists, Joseph Flynn and his brother-in-law Paddy Smyth. The two turned and ran when they saw the gunmen approaching them. A number of shots were fired and Joey Flynn was hit in both legs. He was rushed to hospital where the wounds were found to be not serious.

The following morning's newspapers proclaimed that the city's drug barons had declared war on what they referred to as the 'anti-drug vigilantes'. But the shooting only strengthened the resolve and determination of the Concerned Parents. On the evening of 21 February over a thousand people gathered for a CPAD meeting in Lower Crumlin. At the meeting Whacker Humphrey admitted that mistakes had been made by wrongly accusing people of drug dealing. He told the Crumlin people that Flynn was one of his men and that he would not be deterred by the shooting. He also urged them not to co-operate with the police.

The following day a large group of the Concerned Criminals stood outside Shavo Hogan's house in Rutland Grove. *Irish Press* reporter Andreas McEntee arrived following reports that there had been another shooting in the area. Martin Foley and Shavo Hogan agreed to give an interview although they wished to remain anonymous. Foley complained to the reporter that the Concerned Parents had begun reporting the criminals' nocturnal movements to the Gardaí. Foley stressed that none of the Concerned Criminals was involved in drug pushing. He and Hogan did confirm, however, that the Flynn shooting was the result of 'rising tension in the area'. Cahill's front men would later declare that the Concerned Parents would not be allowed to jeopardise the 'livelihoods of local criminals engaged in illegal activities which were not related to drugs'.

A meeting to discuss peace proposals was convened between the Concerned Criminals and the Concerned Parents. On the criminal side were Foley, Hogan and Tommy Gaffney and on the CPAD side John Noonan, a member of the organisation's central committee. The thirty-two year-old father of four was also a senior Sinn Féin activist and former IRA member who served five years on arms and explosives charges in Long Kesh. Three meetings took place in the Belgard Inn, Tallaght, and the Red Cow Inn, Clondalkin, where it was agreed that future incidents would be sorted out with each side carrying out its own investigation into the source of the problem. The criminals reported back to Cahill at his new Corporation home at Swan Grove in Ranelagh that a truce was now possible. He was happy with the outcome. But the IRA had other ideas. Every Sunday afternoon Tommy Gaffney called into the Park Inn public house in Harold's Cross for a few drinks. On 4 March, while drinking with a relation, he noticed four strangers in the bar watching him. As they left one of the strangers stared hard at Gaffney. The following Sunday, 11 March, the strangers were again in the bar when Gaffney came in. Martin Cahill arrived on a motorbike and strolled into the bar in his leather biker's gear, sporting his customary grin. He talked with Gaffney for a brief period about events in Crumlin. Cahill didn't seem to notice the strangers and promptly left the bar.

Martin Foley also arrived for a few minutes and left again. Two of the men sitting in the bar got up and went outside. As Foley was leaving, he noticed two men acting suspiciously at a red Hiace van outside the pub. He saw one had a gun but thought that the man was selling it to the other person. Around six o'clock Gaffney got up to leave. When he reached the door the two men who remained in the bar grabbed him and marched him outside towards the van. Gaffney shouted to the barmen to call the police. One of IRA men roared back: 'We are the police'. The other two men outside assisted their colleagues and put handcuffs on Gaffney who was by now screaming for help. They bundled him into the van.

As the IRA gang sped away Gaffney was gagged and blindfolded. He was later switched to a second van and driven to a safe house where he was held for the next twelve days. During his captivity he was handcuffed to a chair and a bed and regularly beaten. His kidnappers questioned him about Martin Foley and possible links with drug dealing or the Joey Flynn shooting. But Martin Cahill was their main interest and not drugs. They spent long hours questioning Gaffney about Cahill's activities and movements. They asked about the O'Connor's robbery and what happened with the loot. They connected Gaffney with the discovery of some of the stolen jewellery in Mount Jerome Cemetery because he had worked there. However, Gaffney had no knowledge of the robbery because he had not been involved.

Hours after Gaffney's abduction Martin Cahill arranged a meeting with a number of his associates. He knew that the IRA were behind the disappearance and that they were after the O'Connor's jewellery. He told his hoods that the run-ins between the Concerned Criminals and Concerned Parents had been used as a smokescreen to make the abduction seem like it was drug-related. The General was in a belligerent mood. 'There are more of us than there are of them [IRA] in Dublin and we have the guns,' he told his people.

Cahill was now the most formidable gang boss in Dublin and he was prepared to prove it. He also had the firepower with which to make his point. At the time he had an impressive arsenal – most of it stolen from the Garda Technical Bureau – including a high-powered Uzi submachine gun, a German Schmeisser machine-gun, rifles, pump action shotguns and grenades. He had a network of between fifty and sixty people who would stand by him. Martin Cahill was preparing for war.

The following day Cahill sent a message with Martin Foley and Shavo Hogan who were meeting John Noonan of the Concerned Parents, along with two of Tommy Gaffney's brothers, to discuss the abduction. The message was short and simple. If anything happened to the missing man there would be reprisals and Noonan would be the first to get hit. Noonan knew nothing of the kidnap but said he would make enquiries through his Republican contacts to see if he could get any information and would report back the next evening at four o'clock. The message never came and Cahill mobilised his henchmen.

The next morning, Wednesday 14 March, around sixty members of the Dublin underworld gathered at Gaffney's house for a march to St Theresa's Gardens, the scene of the Joey Flynn shooting, to demand the safe release of Tommy Gaffney. This time Cahill participated in the march but stayed in the background. Foley and Shavo Hogan led the motley crowd most of whom, like Cahill, covered their faces or wore balaclavas. It was an astonishing sight. On the way the marchers stopped outside the homes of Concerned Parents leaders and shouted threats of reprisals. As they continued towards the Gardens a number of shots were fired from within the crowd. As the marchers got near the entrance to the flats a large force of uniformed Gardaí appeared and began escorting them.

The local people had barricaded the entrance to the flats and were waiting with iron bars and pick-axe handles. The atmosphere was extremely tense and senior officers, expecting a full-scale street battle, frantically called in reinforcements. As the stand-off continued scores more officers arrived and formed a thin blue line between the criminals and the CPAD. Angry words were exchanged but the large police presence dissuaded both sides from striking blows.

By this stage Cahill believed that his friend was dead. He moved offside to a hideaway flat to keep out of range of the Provos. From there he directed his men to keep key individuals of the Concerned Parents and Sinn Féin under surveillance. He wanted to build up details of their movements so that, when the time came for retribution, he knew where to find them. In the meantime he would hold his hoods back while the Gaffneys continued their efforts to have Tommy released without a bloodbath. Cahill helped put up £5,000 cash reward for information leading to the recovery of the missing man. Martin Foley was also engaged in his own campaign. He made a number of trips to the country and contacted the head of the INLA, Dominic McGlinchey, who was on the run at the time. He made enquiries on Foley's behalf. However, McGlinchey was of little use to the investigation – he was arrested in a shoot-out with Special Branch detectives in Co Clare a few days later. Foley also called to *Sunday World* columnist, Fr Brian D'Arcy, a respected mediator who had regularly intervened in feuds. But as the investigations continued an IRA active service unit was preparing for further action.

On the morning of 20 March, the Gaffney family received an anonymous letter which read: 'Prepare for a funeral, your little bastard is dead.' The same day detectives investigating the shooting of Joey Flynn arrested Shavo Hogan and Martin Foley for questioning at Kevin Street Station. Foley and Hogan denied any knowledge of the shooting and had alibis for the night in question – they had been in hospital with a relative. Foley was released at nine o'clock on the night of 21 March. Ten hours later at seven in the morning the IRA struck.

Foley was asleep upstairs with his girlfriend, Pauline Quinn, shortly before seven when his brother Dominic answered a knock on the door from a 'postman'. Four armed men burst in on top of him and asked where his brother was. Two of the abductors bounded up the stairs and smashed their way into Foley's room. He had been woken by the noise and he tried to hold them back. A tough street fighter, Foley put up vigorous resistance to the IRA men who beat him with a baton and a sawn-off shotgun. Pauline Quinn was ordered to lie on the floor as the scuffle continued. Foley, who had been hand-cuffed, was wrestled by the two Provos to the landing where all three tumbled down the stairs.

They managed eventually to bundle the screaming and kicking Concerned Criminal into a waiting van and sped off. Driving the van was Sean Hick, a university graduate and self-employed butcher, and beside him, bar manager James Dunne. Sitting on top of Foley in the back were student Liam O'Dwyer and Derek Dempsey, an unemployed carpenter. One of them put a handgun to Foley's head and told him: 'If you don't stay quiet, I will blow your fucking head off. You'll get the same as Tommy if you don't stay quiet.'

Within seconds of the abduction the Garda communications centre got a 999 call from Foley's neighbour. The alert was radioed to all squad cars. At the junction of Crumlin Road and Kildare Road, the van was spotted by the crew of a squad car from Tallaght Station driven by Garda Tony Tighe. As they began tailing the van down the Crumlin Road they heard on the car radio that Martin Foley had been abducted by a number of armed and masked men.

The van stopped at a red light outside the front door of Sundrive Road Garda Station. The Tallaght car remained a safe distance behind. When the van moved off the squad car followed. Another squad car joined in behind the van which was driving at no more than thirty miles per hour and observing the rules of the road. At this stage the four IRA men in the van started to panic. Every time Sean Hick turned onto another road he saw the squad car in his rear-view mirror. As the van drove down the South Circular Road towards the Phoenix Park a third squad car suddenly appeared out of Con Colbert Road and swerved to block it. Hick swung the van up onto the pavement and drove around the police car. The chase began.

The squad cars with their unarmed officers stayed behind the van as it sped at sixty miles per hour towards the Park. By this stage armed units of the Special Task Force and local detective squads were racing to the area from all over the city. The IRA snatch squad cocked their weapons. The van turned into the Phoenix Park at the main entrance from Conyngham Road. One of the Garda cars drove up on the van's right side and Hick tried to ram it off the road. Garda Tighe's car also pulled alongside the speeding van. The side door of the Hiace suddenly slid back and Derek Dempsey took aim with a revolver. He fired a number of shots which hit the squad car. One of the bullets struck the base of the windscreen in front of Garda Tighe.

Tighe began swerving his car from left to right to evade the volley of bullets. The gang were unable to shake the tenacious squad cars off their tail. The rear window of the van suddenly exploded as Liam O'Dwyer blasted his sawn-off shotgun at Tighe's car, showering it with glass and buckshot. The van turned onto Wellington Road where it was forced to stop near the Forty Steps as more squad cars came in the opposite direction to block its path. The gang tried to drag Foley out of the van with them but left him and raced down the steps which led onto Conyngham Road. Foley was grabbed by Garda Tighe and bundled into the back of his car. At this stage over a hundred Gardaí were converging on the quiet city park. As the gang tried to make its getaway they fired several shots at unarmed officers pursuing them down the steps. Dempsey was the first to reach the road. He shoved his gun into his pocket and casually began walking across Conyngham Road. But Special Branch officer Tony Fennessy already had him in the sights of his own weapon. Dempsey turned to face the detective with his hand in his pocket. Fennessy fired a shot over the IRA man's head and Dempsey surrendered.

Meanwhile the rest of the gang had been forced to take cover after detectives began returning fire with Uzi machine-guns and revolvers. Surrounded and faced with overwhelming odds, the gang came out with their hands up. Twenty-five minutes after it had begun the kidnap drama was over. Amazingly no one involved in the chase had been injured. Concerned Criminal Martin Foley emerged slightly battered and bleeding, but safe. The Gardaí had arrested an entire active service unit of the IRA.

The intervention of the police had averted a certain bloodbath on the streets of Dublin. Both the General and his adversaries, the Gardaí, now knew that the abduction was intended to get at Cahill. Buoyed by their success, the police ordered searches across the city that morning involving hundreds of detectives in an attempt to find Tommy Gaffney. Late that evening his captors informed Gaffney about the Foley incident and that they were releasing him on condition that he told the Gardaí and the media he had been abducted by a group 'concerned about the chronic drug problem in Dublin'. Shortly after midnight on the morning of Friday, 23 March, he was released near Abbeyfeale in Co Limerick.

The trial of the kidnap gang began on 5 July, 1984, before the Special Criminal Court. All four faced a number of serious charges including membership of the IRA, false imprisonment and the attempted murder of Garda Tighe. For three months prior to the case the Gardaí kept Martin Foley under close 'protective' surveillance. On one occasion he slipped out of sight to meet with associates in the

INLA. He was informed that the abduction attempt had caused tensions between the INLA and the Provos. He was asked to withdraw his evidence against his four kidnappers. He received further, less subtle, requests which left him in no doubt of the dire consequences of non-compliance.

Ironically, Martin Cahill was inclined to agree with his foes. In his world, wrong-doing was dealt with in the appropriate way and there should be absolutely no co-operation with the police or the courts. During the trial Foley suffered a total lapse of memory about the dramatic events four months earlier. He told the court that he could remember nothing from the time he was in his bed to the time he found himself sitting in the back of a police car. But the state had over-whelming evidence with which to convict the four men. Derek Dempsey got a total of nine years for shooting at Garda Tighe, kidnapping and possession of firearms. Liam O'Dwyer got five years for the same charges. Sean Hick and James Dunne got seven years each. All four were also convicted of IRA membership. The presiding judge, Mr Justice William Doyle, told the four men that unproven claims that they had 'tried to cure the social evil of drug peddling could not justify violent action against Gardaí.'

Following the kidnapping incidents Martin Cahill gave his first interview to a newspaper journalist. Padraig Yeates, then a freelance with the *Irish Times* and the co-author of the book *Smack*, had met Cahill briefly while he was covering the Gaffney story. He approached Shavo Hogan and Martin Foley with a view to getting an interview with the elusive crime boss they called the General. After a number of weeks one of Cahill's minders called Yeates in the early hours of the morning and said the godfather was ready to meet him.

Yeates was met on a public street and taken to a flat where the General was lying low. Throughout his career Cahill agreed to interviews only at times of high pressure when he felt the spotlight might cool things down. During a number of interviews Cahill confirmed that he had intended going to war with the Provos and that the kidnappings were merely a bid on their part to get their hands on the O'Connor's loot. He told Yeates bitterly: 'They can't even go out and rob for themselves any longer. They have to rob ordinary criminals who have done the work and taken the chances. There's nothing lower than someone who robs a robber.'

Cahill and his organisation came back from the brink of war satisfied that he had been the victor. He had been prepared to take on one of the most professional paramilitary organisations in the world. The IRA knew that Cahill would have been a formidable opponent and decided to leave the issue for later – a decade later. When they released Tommy Gaffney the Provos sent a prophetic message to the General. 'Tell Cahill that we will never kidnap him – we'll stiff him on the street.'

CHAPTER 7

The Beit Paintings Robbery

In 1952 Sir Alfred Beit came to Ireland to live in Russborough House near Blessington in Co Wicklow. Among the rich gentleman's baggage was one of the finest private art collections in the world. The collection of Dutch Old Masters included Vermeer's 'Lady Writing a Letter' which alone was estimated at £20 million and the only Vermeer in private hands in the world apart from that owned by Queen Elizabeth.

A financier and member of a wealthy South African diamond-mining family, Sir Alfred had retired from the House of Commons in Westminster as a Conservative MP and parliamentary secretary. He chose to live in his Georgian residence with its imposing granite facade in the midst of breathtakingly beautiful parkland ten miles from Dublin. Although he had no blue blood running through his veins, Sir Alfred had the aloof, upper-crust manner of an aristocrat. One could not have found a starker contrast than that between Alfred Beit and Martin Cahill. One came from the richest, most powerful echelon in society; the other from the deprivation and squalor of a no-hope city ghetto. Beit was a patrician, Cahill a devout philistine. And while the world's most valuable art treasures adorned the mahogany-panelled walls of Sir Alfred's Palladian-style mansion, a single print of swans on a lake, bought in a discount store, hung on the sitting-room wall of Cahill's infinitely more modest abode in middle-class Rathmines, an area in which he was considered something of a social misfit. But the equation was about to be balanced up a little.

In May 1986 the crime lord strolled into the real lord's magnificent stately home and stole eleven of the most valuable paintings in the Beit collection. It was the second biggest art robbery in the world.

The disappearance of the Beit paintings was the beginning of a fascinating and complex story of international intrigue involving police forces and criminal organisations in several countries. The heist would become the stuff of legend in the underworld and earn Martin Cahill a reputation as one of Europe's most accomplished criminals. He would achieve a reputation of almost mythical proportions, displaying an extraordinary capacity to slip the net in the many elaborate police stings aimed at catching him with the paintings. In other ways, however, the Beit haul was to bring bad luck to the General's gang, which was becoming a major source of embarrassment to the Irish government and the Gardaí.

Ironically Cahill again found himself following in the footsteps of the IRA. In the case of O'Connor's, the Provos had looked at the jewel factory and decided against it and Cahill had proved them wrong. The IRA had taken a bolder step twelve years earlier when they robbed the Beit collection. On the night of Friday, 26 April, 1974, an IRA gang led by Dr Rose Dugdale, the daughter of an English millionaire stockbroker, took nineteen paintings valued at £8 million. During the seven-minute raid the armed gang gathered the Beits and their staff at gun-point and tied them up in the drawing-room.

Shortly after the raid a ransom of £500,000 was demanded along with the transfer from English to Northern Irish prisons of the Price sisters who were serving jail terms for car bombings in London. Eleven days later Dugdale was arrested in a cottage in Co Cork with three of the paintings. Subsequently the remaining sixteen were recovered in a hired car. At her trial, Dugdale, who was then aged thirty-three, pleaded 'proudly and incorruptibly guilty' to receiving the paintings. Four other charges relating to the crime were dropped in return.

Sir Alfred, undaunted by the experience, decided to donate his wealth of art treasure to the Irish state under the auspices of the Beit Foundation. He and his wife moved into a wing of the huge house. They lived there for part of the year, spending the rest of their time in South Africa and London. Russborough House itself was opened to the public in 1978 and attracted tens of thousands of visitors.

However, not all those who paid their £1 entrance fee had artistic appreciation in mind. Paddy Shanahan was a case in point. On the surface the well-spoken auctioneer and builder from Co Kildare was a respectable businessman. But Shanahan had been involved with organised crime gangs in Dublin since the seventies. He was described by criminals who worked with him as a Walter Mitty character who loved the sheer drama of violent crime. He got a high dressing up for heists and enjoyed the buzz of carrying weapons even more.

For almost ten years, he had been involved in robbing mailbags from the same Kildare train practically every weekend without being caught. Shanahan had been introduced to organised crime by Henry Dunne, then the most formidable 'blagger' in Dublin. He in turn introduced Shanahan to Cahill who included him in a number of major heists in the early eighties. One of those was a raid on the ADC cigarette wholesalers at Johnstown, Co Kildare. Shanahan, who lived in Johnstown, helped in the planning of the robbery which netted the gang £100,000 worth of cigarettes. He was never convicted of any crime in Ireland and was not known to the Gardaí prior to 1986.

But Shanahan, like many other Irish criminals, regularly worked in England where he had not been so lucky. On 29 May, 1981, he and two London criminals, Alan Wilson and Nicholas Boyd, were jailed for an armed robbery at the Staffordshire home of retired doctor Sam Firman, a well-known antiques collector. The seventy-two year-old suffered a heart attack and almost died as Shanahan's gang ransacked the house. In 1985 Shanahan was released from prison and returned to Ireland where he developed a keen interest in the Beit paintings. He began casing Russborough House and discussed plans with a number of English criminal associates. He also talked to Martin Cahill about the prospect of robbing the place. Cahill did not trust Shanahan but allowed him to believe that he was going along with the idea. In fact, Cahill secretly began working on a plan of his own.

Cahill was excited at the prospect of carrying off such an ambitious robbery. It would be the ultimate 'up yours' to the state he despised. Some who worked with Cahill would later say that, to his strange mind, depriving the state of the paintings was the main objective. The money was almost a bonus. Cahill regarded the wealthy as the real criminals and therefore felt justified – duty-bound in fact – to liberate them of some of their material affluence. He had watched Sir Alfred on television. His well-manicured accent convinced Cahill that he certainly 'deserved robbin'.' Characteristically, Cahill pieced the plan together slowly and meticulously. Every Sunday for two months after Easter 1986, when the house was opened to the public, he drove the ten miles to Blessington and paid his £1 entrance charge to eye up his next major heist. From his discussions with Shanahan he was soon able to identify the most valuable paintings in the collection.

Plenty of information about the collection and the value of each painting was already in the public domain – including the booklet designed to accompany the tours of Russborough House. Cahill brought other members of his gang with him to case the place, posing as art lovers. Some of them advised against stealing the paintings. After all there was a vast amount of other treasure in Russborough that would be easier to turn into hard cash on the black market. There were valuable pieces of antique furniture, clocks and Ming porcelain, which a few members of the gang already had contacts interested in buying.

But when the General had an idea it was like a religious vocation and no-one, with the possible exception of the Gardaí, could change his mind. Any criticism of his plan was deemed disloyal and the person concerned could find himself out in the cold. Cahill believed that the paintings could be off-loaded with little difficulty through his gang's connections in England and the Continent. There were plenty of filthy rich eccentrics prepared to pay millions for the pleasure of hanging a Vermeer or a Goya on a cellar wall away from the gaze of prying eyes.

Four of the masterpieces in the collection were about to be transferred to the National Art Gallery of Ireland as a gift from the Beit Foundation, including the Vermeer, two by Metsu – 'A Man Writing a Letter' and 'A Woman Reading a Letter' – and a Goya – 'Portrait of Doña Antonia Zárate'. These four paintings alone were conservatively valued at £27 million. They were also insured and there was the prospect of a large ransom for the return of the works.

So, while Paddy Shanahan went to England in search of an alarm expert to by-pass the system at Russborough House, Cahill and Noel Lynch, a close friend with whom he had shared a prison cell during the seventies, registered a 'security company' in the Companies Office at Dublin Castle. The plan was that the company, with thirty-eight year-old Lynch as its front man, would approach the Beit Foundation with an offer to 'help' return the paintings.

The company even had its own card with the letters RIP emblazoned in gold on a black background. Apart from the 'recovery' of stolen goods the company 'specialised' in the movement of 'large amounts of cash' and even 'debt collecting'. The fact that Lynch was a notorious criminal with a string of convictions, including possession of drugs and armed robbery, posed no problem. There is no legislation in Ireland to prevent a convicted felon starting up a security business or detective agency, nor are there are any safeguards for the unsuspecting consumer.

A suitable hiding place had to be found for the paintings. Cahill needed a spot in easy reach during the getaway from Russborough House. His favourite location was the Dublin mountains which look down on the city from the south east. The mountains have always been important, particularly to southside crime gangs. Not only do they hide their loot there but the windswept mountain-top has been the venue for many underworld punishment shootings. It is well-known among the criminal fraternity that colleagues have been murdered and buried there. The very suggestion that someone should 'take a trip to the mountains' is enough to instill fear.

Cahill began digging a bunker in a dense forest on a mountain-top two months before the robbery. He allowed only two gang members to help in order to minimise the number who knew where the treasure was to be hidden. The makeshift bunker was situated ten feet from a roadway. It was six feet deep and five feet wide.

Materials were brought up to the spot gradually to avoid unwanted attention. The walls of the bunker were lined with blocks and plastic sheeting. A crude air vent was installed and the top was covered over with wood and plastic sheeting. Access was through a manhole cover and the area was camouflaged with moss and pine-needles from the trees overhead. A second location was found in the wall of an attic in Tallaght.

Towards the end of April 1986 Cahill began forming his team. Like the O'Connor's heist the Beit robbery would be a labour-intensive exercise and he needed a dozen men. By now the General had gathered a close-knit team of loyal, level-headed criminals who placed complete trust in him.

At the same time he continued his reconnaissance missions to Russborough House. On a number of occasions he 'borrowed' a van belonging to a legitimate security company (not the one he and Lynch had set up). During one of the visits he spotted Paddy Shanahan rambling through the House, deciding which paintings he wanted to liberate for himself. Members of Cahill's gang dressed up as security men and scared Shanahan's people away. He also discovered that Shanahan had an alarm-cracking expert travelling from the East End of London and decided to bring his plans forward. The gang robbed two four-wheel-drive jeeps on the weekend of Saturday, 17 May. They would hit Russborough House on the night of Wednesday, 21 May.

The hallmark of the General's planning was its military precision and the principle was to keep the plan simple and uncomplicated. The gang gathered at a pre-arranged rendezvous in the Dublin mountains shortly after midnight on 21 May. Cars were left at a number of locations for a speedy getaway after the job. Sir Alfred Beit and his wife had gone to London at the weekend. The House was occupied by the administrator, Lieutenant Colonel Michael O'Shea, the chauffeur Tom Brosnan, and their families. Cahill had decided to hit the House at its most vulnerable point, the back. The two jeeps and the rest of the gang waited just off the Ballymore Eustace Road which runs along the boundary of the 600 acre estate several fields away. Cahill and two of his men walked carefully towards the House in the pitch dark. To guide the vehicles up to the rear of the House, Cahill stuck sticks in the ground at fifty yard intervals. At the top of the sticks he attached ordinary white plastic bags which acted as markers for the gang. Despite the installation of a sensitive alarm system in the House after the IRA raid twelve years before, Cahill had little difficulty in entering. The gang cut a small pane of glass out of a large French window and forced the shutters open. In front of them was their goal. Cahill deliberately stepped in front of the passive infra-red sensor, activating the alarm system which was directly connected to the Garda station in nearby Blessington. In the seconds after the alarm was activated one of Cahill's men tampered with the sensor so that it would not set the alarm off a second time.

Cahill and his henchmen carefully retreated leaving almost no sign that there had been a break-in and lay silently in the field outside. Lt. Col. O'Shea who was living in another part of the House got up and checked for any sign of intruders. As the Gardaí arrived he was able to tell them that everything seemed in order. Cahill watched the squad car leaving and radioed his waiting gang to drive up to the steps outside the French window. But the plan almost came unstuck as the gang drove across the fields when the driver of the first jeep, a criminal from Ballyfermot, narrowly avoided driving into a ditch.

This time the gang strolled into Russborough House undetected. Equipped with the booklet from the guided tour Cahill instructed his men what to take off the walls of the salon, music room and library. The raid took just six minutes and the gang left through the soggy fields with eighteen paintings. They drove ten miles to Blessington Lake at Manor Kilbride where Cahill and one of his men discarded the seven least valuable paintings of the haul and one of the four-wheel drives, a Nissan Patrol.

Among the eleven he kept were the two Metsus, the Vermeer and the Goya which were destined for the National Gallery and worth almost £30 million. The Vermeer was also one of the paintings unsuccessfully stolen by the IRA. The rest of the haul was made up of two Rubens, 'Portrait of a Monk' and 'Portrait of a Man'; a Gainsborough, 'Portrait of Madame Bacelli'; Guardi's 'View of Grand Canal, Venice'; Vestier's 'Portrait of Princess de Lambelle' and an untitled Palamedesz. The gang split off in different directions leaving the paintings with Cahill who hid them in the bunker further up the mountains.

Cahill had worked very fast that night. At 3.15 am – an hour and a quarter after the alarm had been activated at Russborough House – he was stopped by uniformed Gardaí on Terenure Road East on his way home from the mountains. When the Gardaí tried to search him Cahill began peeling off his clothes and shouting at the top of his voice, 'I'm being harassed by the police ... I don't want to talk to youse ...' Later he walked into nearby Rathmines Station and made allegations of ill-treatment against the officers on the checkpoint. It was the perfect alibi. In the years up to his untimely end, whenever Cahill walked into Rathmines Garda Station the alarm was raised to expect a serious crime – with his *modus operandi* written all over it.

The alarm was not raised until just before nine in the morning, more than five hours after Cahill's visit to the police station. The planning and precision of the job immediately led Gardaí to believe that a highly-organised gang of international art thieves was responsible. There was even speculation within the first days that the gang had flown out in a light aircraft. On Friday morning Cahill did something unusual – he bought all the papers to read about his second master stroke. He enjoyed reading the media speculation about who was involved.

In an interview, Sir Alfred, who was in London when he heard about the robbery, blamed paramilitaries for the theft. 'I cannot think other than that one of these sort of revolutionary movements are behind the theft and they are seeking a ransom which they won't get. It is not me that has been robbed this time – it is the Irish people, since the collection is now in trust for the state,' he said. But Martin Cahill was no revolutionary, he was firmly apolitical.

Reading that quote alone made the whole risky business worth-while as far as the General was concerned. Sir Alfred wasn't the only one upset. Paddy Shanahan was incensed that he had been duped by Cahill. The General calmed him down by agreeing to give him a cut of the action – Shanahan was to seek buyers for the haul.

The newspaper coverage of the robbery described a gang of

sophisticated art connoisseurs who had probably already placed the paintings in a special storage facility somewhere on the Continent. Art lovers convinced themselves that the paintings would at least be looked after. In fact, the way Cahill was treating the paintings would have been enough to bring tears to the eye of a professional art thief. Reading the reports he expressed a doubt to his associates that the bunker might be the most suitable resting place for the 'paintin's'. Some days after the robbery Cahill and an associate took a trip up to the mountains.

By the time they got to the bunker it was already dark. Under the dense tree cover it was impossible to see without the aid of a torch. Cahill reached into the hiding place and dragged up one of the priceless pictures. He sat on his backside to cherish his treasure. He told his associate to shine a light on it. Inside the frame, where the picture should have been, was completely blank. Cahill looked closer and frowned. 'Someone's whipped the fuckin' paintin'. Now what fucker would do that?' he asked the associate as he got into the kind of temper that might give a double-dealer fears for his well-being.

The associate looked closer. A crusty coat of powdery efflorescence caused by the dampness in the bunker covered the canvas. Cahill, still frowning, looked suspiciously at his associate. He looked back at the white canvas on his lap and gave it a rough wipe with the sleeve of his denim jacket, uncovering part of the picture again. 'Ah Jaysus, there it is,' he exclaimed with a big smile like a child who has found a bag of sweets. The associate was also relieved. As one of the three people, including Cahill, who knew where the stash was hidden, he could have found himself facing one of the General's absurd courts-martial had the picture been stolen.

The two men pulled the rest of the paintings out of the hole and began removing their frames and wrapping the canvasses in plastic sheeting. At one stage, while the collection was lying on the mossy earth, Cahill accidentally stepped backwards and put his foot through a painting. 'Help me get this fuckin' thing off,' he snarled at his associate, holding up his foot which had a £1 million picture dangling from it. When they had finished, Cahill and his associate put most of the pictures back in the bunker and moved a number of smaller ones to a safe house in Dublin.

Cahill then began planning how to turn his haul into hard cash. The first difficulty came within a week when detectives in Dublin, working on intelligence reports, targeted Cahill and his gang. He cautioned his people that they must lie low and allow him take care of the negotiations to off-load the paintings. 'Everyone who comes with an offer to buy the paintings could be a cop and ya must never forget that,' he instructed them.

Art historian Dr James White, the former director of the National Gallery of Ireland and trustee of the Beit Foundation, offered a reward of £50,000 for information leading to the recovery of the paintings. But Cahill and his mobsters had little interest in what they considered a derisory offer. From the outset they had aimed at making millions out of the haul. Contact was made with a Drogheda-based fence who had well-established links with paramilitary and criminal gangs on both sides of the border. A week after the robbery the fence flew to Paris to discuss a possible deal with an Irish paramilitary. This came to nothing.

Cahill used intermediaries to make a number of early ransom demands. On one occasion, within a few months of the robbery, the Gardaí were led on a wild goose chase by Cahill. He tested the waters by making a ransom demand for £100,000 in cash which was to be left in a tar barrel on the Kilcullen Road, Co Kildare. Gardaí launched a major operation but failed to get any details of the gang which picked up the 'ransom money' – a bunch of old papers. Next Cahill tried the 'security company' approach. He sent Noel Lynch to visit Dr White, purporting to be a private investigator. Lynch talked about 'helping' White in private investigation and about the huge sums of money being offered to the gang for the paintings. Dr White refused to have any dealings with him.

Garda chiefs in Dublin decided that the only way to trap Cahill and the paintings was to set up a sting operation. They knew how slippery Cahill was and that the sting would need to be credible. In July 1986, two months after the robbery, Operation Moonshine was launched jointly by Gardaí – from the undercover surveillance squad of the Serious Crime Squad led by Detective Inspector Gerry McCarrick – and Scotland Yard to trap the gang. An experienced detective with a flair for secret surveillance, McCarrick had formed a unit in 1982 to help smash the Dunne family's grip on the heroin market and had been very successful. English officers, posing as London art crooks, made contact with the Drogheda fence with a view to buying the paintings. He had put the word out through the British underworld that the Beit paintings were for sale. Over two days a series of meetings was organised in Jury's and Bloom's hotels in Dublin between the interested parties. The Drogheda fence had made efforts to get the paintings from Cahill to show to the Scotland Yard men. At the last minute Cahill decided that something was amiss and refused to hand over the pictures. In January 1987 officers from the Crime Branch in Garda Headquarters in Dublin flew to America to meet with FBI chiefs in Washington. The plan was to put forward two Federal agents posing as wealthy US art dealers anxious to buy the stolen treasures. The operation failed to get off the ground.

The Beit story continued to unfold on the international stage, this time moving to Holland, the home of organised crime in Europe. Irish criminals have extensive contacts in Holland through their dealings with the main cannabis and heroin smugglers based in Amsterdam and Rotterdam. Every major criminal in Holland knew about Cahill's master stroke. In July 1987, a big-time criminal called Paul Wilking had a meeting with representatives of the Cahill gang in London. A flamboyant and obese arms dealer, Wilking was known as 'Pistol Paul' and had been a bit-part movie actor.

Pistol Paul also had a love of art – stolen art. He had been prepared to pay three million Dutch guilders or £1 million for the Beit collection. In July Wilking travelled to Dublin with the money. He was closely monitored by Dutch and Irish police. But after a long delay a member of the gang returned to him with an apology, saying that they were unable to get the paintings because the 'man looking after the paintings was on holiday'. But no-one was on holiday. Martin Cahill's survival instinct had told him to back off.

Six months before Pistol Paul's wild goose chase the first serious attempt to catch the General and the paintings was also being mooted in the Dutch town of Arnheim. Kees Van Scoaik, a fraudster, met an associate of the General to discuss a possible deal. The associate was a major player in the Irish underworld and had been involved in armed robbery, fraudulent compensation and protection rackets. He was paid £10,000 by Van Scoaik for the stolen Francesco Guardi painting 'View of Grand Canal, Venice'. After handing over the cash Van Scoaik found the painting in the boot of a car in Dublin. Later it was claimed that the money for the purchase had been put up by the Gardaí, but they flatly denied the claim.

Months passed without any developments. Meanwhile Van Scoaik had problems of his own with the Dutch police and agreed to take part in a major sting operation to snare Cahill. For his part the Dutch gangster was to receive £50,000 from the Gardaí. Several meetings took place between Van Scoaik and members of Cahill's gang.

Already hungry for the pay-off the gang members were putting pressure on Cahill to do a deal. At last he was taking the bait. Early in August, Deputy Garda Commissioner John Paul McMahon travelled to Holland where he met Van Scoaik and senior Dutch police officials. Van Scoaik arrived at the meeting and produced the Guardi painting from a folded newspaper to show the Irish policeman.

McMahon set in train an international operation involving Van Scoaik, his Dutch police handlers, Interpol and the Gardaí. When he returned to Dublin, McMahon organised a special unit for the sting. One of the features of the operation was the strict secrecy. In fact, it was so hush-hush that only detectives from the Special Detective Unit (Special Branch) and the Crime Branch of Garda HQ were to know about it. The Serious Crime Squad who were investigating the robbery were not informed. An office was set up in the Technical Bureau at the Phoenix Park HQ a week before the undercover operation was to take place on Tuesday, 29 September.

The plan was that Van Scoaik would meet with Cahill and produce £100,000 in 'show money' to satisfy him that the cash was there to do the deal. The asking price was £1 million for the four pictures. If both parties were happy, the deal was to be finalised by Tuesday, 29 September. But the squad did not know where or how the deal and the handover would take place – unpredictability was one of the General's characteristics. It was suspected that the most likely venue would be the Dublin mountains.

A surveillance squad from the Special Detective Unit (SDU) was put on standby. A specially-equipped plane borrowed from Scotland Yard and fitted with sensitive tracking equipment would follow the 'art expert' to the rendezvous. The plane would stay in constant contact with the surveillance team on the ground. The SDU team would alert a squad of thirty heavily-armed detectives, which would swoop at the crucial moment, arresting the General's gang and recovering the paintings.

On Thursday, 24 September, 1987, Van Scoaik, accompanied by two Arnheim police officers, arrived in Dublin. A surveillance team was to watch the Dutch criminal's every move. He checked into Room 722 in Jury's Hotel in Ballsbridge. Unknown to Van Scoaik the room was being bugged by an SDU team who had planted hidden cameras and microphones there in case the meeting with Cahill took place in the hotel.

Van Scoaik was given £2,000 pocket money. He received a call that he was to meet a member of the gang later that day. It was arranged that he would meet Cahill the next afternoon. All the time he was being monitored by Gardaí. So far everything was going according to plan and the slipperiest gangster in Ireland was sniffing around the door of the trap. Cahill and the criminal were to discuss the show money. Cahill never showed.

Unknown to the General events in Garda HQ were inadvertently working in his favour. For just as the situation was beginning to look hopeful for the police, the operation hit its first snag. John Paul McMahon and the Garda Commissioner at the time, Larry Wren, had a late-night meeting at the Department of Justice. They requested the £100,000 show money which included a £50,000 payment to Van Scoaik. The government flatly refused to give the money on the grounds that it could not risk the embarrassment if Cahill got his hands on the cash and slipped the net. The officers were devastated. The Dutch police and Interpol were furious at such a lack of support.

With no show money the Garda operation was a non-starter and their adversary would again give them the two fingers. A member of the investigation team contacted a bank manager who gave him a lodgement slip which Van Scoaik could show Cahill as evidence that he had cash with him for the deal. The plan now had to be radically overhauled and brought forward to the weekend. The pictures would have to be viewed on Sunday instead of Monday when the banks were closed, otherwise Cahill would demand to see the show money. But there were other cash flow problems.

By Saturday morning, 26 September, the Dutchman had blown his pocket money. He had swilled champagne in the clubs and pubs around the city since his arrival. That morning, Van Scoaik got a call at his hotel to meet with the General and his men at the Four Roads pub in Crumlin. At one stage he threatened to pull out of the meeting unless he got more pocket money. A detective visited a friendly publican who lent him £1,000. The Dutch police, already flabbergasted at the official reluctance to produce show money, could not believe that their colleagues were being forced to take such steps to keep an operation alive.

That afternoon Van Scoaik arrived at the Four Roads pub around four o'clock. Waiting for him was a grinning Martin Cahill with three of his gang – Noel Lynch, Shavo Hogan and Eamon Daly. Twenty-nine year-old Daly from Crumlin was one of Cahill's cherished protégés. The adopted son of a school teacher, he was unlike the rest of his colleagues in crime in that he came from a moderately well-off background with plenty of opportunities. He was first arrested at the age of thirteen for house-breaking. Gardaí were astounded when he appeared in a Children's Court represented by a junior counsel paid for by his father. But despite efforts to reform him, Daly went on to earn himself a formidable reputation as an armed robber and as one of Cahill's most respected lieutenants.

Lynch stood outside the pub co-ordinating an elaborate counter-surveillance operation to see if the Dutch criminal had been followed. Women pushing prams and men walking their dogs in the park across the road were part of the operation. As it happened the criminal *was* being followed by a surveillance team from the SDU who were actually inside and outside the pub eavesdropping and taking photographs of everyone who entered or left the premises. They were not spotted by the eagle-eyed 'private eye' Lynch or his lookouts.

Inside, the gregarious Dutchman ordered a round of drinks. When Cahill asked about the show money Van Scoaik produced the lodgement slip, explaining that he had put the money in the bank for safe keeping when Cahill had failed to turn up on Friday. He also informed the General that his 'art expert' had to fly back to Paris on the Monday and therefore he would have to view the paintings the next day, Sunday. Cahill was suspicious of Van Scoaik, who seemed nervous, but accepted the explanation and said he would arrange a meeting later that evening along the Grand Canal to discuss the final arrangements. A few hours later, Cahill met Van Scoaik near Portobello Bridge in Rathmines. The General informed Van Scoaik that his 'art expert' would be picked up at the Burlington Hotel at one o'clock the following day and taken to view some of the paintings. The deal would now be finalised on Monday instead of Tuesday. Cahill also said that, depending on the weather, the viewing would take place outdoors.

At noon the following day the team of detectives received their final instructions in Garda HQ. On Friday they had been introduced to the Interpol agent who was checked in under a false name in the Burlington. The surveillance teams from the SDU would tail Hogan and the Interpol man. The thirty-strong snatch squad would stay a safe distance behind until the order was given to move in. They would remain in constant touch with the surveillance plane one mile up in the sky and, to avoid being picked up on a scanner, would not use the normal police frequencies. At exactly one o'clock Shavo Hogan, wearing a false beard, arrived in his red Ford Escort to collect the Interpol agent from the Burlington. The car was followed. The operation was on.

Hogan spent over an hour driving around the southside of the city and county in a bid to lose a possible tail. Just as on Saturday the surveillance people were not spotted. He drove out to Dun Laoghaire and across to Shankill where he finally made his ascent into the mountains. In the meantime the back-up squad went to a staging point at Brigid Burke's pub at Firhouse in the foothills of the Dublin mountains. It was now after half past two in the afternoon. The 'surveillance team and the snatch squad were beginning to experience difficulties with their radio equipment.

Meanwhile the Ford Escort was arriving at a spot three miles away from the massed Garda force at Kilakee Wood. The 'art expert' was met at the edge of the forest by Cahill and Eamon Daly. The SDU surveillance unit saw them disappearing into the trees. They continued frantically trying to make contact with the support teams now sitting outside Brigid Burke's. Four of the Beit paintings were produced for the 'art expert's' inspection. They had been removed from their frames.

The Interpol man had a special torch which he used to flash signals to the surveillance plane above. The 'art expert' exclaimed very loudly, 'They are the real thing, the real thing!' Already suspicious, Cahill's extraordinary survival instinct took over. The deal was off. He and Daly hurriedly packed the paintings into the back of a car and drove off. Hogan pushed the Interpol man into the car and headed out of the mountains towards Shankill, followed by the surveillance unit which at this stage had no idea what was going on.

At the crucial moment when the back-up teams should have been surrounding the General, a detective was calling the operation control room at Garda HQ on the pub phone. He was told that the gang were 'in a wood a half mile above Brigid Burke's'. Unfortunately for the detective who made the call, everywhere for a half mile and further up the mountains from the pub was forest. Where were they to go?

Simultaneously, Cahill and Daly drove towards Tallaght and Brigid Burke's pub. 'Take it nice and easy,' Cahill cautioned as they suddenly found themselves driving through a large force of detectives and squad cars parked along the side of the road. However, in the confusion, none of the waiting cops noticed Cahill – they were trying to find out what was going on.

They drove slowly past. 'We're all right. They must be lookin' for the IRA or somethin'. I thought we were nicked there,' said Cahill. Half an hour later the four precious Beit paintings were being concealed in the attic wall of a house in Tallaght.

Minutes after Cahill and Daly drove past Brigid Burke's, the force moved off and converged on the spot where Cahill had taken the bait. They found nothing. There was despair and anger all round. In the following days an intensive search of the area was carried out by Gardaí. Nothing was found except the body of a criminal who had been missing from Crumlin since he was caught having an affair with another hood's girlfriend. It was the nearest the Gardaí would ever come to enticing the General into the open.

As Hogan passed Shankill with the Interpol man he was stopped outside the Silver Tassie pub and arrested under the Offences Against The State Act. After being held for forty-eight hours he was released without charge. The Interpol man had not formally identified the picture. There was no evidence that a crime had been committed. The whole debacle was a dreadful blow to Garda morale and during the post mortem there were bitter recriminations.

Both Interpol and the Dutch police expressed their anger at the way Operation Kilakee had been executed. Interpol was especially annoyed and claimed that the life of their agent had been at risk. The Serious Crime Squad boss Chief Superintendent John Murphy was also furious about the operation. The investigation was the responsibility of his men and they knew Cahill and his gang better than specialist units from the anti-terrorist SDU or the Park. Indeed Cahill was to tell *Magill* journalist Michael O'Higgins a year later that he would have been caught had it been the Serious Crime Squad on his tail.

There were other reasons for criticism. The local Garda commander in the Tallaght M district, Superintendent Bill McMunn, was called by his station around lunchtime on the Sunday afternoon and told of the Garda activity around Brigid Burke's. An aircraft had also been seen circling the area and the local units did not know what was going on. But McMunn had not been informed either. When he arrived, he was told that the squad's radio equipment had not worked. McMunn could have told them that radio blackspots were a regular operational headache for squad cars in the M District. The Superintendent had recently called out communications experts from Garda HQ and they had identified the black spots.

When Martin Cahill discovered how narrowly he had escaped a cosy one-bed cell in Portlaoise Prison, he was ecstatic with relief. Inadvertently he had humiliated the police at the very top. It did not seem to register that the more he irritated the system, the more likely it was to come down on him with all its force. Never again, he swore, would he walk into a trap like the one which had exposed him on a mountainside. The gang, anxious for the pay-off, now listened to the General when he advised extreme caution. He vetoed a suggestion by members of the gang to take a painting, or a share in a painting each, and try to sell them individually.

For now he was going to enjoy his triumph. Every day Cahill drove from his home past the permanent Garda security post outside the house of former premier Garret FitzGerald. Normally he held his hand over his face or wore a balaclava. In the days after the debacle in the mountains, however, Cahill would stop on the road and smile at the cops inside. On occasions when he was stopped at checkpoints he would actually refer to the mistakes made in Operation Kilakee. A week after the incident he told a detective from behind the hand covering his face: 'Youse made a mistake. Youse brought the wrong Gardaí. Youse had a right to bring the Rathmines Gardaí.'

Cahill's luck and the Gardaí's lack of it had contributed to another victory for the godfather of Irish crime – and an almost intolerable defeat for the forces of law and order. The saga of the Beit paintings was far from over. For the moment circumstances would force the General to suspend his efforts to sell off the paintings. But his outwitting of the Garda trap at Kilakee had made him cocky to the point of recklessness.

The General was now attracting the attention of the media and was beginning to believe he was invincible after slipping the police net. He had smashed holes in the morale of the Force. The ordinary cop on the beat was angry that such an apparently insignificant criminal was making fools of them. But what Cahill didn't realise was that the police were learning the 'game' from him. Slowly they were beginning to regroup and prepare for a new offensive against their hated enemy. The cops would soon be fighting back on his terms.

CHAPTER 8

The Untouchables

The fiasco in the Dublin mountains could not have come at a worse time for a police force already struggling to curtail an increasingly sophisticated organised crime network. In 1987 there were almost six hundred armed robberies in Ireland – five hundred of which were in Dublin – with only one hundred solved. There had also been the startling discovery that the IRA had smuggled enough weapons into Ireland to equip an army. And a paramilitary renegade, Dessie O'Hare, created havoc for over a month when he kidnapped a Dublin dentist.

But it was the General's obsession with fighting the law which earned him the top position on the Gardaí's most wanted list. No criminal in the history of Irish crime had gone to such lengths to bring the fight to the state. Exhilarated by his lucky escape and two of the biggest robberies in the history of the state, Martin Cahill and his gangsters saw themselves – and were seen by others – as the untouchables of the Dublin underworld.

His gang were by far the most active in the country, robbing with apparent impunity, sometimes at the rate of three or more big heists a week. Terror, threats and kidnapping were the trademarks of the General's gang. In the long dark winter nights, Cahill's favourite time of the year, the typical jobs were 'tie-ups' in which the wealthy occupants of large houses around the country were tied up while the gang made off with cash and valuables.

His old adversaries in the Gardaí had tried every trick in the book to catch Cahill but failed. It was impossible to get information from inside the gang, for there was tremendous loyalty among the General's men – something unusual in large criminal groups – and the possibility of planting an informant was practically non-existent. In addition, Cahill was such an unpredictable, secretive character that traditional methods were useless. In the aftermath of Operation Kilakee there was increasing dissension and anger among the rank-and-file Gardaí in Dublin, especially in the divisions on the southside of the Liffey, Cahill's stomping ground. The Gardaí wondered why new, more imaginative tactics were not being employed to turn the joke on the crime boss. They needed a victory very badly and Cahill was pushing them to the limits of their endurance.

Three weeks before Operation Kilakee, in August 1987, the General dealt an even more humiliating blow to his foes. He broke into the offices of the Director of Public Prosecutions (DPP) and stole files and books of evidence pertaining to some of the state's most sensitive criminal cases. It was the ultimate act of effrontery.

The DPP is the state's chief prosecutor and decides on what criminal cases should be brought before the courts. The Gardaí, who act as agents of the state, submit detailed background reports and recommendations about indictable crimes for the DPP's consideration on whether there is a case to answer. From these reports books of evidence are compiled which contain the case against the accused. Some of the Garda files sent to the DPP contain background information which is never disclosed in court. The identities of informants and such matters are not included in such files and are known only to the officer involved directly in the case.

In the years after this burglary Cahill claimed to associates that he had been breaking into the DPP's offices on Saturday nights for the previous two years without being detected. When he told them this he did so matter-of-factly and his associates say they had no reason to disbelieve him. The General claimed that he let himself into the offices with a stolen key. The office security system was such that Cahill had little difficulty getting around. He claimed that he would go in late on a Saturday night and actually read files while sitting in the chair of the Director of Public Prosecutions himself.

There is, however, no proof of Cahill's nocturnal visits to the DPP's offices, although it was certainly not beyond him. The General was primarily a very capable creeper or burglar and worked mostly alone. No-one, not even his closest family, knew what he got up to on his nightly forays. But whether or not he had ever been in the offices before became unimportant when he carried out the audacious burglary in August 1987. Two incidents were to precipitate this provocative crime.

The first was an unexpected sequel to the O'Connor's robbery of 1983. On the afternoon of Friday, 15 January, 1987, Eileen Egan, the wife of Michael Egan who had assisted the robbery gang, walked into Sundrive Road Garda Station and asked to see Detective Sergeant Gerry O'Carroll. O'Carroll, a gregarious but uncompromising policeman, had pursued Martin Cahill and his underworld associates since he joined the force in 1967. A burly Kerryman, he first met the General when Cahill was still a petty thief living in the slums of Hollyfield Buildings. O'Carroll had been a member of Ned Ryan's tough, controversial team of detectives which began tailing Cahill after the Semperit factory robbery in 1977. He was also one of the men who arrested the General following the bomb attack on Dr James Donovan. Once described by a judge as one of the country's most distinguished detectives, O'Carroll was also a member of the Murder Squad and played a key role in the investigation of dozens of the state's most serious criminal and terrorist outrages during the seventies and eighties.

When Eileen Egan blurted out her husband's involvement with the Cahill gang, O'Carroll could not believe his ears. It was the first chink in the wall of silence which had surrounded the country's biggest jewellery robbery. Over the next few hours she gave the detective a detailed account of the events in her home after the jewellery robbery, including the role played by her husband. She said that she could no longer live with the tension her husband's association with the gang had caused. The tension had split up their marriage and they were involved in a particularly acrimonious separation.

When he had listened intently to her story, O'Carroll phoned his boss, Detective Inspector Michael Cannavan, another one of Cahill's hated enemies. Cannavan and O'Carroll had worked together for many years. Cannavan was considered to be a thorough investigator and had been one of the youngest detectives ever appointed in the Dublin Metropolitan Area. He had investigated over 170 murders around the country, most of which were solved. He first had a confrontation with Martin Cahill when he went to arrest Anthony Cahill after the murder of John Copeland in 1975. He and O'Carroll also played crucial roles in bringing two Englishmen, John Shaw and Geoffrey Evans, to justice in 1976 for the murder of two women.

Both men, who were now stationed in the Crumlin G District, took an immediate interest in the O'Connor's case and arrested Egan in the hope that through him they would find a chink in the General's armour. In a statement of confession Egan said that he had been too scared to object to the gang using his lock-up garage after the O'Connor's heist. He revealed that he was robbed of his share of the proceeds by one of Cahill's associates and that he got only £5,000. 'I have ended up with no financial gain of any kind from this incident. All I have had from this is trouble and threats,' he told detectives.

When Cahill got word of Egan's arrest and learned that Egan had been ripped off in his share of the loot he was furious. All it took was one disgruntled criminal facing a jail term to spill the entire can of beans. Cahill was firm when it came to the share-out – everyone, even the look-outs on a job, got an equal share. Now the greed of one of his people was jeopardising the whole gang.

Cahill also suspected that the same gang member had conned him out of his fifty percent share of a business transaction. This later transpired to be untrue. On the night of 26 March, he went looking for the suspect. Cahill had a gun and intended using it but fortunately for the associate he had skipped town.

The file pertaining to Egan's case was forwarded from Sundrive Road Garda Station to the DPP's office in March. The O'Connor's file was now a source of intense interest to Cahill. But there was an even more pressing reason for the eventual burglary.

On 14 December, 1986, Martin's younger brother, Paddy, died from stab wounds in Ballyfermot. The twenty-nine year-old single man suffered knife wounds in the chest and upper body following a row that he had started with a neighbour, Anthony Quinn. Paddy

Cahill had been a paraplegic since falling off a motorbike during a getaway from a robbery in the early eighties. He got around with the aid of crutches and despite his handicap was a notorious burglar in the Ballyfermot area. He was also a drug abuser and a major thorn in the side of the local community and the police. Paddy Cahill had been having an ongoing row with the Quinns who lived in Raheen Park, a large working-class estate. Quinn, a petty criminal, was the oldest of four children born in London. The family returned to live in Dublin in 1974.

On 2 September, 1986, Anthony Quinn's father, Shay, was stabbed in the back at the family home. Paddy Cahill and a friend, Alan Doran, were taken in for questioning in relation to the offence and a file was sent to the DPP's office for a decision on whether to prosecute them. Subsequently Shay Quinn was unable to identify his attackers and charges were withdrawn. Since then there had been a number of violent altercations between the Quinns and Cahill.

On the night of 14 December, 1986, Paddy Cahill arrived outside the Quinns' house and began shouting 'Youse bastards!' There was a fight in the front garden of the house between Anthony Quinn and Cahill, resulting in the death of the General's brother. That night, he was found lying on his back on the lawn of the Quinns' home with his crutches across his chest. Later, the man heading the investigation, Detective Inspector John McLoughlin, asked the family to identify the body. They refused. It was one of those bizarre traits which Martin instilled in the rest of the family. He had done the same in 1983 when his brother Anthony died in prison. Helping the police in any way, even by identifying the corpse of a murdered brother, was strictly prohibited.

Quinn was arrested at the home of a girlfriend after a four-day manhunt. Over the next six months, while his trial was pending, the local Gardaí braced themselves for a backlash against the Quinn family from the General. It never came. Martin Cahill, although deeply upset by the death of his brother, did not allow retribution. In a way Paddy had been the author of his own destiny and, furthermore, the cops were expecting him to retaliate. Cahill always did the opposite to what they expected.

In July 1987 Anthony Quinn stood trial in the Central Criminal Court on a charge of murder. During a four-day trial, Quinn testified that he had killed Cahill in self-defence and because he feared his father would be attacked again by the General's brother. At the end of the hearing, the jury unanimously acquitted him of the charge and he was freed. But far from celebrating, Quinn and his family rushed home and packed their belongings. That night they took the ferry to England and went back to live in London where they felt safer. Within twenty-four hours of the acquittal the Quinns' home was burned to the ground.

Martin Cahill was a world-class conspiracy theorist. In fact, both his associates and the police considered him paranoid to the point of being insane. For a number of years after he robbed the Beit paintings he lived in fear that the South African secret service, BOSS, would assassinate him simply because the Beit family was South African. Cahill wrongly believed Quinn's acquittal was the product of a conspiracy between the police and the DPP. He imagined it was another attempt to get at him. So he decided to get at them.

On the night of Saturday, 29 August, a Garda patrol car spotted Martin Cahill and a member of his gang sitting in a car opposite the four-storey Georgian building that houses the DPP's office on St Stephen's Green. The sighting, like all the others of Cahill, was logged with the criminal intelligence section. The officers were not to know that a few hours later Cahill and his gang would be rummaging through the most important law office in the country.

Cahill had little difficulty getting around the security arrangements at the DPP's office. Some of his associates later claimed that the General had studied the security system during his regular night-time visits. The gang gained access to the building from the back. They knew exactly what was alarmed and what was not. They climbed over the back wall and into the rear yard which was not alarmed. Cahill knew that the back door was alarmed. His men merely cut out a panel in the door and crawled through. They ran up the four flights of stairs to the DPP's floor at the top of the building. The door to the offices was locked. Despite his later claims to have had a key, Cahill drilled through the door, perhaps as a deliberate challenge to the Gardaí, and walked in.

The files and legal documents were stored in a rooftop penthouse above the DPP's office. Cahill and his men drilled through two more doors and found themselves in the midst of criminal files from all over Ireland. The files, which were numbered, were kept on open shelving. But Cahill was able to put his hands on the reference books and took his time selecting the ones he wanted. Among the files he looked for were those pertaining to the O'Connor's case against Michael Egan and the murder of his brother, Paddy. Also taken were important files on major armed robberies, assault and drug cases. Included in the files were documents on a number of Garda corruption cases and the file on the controversial death in 1986 of wealthy midland priest, Fr Niall Molloy. Officially, 145 files were stated to have been taken, but some underworld sources have since claimed the number was over three hundred. When they were finished Cahill's gang defecated on the floor of the office.

Cahill and his team left the way they had come in. The files were hidden in a back lane and the team dispersed. The following night when Cahill came back to retrieve his haul he found that a homeless wino had uncovered them while looking for shelter for the night. He gave the tramp £20 and thanked him for looking after the stuff for him. Four years later when Cahill moved into the hot-dog business one of his regular free customers was the same tramp. The files from the DPP's office were to become currency in the underworld where criminals hoped they could be traded in return for the dropping or the reduction of charges against them. Some of the files were considered so valuable that a value of £100,000 was being put on them by members of Cahill's gang in April 1995.

When the burglary was discovered there was consternation and extreme embarrassment in the Department of Justice and among the Gardaí. Very soon, information started coming back that the General had been behind it. In fact, Cahill, who had the files well-hidden, wanted the DPP to know that he had the files and ensured that the word filtered back. It was to give added impetus to the Beit sting operation, by now in its final stages. When Operation Kilakee failed the embarrassment for the Gardaí was almost too much to bear.

In the weeks that followed the sting Cahill began to lose his cherished anonymity. On 10 October, 1987, the *Sunday World* was the first newspaper in Ireland to expose the life and crimes of Martin Cahill and his gang. This led to other newspaper articles. The Irish public began to develop an interest in the elusive General

In early November a new Garda Commissioner, Eamonn Doherty, was appointed. He called a meeting of all divisional commanders in the Dublin Metropolitan Area and ordered that each detective unit in the city draw up a detailed intelligence list on the personalities involved in organised crime. In the meantime the new Garda boss was receiving a baptism of fire.

Renegade INLA man Dessie O'Hare had kidnapped Dublin dentist John O'Grady. During the kidnap drama, O'Hare spent four weeks running riot around Ireland. There were a number of shooting incidents as the gang and the Gardaí engaged in a Keystone Cops chase across the country. In a particularly brutal episode O'Hare chopped off one of the dentist's fingers and left it in a church for an intermediary to find. A detective was shot at point-blank range and almost died. Eventually the police rounded up the gang and rescued O'Grady. O'Hare himself was captured after an ambush in Co Kilkenny when Irish soldiers opened fire on a car in which he was a passenger. The stolen BMW was riddled in a hail of high velocity bullets which killed the driver of the car outright. Amazingly, the INLA renegade, although seriously injured, survived.

No sooner had the kidnap drama ended than French police intercepted the gun-running ship, the *Eksund*, with a huge cargo of arms and equipment – a present from Colonel Gadaffi of Libya, destined for the IRA. Dublin-man Adrian Hopkins, was the skipper of the ship. The government was rocked by the discovery. A national emergency was called in November and almost 8,000 troops and police searched 50,000 properties throughout the Republic. Operation Mallard did not uncover any substantial haul of weapons except for two empty underground bunkers. The crisis had, for a time at least, deferred the state's showdown with the General.

While the crisis continued, Cahill and his gang went on with their armed robbery activities. In fact, they had become so business-like that they held weekly meetings to discuss future jobs. On 1 December, 1987, however, they pushed things too far. The previous evening, 31 November, armed and masked men burst into a house in Inchicore on the west side of the city. Anne Gallagher, the postmistress at Kilnamanagh post office, lived in the house. She and her landlady, Nellie Whelan, were taken to a house in Tallaght, where gunmen had also taken the householder, Myles Crofton, and his family hostage.

The next morning Anne Gallagher, Myles Crofton and his eighteen-month-old daughter were ordered to go to the post office and withdraw stamps and cash worth £30,000. Cahill's men attached a radio-controlled bomb to Crofton's chest. The money was duly handed over and the hostages released unharmed. The crime was a replica of another post office robbery exactly two years earlier at Killinardin in Tallaght.

On 3 December, 1985, armed men had burst into the homes of Killinardin post mistress, Anne Whelan, and her neighbours, Brian and Linda Comerford. The gang held the families, which included six small children, hostage. At half-past five in the morning, Cahill's men bundled the terrified children and other hostages – except Mrs Whelan – into a van and brought them to a derelict house on Leinster Road in Rathmines where they were tied and gagged. Anne Whelan was instructed to go to the Killinardin post office and take £83,000 in cash which was on the premises for social welfare payments. 'We want the money and if you don't carry out the instructions two of the children will be shot so the next time they know we mean it,' she was told. The post mistress later handed over the money near the Embankment on the Saggart Road outside Tallaght.

Within two weeks detectives had traced some of the cash from the raid to the home of a member of the Manchester mob, the Quality Street Gang. Manchester police had found a hidden biscuit tin full of cash from the Tallaght robbery in a house search while investigating the attempted murder of a police officer. The house-owner and gang member had served time with Cahill's friend, Noel Lynch, in an English jail.

Gardaí also discovered that members of the Quality Street Gang had exchanged some of the proceeds from the O'Connor's robbery for drugs. And one of the gang had flown to Ireland in early 1987 to bid for the Beit paintings. In fact, the General had regularly sent cash from robberies in Ireland with a trusted courier to a member of the Manchester gang who placed it in a safety deposit box in St James's Building on Oxford Street in the city centre. Cahill, using the name Brian Ferguson, would then travel to England by ferry, change the Irish money into English currency and bring it home again.

The Kilnamanagh raid was the last straw for Detective Superintendent Ned Ryan, who had warned his superiors thirteen years earlier that one day Cahill would be a major criminal. Intelligence had known that Cahill was planning another job in the Tallaght area but not when or where it would take place. Now he had pulled another terrifying robbery right under their noses. The Donovan bombing, O'Connor's, the Beit paintings and the DPP files had fulfilled Ryan's prediction. He was furious at the apparent free hand Cahill had to commit serious crime. Members of Cahill's organisation had also threatened one of Ryan's young detectives when he began investigating the activities of the General's associates in Crumlin. They had visited the policeman's home and told him they were going to shoot him and his family. They knew the times his wife picked the kids up from school and even knew their names.

By the time of the Tallaght robbery, however, Ryan had no difficulty convincing the Garda hierarchy that urgent action was needed. When Ryan's boss, Chief Superintendent John Hughes, called Garda Commissioner Eamonn Doherty at Garda HQ in the Park he found an open door. A meeting was called for the next morning, 2 December, 1987, at the Commissioner's office. Present were the chief superintendents commanding the five divisions in the DMA and Detective Chief Superintendent John Murphy of the city's Central Detective Unit (CDU) which incorporates the Serious Crime,

Drug and Fraud squads. They reviewed the intelligence reports Doherty had ordered. It was clear that the organisation causing the most trouble was Cahill's.

Doherty sat back in his chair, looked around at the assembled brass and asked the question that was to change the General's life: 'What are we going to do about this man Cahill?' Chief Murphy was first to reply. He said if he and his detectives were given the resources they could put Cahill out of business within six months. Surveillance, it was agreed, was the most effective tactic. But they disagreed on whether this should be undercover or open. Murphy argued that the most effective method was to put long-term undercover surveillance on Cahill. Murphy had been a city cop for thirty years and had known many of the big league criminals since they were kids picking pockets and stealing sweets. Eventually it was agreed to devise a method of open close-up surveillance designed to harass and antagonise the target as much as possible. Scotland Yard had used similar tactics against the Krays in London in the late sixties. They sat on Ron and Reggie for two years until an informer came forward and helped to put the brothers behind bars. A second meeting was scheduled for Friday, 4 December, at Harcourt Square, the headquarters of the DMA.

At the outset, no-one in the Garda top circle knew exactly what the overt surveillance or targeting operation was supposed to achieve. In the seventies Ned Ryan and his detectives in the CDU had used similar tactics against Martin Cahill. But the operations were sporadic and the Troubles in the North had swallowed up resources needed in the fight against ordinary crime. This time the plan was to form a large group of detectives to watch and follow their targets for twenty-four hours a day indefinitely. Many in the police still argue that it was a waste of time, money and manpower.

There was also a political motive for a highly visible operation. At least the police would be seen to be doing something about the General the public had been reading so much about in the papers. And – playing the game Cahill's way – it was the last thing in the world he expected them to do.

At the second meeting each of the five divisional commanders was asked to produce around fifteen officers to augment a surveillance squad from Chief Superintendent Murphy's CDU. Those selected were to be young, hard-nosed officers, most of whom had been in uniform for as little as a year. None of them had experience in surveillance. All they had was energy and enthusiasm.

On Monday morning, 7 December, ninety policemen and women gathered in the conference hall on the third floor of Block One at Harcourt Square. Detective Chief Superintendent Murphy addressed the crowd of fresh-faced cops and gave them a rough idea – for that is all the plan was – of what the overt operation was supposed to achieve. Detective Chief Superintendent Murphy was in overall control of the operation along with his deputy, Detective Superintendent Noel Conroy.

The new squad was to be called the Special Surveillance Unit (SSU). It would be divided into four teams. Each team was headed by an experienced detective sergeant from CDU – Felix McKenna, Noel Keane, Martin Callinan and Denis Donegan. The targets were Martin Cahill and six of his closest associates, Eamon Daly, Christy Dutton, Martin Foley, Shavo Hogan, Noel Lynch and Cahill's brother-in-law, John Foy. The number of targets would vary with surveillance being extended to other criminals as they came into the picture. The object was to stick to each target, cut them off from each other and convince other criminals that it was unwise to associate with them. The gangsters had been winning the game on their own rules; now the Gardaí were preparing to give them a match to remember.

Murphy, Conroy and Ned Ryan gave the SSU men and women a profile of each target, including the individual's idiosyncrasies, haunts and habits. Ned Ryan told them what to expect. 'They'll put everything up to you and you must be prepared to give as good as you get. They can not see that you are afraid of them.'

Detective Garda Frank Madden also spoke. As a member of CDU for twenty years he knew all the targets personally. 'This job is not going to be easy. It is going to be cold, tedious and soul-destroying work. You will have to learn their tricks because they'll try every one in the book to get away from you and to get at you and break you down. They will intimidate and threaten you and may even try to follow you home and threaten your families. You must think like them. These boys will exploit every loophole, legal or otherwise, to beat you. You can expect to find yourselves isolated and you'll find at times that our own authorities are not too enamoured with us, but if it is to be done right, you've got to stick with it and not back down.'

In the following three weeks the 'rookies', as Cahill would call them, underwent intensive training in firearms and driving techniques. By mid-December the unit had been reduced to just over seventy – the rest either didn't make the grade or had to bow out for other reasons. Each target was to be given a codename. Cahill was T One or, in police-speak, Tango One. The eager new units were ready for action. The Tango Squad was born.

CHAPTER 9

The Tango Squad

Martin Cahill had never seen the likes of the Tango Squad before. The police had been prowling around in his shadow for the past fourteen years and he was well-accustomed to surveillance. But when he looked out his front window two weeks before Christmas 1987, he sensed that the Gardaí had something new in store for him. There were two fresh-faced policemen sitting in a car directly opposite his Cowper Downs home. They just sat there and watched. Whenever he looked out at them they gave a little wave with cocky grins on their faces.

While the SSU was being set up, Cahill was approached on the street by a senior officer from CDU sent by Detective Chief Superintendent Murphy with a message. The officer told the General that the Beit paintings and the DPP files were to be returned within a matter of days. They were to be left at a pre-arranged location. If Cahill didn't comply then further action would be taken. There was no more conversation, no small talk, no deals. The officer got into his car and drove away. There was something in his tone which annoyed Cahill. The officer seemed confident, as if he had something up his sleeve, as if he was almost hoping Cahill wouldn't comply with the demand. The gangster's instinct told him there was trouble ahead.

The first shot in the war of wits came on Christmas Eve. Eamon Daly was stopped coming out of the Rathmines Inn pub by uniformed Gardaí and breathalysed for drunk driving. The test proved negative and when he went back to collect his car, the tyres had been slashed. In the past whenever a member of the Cahill gang had been in trouble with the law, there would be spates of tyre-slashing in middle-class estates as a retaliatory gesture. This was designed to create friction between the well-off and the Gardaí who were supposed to protect them. Now someone, somewhere, was playing the 'game' the General's way.

On Christmas Day Martin Cahill, accompanied by his wife Frances and the children, was driving to the home of his sister-in-law, Tina, at Swan Grove. An unmarked car from the Tango Squad pulled alongside. The officers inside began jeering and laughing at Cahill. He became angry. When he neared Swan Grove he jammed on his brakes and the squad car slammed into the back of him. Cahill, complaining of whiplash, insisted on being brought to hospital. His wife and children continued their journey on foot. He was later to claim that he got a cheque for the damage to his car – a claim which the authorities denied. For the young cops it was the first tangle with Tango One and already he was playing the game.

On 1 January, 1988, the Tango Squad began surveillance in earnest. Tango One walked out the front door of Swan Grove to find three unmarked squad cars waiting for him. At the homes of Daly, Dutton, Foley, Lynch, Foy and Hogan there were similar scenes. It was the beginning of a bizarre 'cops and robbers' caper on the streets of Dublin, the drama unfolding in full view of an astonished public. Over the next six months, the drama would often descend into farce as Cahill, who had shunned the limelight for so long, became an object of intense media attention. Through his sheer cheek and outrageous sense of humour, he would establish himself as a household name and Joker of the Irish underworld.

Cahill's defence was to ignore the Tango Squad. It was a psychological tool he had learned in the harsh industrial school. 'You must never, ever look at them. They must never be allowed to see they are getting a reaction,' he would tell associates. 'The reason they sit outside my house is because they think it will embarrass me in front of my neighbours, but it won't, they're wrong. They are thinking about what would upset them. I'm not like them, I don't care about these people.' He removed the wing mirrors on his car so he didn't have to look at the cops behind. As he drove off the squad cars would follow, one in front, one behind and, occasionally, one alongside.

From the start the conflict was personalised, with teams of detectives 'adopting' a criminal and staying with him twenty-four hours a day. It was a device intended to unsettle the gangsters. When Cahill walked on the street, the cops walked behind him. Others cruised in a car along the kerb. The insults and the taunts came fast and furious. But Cahill never responded or acknowledged the police presence.

He seemed to have little difficulty slipping the net. Like an alley cat he had a myriad of escape routes and tricks. He bought a second anorak and balaclava, identical to his own, which he often put on a decoy. When the decoy left the house the cops would follow and Cahill would go about his business. He would hop across the wall at the back of Cowper Downs and vanish. But the 'rookies' soon learned to identify the hooded joker by his mannerisms and his hands. Cahill gave up when the Tango Squad began sitting on top of the wall looking into his back kitchen.

No matter how many times Cahill tried to shake off the watchers, the 'rookies' caught up with him and continued their 'game' of patience. On practically every journey Cahill or his men took, they were stopped and searched. It was not unusual for one of them to be stopped and searched, then allowed to go on only to be stopped again two hundred yards up the road. When the targets went to the pub for a drink the grinning 'rookies' sat beside them, interrupting their conversations with friends. Visitors to their homes were invariably stopped and questioned about their association with the particular target. It wasn't long before the tenacity and taunts of the Tango Squad began wearing down members of the gang – all, that is, except Tango One.

In the first days of the operation, Cahill's concerns about the new offensive were confirmed. Detective Garda Frank Madden stopped the General's car while he was being tailed by a convoy of Tango cars. Cahill seemed almost glad to see an old adversary. He didn't know the cops in the Tango Squad and that unsettled him. Madden walked over to the car and smiled in at Cahill. 'Martin, me auld flower, it's only a matter of time now before we have you. But fair play to ya, you had a good run of it,' said Madden, wearing that same disconcerting grin. Cahill's lip curled up behind his balaclava, by now his symbolic head dress. 'Youse are all criminals. Youse are worse than the fuckin' robbers themselves,' he snarled and drove on.

Cahill could not figure out why the police were so confident. It never dawned on him that the detectives, after all the years he had tormented them, were now playing a first-class game of bluff. They hadn't a clue where their operation was bringing them, but they were pushing the right buttons. Cahill's paranoia took over. He began to think that the 'rookies' were a smokescreen for some nefarious plot against him. One night his fears were confirmed when he slipped his surveillance team and went up the mountains to view his collection of stolen Beit masterpieces.

He later claimed that when he got within a few hundred yards of the bunker he heard the voices of two men who were hiding behind the trees. He was convinced for several months that the cops had found the paintings and were waiting for him to show up and then shoot him dead. He also feared that they would abduct him, take him to the haul and then murder him. His suspicions were the product of the mind games the detectives were indulging in. It transpired that the Gardaí never found the paintings in the woods. If they had been found there is no doubt that the morale-starved police force would have immediately put them to use as a much-needed publicity coup.

Within a few days of the start of the surveillance operation, Cahill called a meeting with the other marked men at his home in Cowper Downs. There was a traffic snarl-up in the small private estate as each criminal arrived along with two or three Tango cars. Inside, Cahill wouldn't allow anyone to speak until he closed the curtains for fear that the detectives outside were using eavesdropping devices. He advised his associates to keep their heads no matter what happened. Most of the planned robberies were to be deferred until they got a handle on what was going on.

The men at the meeting were confused and angry at the level of police attention. They wanted to hit back. 'Treat it like a game and don't let them get to ya, 'cause all they want to do is wind you up so ya do somethin' stupid and they'll nick ya for it or shoot ya,' Cahill admonished them.

A subsequent meeting was held at Christy Dutton's house in Ballyfermot, accompanied by the inevitable traffic jam of squad cars and gang members' cars. None of them had seen the likes of it before. When they looked outside Dutton's window there were at least fifteen squad cars and thirty of those smirking faces. Dutton was angry about the heat Cahill's more audacious strokes had brought down on the gang, without gaining them a single penny. Noel Lynch wasn't enjoying the heat either. Others at the meeting spoke of the bad luck the Beit paintings had brought them.

The marked men complained to Cahill that other criminals were steering clear of them because of the Garda attention. Men like Dutton preferred to keep a low profile. Apart from times when he went on his infamous drinking binges, Dutton was quiet-spoken and, superficially at least, genial. An old-fashioned criminal, he steered clear of drug dealers. Now, with cops crawling all over his road, he was feeling smothered. It was decided that the gang would have to meet surreptitiously in future – without the Tango Squad. Cahill urged his men to play cool. Martin Cahill avoided face-to-face confrontations. If someone, criminal or other, tackled him he would smile and walk away. He preferred returning unexpectedly with a gun to put across his side of the argument. He instructed his people to find out where some of the more enthusiastic Tango Squad members lived.

The game was getting serious. By late January, five members of the Tango Squad had been threatened openly by Cahill's men. Those directly threatened were given disturbing details of their addresses, the schedules of their wives, the names and ages of their children, the schools they went to, all of which showed that the Tango Squad men themselves were also under surveillance. One member of the gang actually visited the DMA HQ at Harcourt Square wearing a balaclava and invited a senior officer to a fist fight.

Cahill would drive into estates where members of the SSU lived. He would flash his hazard warning lights as he passed the homes of the detectives tailing him. He also began taking photographs and videoing them. Many of the Tango men began to wear hats and dark glasses and grew beards so that Cahill or his people could not recognise them. Members of the squad began sleeping with guns under their pillows and had to check beneath their cars before going to work. At the height of the drama, the wives and families of some officers moved out of their homes. One of the more persistent Tango men who sat beside his target in the pub was told in great detail the difference a bullet makes to a face when shot through the back of the head. The cop smiled and said: 'This is it. This is what you're up against.'

Cahill sanctioned the use of a hot-shot getaway driver to ambush the Tango cars. Tango men would be lured into pre-arranged estates where twenty year-old Mark Fitzgerald was waiting to ram them. The General had taken the youngster under his wing. He liked to nurture 'new talent' – it was good for the 'business'. A son of Seán Fitzgerald, the man who fronted the infamous pool club for the Cahills in the seventies, Mark was seen as one of the underworld's most talented 'wheels men'. For Fitzgerald had a unique ability to disable a Garda car by hitting it in such a way that the stolen car he was using could still be driven away.

The most serious indication of the General's annoyance came via an informant who gave details of a planned assassination of Detective Superintendent Ned Ryan early in January 1988. Cahill had hated Ryan for over fourteen years and blamed him for the surveillance operation. The informant claimed Cahill had hired two hitmen from London to carry out the contract.

At first Ryan laughed at the suggestion that he needed protection and considered it a total waste of time. Nevertheless an armed Special Branch man was posted outside his home. On the night of 29 January, Ned Ryan, a teetotaller, returned home after a night playing cards with friends. He invited the Special Branch officer in for tea. Before going into the kitchen the officer looked through the blinds of the front-room window and left his Uzi sub-machine-gun on the table. He went to the kitchen. Minutes later the two hitmen crept up to the front window. They were unaware of the security at the house and peeped in. A chink of light from the partially-opened door caught the reflection of the weapon sitting on the table. The hit team backed off.

Within a few days a senior detective in Ballyfermot received information about the incident at Ryan's home. The detective, Mick Carolan, had a number of reliable informants in the underworld and the matter was taken seriously. It was strengthened by the fact that neighbours living near Cahill's old enemy had spotted two men acting suspiciously in the area. Ryan also took this new information seriously. He was offered a bodyguard from the Special Detective Unit but insisted on Detective Sergeant Gerry O'Carroll getting the job. O'Carroll, equipped with a machine-gun and a .38 revolver, moved into Ryan's house and stayed by his side for the next two months. In later years Cahill denied to associates that he had plotted to kill Ryan or that he had hired gunmen for the job. He did, however, admit to prowling around Ryan's house at night.

As the war of wits continued, Cahill developed new methods of slipping the surveillance net. On some occasions his wife, Frances, would reverse his car up to the garage door to bring in the groceries. While she was emptying the car boot, Cahill, out of view of the cops across the road, would creep in and hide for hours. Later, when Frances drove off on her own, the cops wouldn't follow, thinking Cahill was still in the house. At other times, Cahill would stay inside for days at a time so that the Tango Squad got bored waiting for him to emerge. And whenever the police parked outside any of the homes of his gang frantic calls were made from 'worried housewives' to the local Garda stations reporting 'strange men' in cars trying to molest the children playing on the streets.

One night in early February a detective was sitting in a tree at the back of Cahill's house with a pair of night-sight binoculars. There had been a snowfall and the garden behind Cowper Downs was covered in a white blanket. A black object moving slowly along the ground caught his eye. The detective shone a torch on the object. It was Cahill crawling along the ground to get back into the house after slipping out several hours earlier. The Tango men kept the torch on him. He never moved as he lay face down in the snow-covered muck. Cahill just lay there for the next six hours without moving. As the batteries of one torch ran out, another torch was trained on the motionless General. Abuse was hurled at him from all directions but there was no response. At daybreak he simply got up and hopped across the wall without a word.

On another occasion a detective was sitting in a tree watching the house when Cahill crept up behind him. He shouted 'Boo' and the startled policeman fell out of the tree. Before he could get to his feet to do something about the source of his disturbance the giggling General was safely back in his house.

A wave of mystery fires began to hit the once quiet Cowper Downs estate. Three unfinished houses further down the road from Cahill's house were set on fire. One night, as detectives were sitting on a wall at the front of the house, Cahill appeared from behind them with a smile on his face. 'It's a bit cold tonight, lads, isn't it?' he said, as he skipped past. 'Ye'd need a fire to warm ya up.' When they turned around a house was in flames a hundred yards away.

Cahill seemed to have an inexhaustible collection of tactics to frustrate his watchers. One afternoon the 'rookies' were strolling beside Tango One on the street. Another car was driving alongside him. The cops were being particularly boisterous. He stopped to rummage in a bin. The cops shouted over at him, calling him 'a dirt bird' and taunting him about rooting in the bins.

Then Cahill found a half-eaten, blue-moulded sandwich among the discarded rubbish. 'It was the horriblest, sloppiest thing ya every put yer hand on,' he later recalled. He took it out and began munching it through the hole in his balaclava like it was a fresh cream cake. He broke one of his own rules and turned to the policemen, offering them a bite. They were repulsed and backed off. Cahill finished the sandwich and walked to Swan Grove. When he got in the door he threw up for the next few hours. He told associates it took days to get the taste out of his mouth.

On another occasion while walking down Rathmines Road he again rummaged in the bins. Passers-by must have wondered at the sight of a man with an anorak and balaclava rifling a bin and being watched by three men in a car. On this occasion the police threw pennies in his direction. Those that fell in front of him Cahill picked up and placed in his pocket. He felt that was bound to annoy them. The pennies which dropped behind him he ignored. If he turned to pick them up he would have had to look in the direction of the cops and that wouldn't be playing the 'game'. Another coin was thrown and Cahill went to pick it up. The Garda car rolled forward to cover it with a tyre but missed. Cahill bent down to pick the penny up. A cop stepped out and put his foot on the coin. Cahill straightened up, turned and walked away without acknowledging the presence of the detective standing over him.

The gang also used motorbikes to lose their tails in the traffic. Like Cahill, most of his men were bike enthusiasts and used them regularly on robberies. Cahill would start his 1000cc Kawasaki in the garage at Cowper Downs. One of his children would lift open the door and Cahill would race out onto the road like a greyhound leaving a hatch, disappearing before the Tango men could start their engines. One afternoon he was less fortunate. As he turned onto Cowper Road, the bike slid across the road, hitting the kerb and throwing him off.

Eight Tango men walked up feigning concern and asking if he was OK. Trembling and shaken, Cahill told them to fuck off and limped back to his house. The Tango Squad then recruited motorbike cops who were much more skilled than the criminals. The General's men couldn't get away from them. Eventually they stopped using bikes.

On Wednesday, 10 February, 1988, the 'game' took on a new importance when RTE's *Today Tonight* programme broadcast a documentary about organised crime in Dublin. For weeks, reporter Brendan O'Brien and a camera crew tailed the Tango Squad as they tailed the General's men. The programme listed a catalogue of crimes Cahill's gang had been suspected of, including the bombing of Dr Donovan and the Beit, O'Connor's and DPP robberies. Although criticised as 'trial by media', the programme grabbed the imagination of the nation and the General became a household name overnight.

Brendan O'Brien approached Cahill outside Werburgh Street employment exchange where he collected his £92 unemployment assistance every week. Cameras in a van across the road filmed O'Brien walking beside Cahill, who had a hood pulled tight around his head and his hand over his face. Two members of the Tango Squad walked immediately behind him. An unmarked car with three detectives inside drove slowly along the kerb. After a few minutes Cahill stopped and agreed to talk with O'Brien. He was genial and talkative. There was no threatening behaviour, no sinister undercurrent.

O'Brien asked him about the police following him. He replied: 'I never see them. I never see them. Seriously, I don't see them at all.'

When O'Brien put it to Cahill that he was the crime boss known as 'the General', he replied that 'there must be another Martin Cahill somewhere else'.

'I am sure there is another Martin Cahill. Well, who do you think "the General" is?' O'Brien asked.

'I don't know. Some army officer, maybe!' replied Cahill vaguely.

'I am sure there is an army officer somewhere called "the General",' O'Brien laughed.

'Ah, sure the way the country is these days ya wouldn't know,' offered Cahill.

'Then why have the Gardaí circulated notices about Martin Cahill, known as "the General", wanted for armed robberies in Mallow and Clonmel and other places. Why have they done that?' asked O'Brien.

'I suppose they're tryin' to blacken me for some reason. Ah, I know why they're blackenin' me, it's Ned Ryan.'

'Then what do you know of the senior police officer who is under armed protection?' O'Brien continued, referring to Ryan.

'I have no interest in the police, to be honest with ya. No interest at all.'

The programme then focused on Christy Dutton who was less communicative. O'Brien and his camera crew cornered him on Meath Street. Dutton, wearing a blue anorak with the hood pulled around his face, was coming out of a bookie's shop. Before O'Brien got a question out, Dutton said, 'Fuck off.'

O'Brien: 'I just want to ask you –'

Dutton: 'Go away – go away, I said.'

O'Brien followed him across the street, still trying to finish his question.

'Go away, I said,' Dutton snarled and gestured that he was going to hit the reporter. 'Go away or I'll fuckin'–'

'I just want to ask you about the crime –'

Dutton swung round, pushed O'Brien and ran across the street with the stubborn reporter on his heels. In an alleyway O'Brien and the camera crew caught up with Dutton.

'I know nothin' about any crime scenes. Righ'?'

'But what do you know about the Garda surveillance on you?'

'I know nothin' about it, righ'? If they have surveillance on me it's–' Dutton didn't finish what he was going to say. He lunged forward and dragged the cameraman to the ground. He shuffled off down the road flexing his arms menacingly and warning: 'Now, don't get me annoyed.' If Martin Cahill came across as the innocent victim of a misdirected campaign of vilification, Dutton looked like the nasty villain with something to hide. The scene spoke for itself.

The camera then focused on Shavo Hogan and Eamon Daly on their way into the Circuit Criminal Court where Daly was facing a charge of receiving stolen money along with Michael 'Styky' Cahill. The cash was taken in an armed robbery at St Stephen's Green in 1985. Five days after the programme was broadcast, Styky Cahill pleaded guilty to the charge and got five years.

The programme returned to a more talkative Martin Cahill. In fact, as the seventy-five minute interview continued, O'Brien could hardly get a word in. On the subject of the Beit paintings, Cahill was anything but circumspect. He said that he knew of a private detective who was looking for the paintings. He was Noel Lynch. Cahill said that 'Mr Lynch' made him a private detective and that he was on 'standby for a job' along with Eamon Daly and Martin Foley. 'I have asked people and no one knows and I don't know anythin' more about them [paintings],' he told O'Brien.

When O'Brien asked if the cops had been out-smarted in Kilakee, Cahill waved his right hand: 'The police are never out-smarted. Those police are very, very clever. It's been rumoured that Martin Cahill says that ... that I said it, Martin Cahill, are ya righ', that the police are thicks and all like that, no such thing. I never said anything like that 'cause they aren't, d'y'understand? They want to give the impression that there's a big gangster somewhere. D'y'understand? A dangerous man. That he's frightenin' everyone and they're probably believin' it themselves.' And in response to the threats the SSU had received he had little to say. 'They are probably of their own makin'.'

During the interview, Cahill was, by and large, almost convincing. But he made an uncharacteristic blunder on the subject of the Beit paintings when, after claiming that he was unemployed, he casually disclosed that he was working for a 'company'. The contradiction made him appear, at best, untrustworthy. Cahill later confided to a friend who had been away during the surveillance operation: 'I thought, "Good Jaysus, so much for keepin' things quiet." Me and me big mouth, the bastards were all over me.'

The programme also caused divisions among the gang. Noel Lynch and Christy Dutton were enraged at the unwelcome publicity. On the other hand, Cahill, after a lifetime of anonymity, seemed to relish his infamy. His obsessive personality, with its streak of eccentricity, meant that he could endure the wrath of Irish society. After all he had been alienated from the time of his birth. The extra pressure created unwanted risks, but it was part of the 'game'. If he kept his head he would come out smiling.

The programme provoked angry scenes in the Dáil the following day which guaranteed that Cahill stayed in the headlines. Des O'Malley, leader of the Progressive Democrat party at the time, forecast a 'new level of public cynicism' when it became known that Cahill had a private house worth £80,000 and possession of a £50,000 Corporation house, while drawing the dole with no visible means of income. 'I'm not entirely clear as to the reason for this, except perhaps neither property is big enough for him to hang his collection of paintings. Perhaps he needs the two houses so that he can gaze at his collection of seventeenth-century Dutch Masters,' mused the PD leader. O'Malley also complained that Department of Social Welfare investigators spent more time 'hounding' little old ladies who were probably earning a few pounds more than they should. Other deputies called for a special debate to discuss fully the disclosures in the *Today Tonight* programme.

The then Minister for Social Welfare, Michael Woods, announced that Cahill's unemployment assistance was being cut, pending an investigation into the fact that Cahill had two houses. The General had left himself wide open for a backlash as a result of his bravado. Martin Foley's social welfare payments were also queried. When he went to collect his dole the following week he was questioned about Cahill's comments on the *Today Tonight* programme. He said that they weren't true and he was going to sue Cahill. Later, when he met the General and expressed his anger, Cahill simply smiled and made up names for the two of them. 'You can be Magnum and I'll be Cannon, what d'ya think?'

The 'game' was moving into a new phase.

CHAPTER 10

Confrontation

After the *Today Tonight* programme and the inevitable media circus that followed, the Tango Squad were given fresh determination to interrupt the lives of Tango One and his friends. Their targets were equally resolute. Tempers soon began to flare.

On the afternoon of Friday, 19 February, 1988, Martin Foley and Shavo Hogan were driving from the tax office in the city centre. Surveillance cars were in front, behind and alongside. The Tango car in front had suddenly to jam on its brakes on Church Street bridge and they ran into the back of it. There was an argument between the detectives and their targets as they stood beside the two cars, disrupting the busy afternoon traffic.

An ambulance was called and Cahill's two men and two of the Tango Squad were fitted with surgical collars and brought to St James's Hospital. The rest of the Tango cars followed in convoy. In the hospital Foley was visited in an interview room by Detective Garda Gerald O'Connor. During a heated conversation Foley jumped up and punched O'Connor in the face, smashing his jaw and leaving him unconscious. Foley was arrested and charged with assault.

On Saturday night the Garda golf club in Stackstown was attacked by vandals. Hundreds of holes were dug in the greens, costing several thousands of pounds to repair. The tyres of twenty-three cars belonging to Gardaí at the club were also slashed. At four o'clock the following Monday morning, Cahill's car was attacked outside his home at Cowper Downs. The windows were smashed and the tyres slashed.

At the same time the tyres of Eamon Daly's car were slashed outside his home in Terenure. Daly had given the Tango Squad the slip a few days earlier on his way to court where he was due to stand trial along

Martin Cahill and the face he hid for over twenty years

THE SUNDAY WORLD

A prison officer escorts Martin Cahill to jail

The hooded General is taken away to serve a four-
month sentence on Spike Island

Martin Cahill in characteristic balaclava and tight hood

Cahill leaving court to face the media

'It's Mickey Mouse,' Cahill outside the Dublin courts where he appeared on a breach of peace charge in 1988

The Tango Squad try to relieve the General of his notorious head-
dress after his impromptu strip-tease outside the courts

THE STAR

Cahill's car is winched away from the murder scene

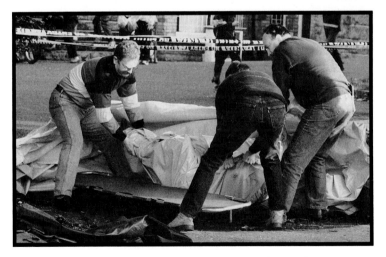

Detectives remove the bloodied remains of the General in a body bag

A floral tribute to a much-loved gangster

Cahill's funeral procession winds its way through the streets of Dublin

with Michael Cahill. The General had also vanished out of sight.

The police rejected suggestions that they had wrecked the men's cars in retaliation for the damage at the golf club. The Tango Squad had been pulled out of the area where Cahill and Daly lived because the two men were missing. One man who did manage to get in touch with Cahill during the week, including the night of the attack on the Garda golf club, was Michael O'Higgins. A journalist for *Magill* magazine and a barrister, O'Higgins had tenaciously pursued Cahill for an interview since the first major story was published about the Cahills in the *Sunday World* in October 1987. Now Cahill was under pressure and he sent a message agreeing to meet O'Higgins in the journalist's flat in Harold's Cross. It was the second interview he had given to a newspaper journalist, the first being at the height of his problems with the IRA in 1984 when he spoke at length to *Irish Times* freelance, Padraig Yeates.

On Sunday, 21 February, 1988, Martin Cahill turned up at O'Higgins's flat. The journalist was expecting a sinister figure in balaclava and anorak. Instead he met a plump, balding man in an ill-fitting suit and even more awkward-looking black leather gloves. He was a comical sight. To O'Higgins he didn't look like a big bad General of organised crime. Cahill was also surprised with what he found. O'Higgins, with his modest bedsit and electric coin meter, was an ordinary guy with no airs and graces, unlike the person the General had expected. Both men, after an initial period of wariness, got on well. In fact, they were to meet on several occasions over the next six months during which O'Higgins wrote a series of incisive articles for both *Magill* and the *Sunday Independent*.

'Now they [the Gardaí] are coming down to my level. They are now breaking the law,' Cahill told O'Higgins. He seemed chuffed with himself. 'Where is the surveillance? I am supposed to be watched twenty-four hours a day.' Over the following week he made himself available for three interviews at O'Higgins's bedsit, each one lasting an average of five hours.

On Thursday morning, 25 February, however, he had other things occupying his mind. At ten o'clock Martin Cahill was meeting Shavo

Hogan and John Foy near Walkinstown roundabout. They had also given their watchers the slip. The plan was to hit a security van which was expected to deliver cash to three banks situated close to the roundabout. The van was carrying over £50,000 in cash.

Even if the Tango Squad had passed by they would have found it difficult to recognise their targets. Shavo Hogan, in a suit and wearing a false beard, moustache, blond wig and gold-rimmed glasses, was standing in a lane at the rear of the Cherry Tree pub near the Walkinstown roundabout. Martin Cahill emerged from the gateway of St Peter's Industrial Estate. He too was wearing a blond wig and false beard. He also wore a dark blue crombie and a big hat which came down over his forehead. Under his arm he carried a gripless blue sports bag containing three firearms for the job.

Hogan and Cahill walked into the car park of the Cherry Tree pub which faced onto the roundabout. Foy was sitting in the gang's getaway car, a blue Mazda 323 which had been bought in an auction under a false name three weeks earlier. Cahill opened the door of the car and threw the bag in. Foy took off slowly in the car around the roundabout and down Walkinstown Road. Cahill meanwhile walked across the road towards the Kestrel pub which also faces onto the roundabout. Hogan went around on the other side of the roundabout, walking on the opposite side of the road to Cahill. Uniformed Gardaí Pat Flynn and Gerry Carney were on routine patrol in the area. A passer-by informed them that three men had been seen acting suspiciously and they went to investigate. As they drove down Walkinstown Road and onto the roundabout, they spotted Hogan jumping into the passenger seat of the car driven by Foy. Their curiosity was aroused because the car was still moving as Hogan got in.

Foy had spotted the police car and decided to drive on. Cahill also saw what was happening and turned and walked briskly in the opposite direction. Foy and Hogan turned left into Walkinstown Drive. The squad car followed. They picked up speed and so did the cops. As the car swung left on to Walkinstown Parade, Hogan reached out of the passenger window and fired a shot at the two unarmed officers with a Smith and Wesson .45 revolver. As the squad car continued to follow, Hogan fired a second shot.

Foy turned at high speed onto the Long Mile Road dual carriageway, Shavo again leaned out the window and fired two more shots, this time from a different weapon, to shake off the police car. As the chase continued Garda Carney radioed for assistance. The car swerved left onto Robinhood Road and Hogan fired a fourth shot at the cops. Foy turned right onto Club Road, a *cul de sac* with bollards at the end separating the road from the Naas dual carriageway.

The two criminals jumped out as the squad car pulled across the top of Club Road to prevent them reversing. Foy threw a Lama semi-automatic pistol into a garden as he dashed towards a second getaway car which had been left in the car park of Joe Wong's restaurant. Hogan, meanwhile, fired another two shots at the unarmed officers as he raced towards a wall. He dived across and out into the dual carriageway. Garda Carney ran after him.

Meanwhile detectives Greg Sheehan and Anthony Scully from CDU, who were patrolling in the area, arrived in Joe Wong's car park just as Foy was trying to start up the second getaway vehicle. They spun their car around in front of the getaway car, jumped out and pointed their weapons at Foy. They ordered him to get out of the vehicle and lie face down on the ground. They pulled off his wig and false beard and arrested the General's brother-in-law.

At the same time Shavo Hogan was making a spirited attempt to get away. Uniformed officers Patrick McNicholas and Anthony McCarthy were coming towards him in a police van. When he saw the police, Hogan aimed his gun at them. McNicholas, who was driving, did a U-turn in the road to avoid being shot. Hogan ran behind the van to cross to the other side of the dual carriageway. McNicholas completed the turn and continued pursuing Hogan who ran up onto the grass margin.

As the van got within ten yards of Shavo, he turned to face them, raised his right arm and took aim. The weapon appeared to fire. McNicholas and McCarthy ducked down in the van to avoid being shot. Hogan was about to turn and run when the van hit him. He was thrown in one direction, his gun in the other. The two officers jumped out and found him lying on the ground dazed. McNicholas arrested Hogan and recovered the weapon.

When Garda McCarthy got into the back of the van, Hogan recovered and jumped suddenly on the policeman. 'You'll never reach the courts with me, ya bastards. I'll have ye done if ye don't let me out now.' Hogan tried to choke McCarthy by grabbing the strap of his walkie-talkie radio and wrapping it around his neck. He also punched the officer around the head and broke his nose. Other officers arriving on the scene piled into the back of the van. Within a few minutes Hogan had been subdued.

Within twenty-four hours, John Foy and Shavo Hogan, two of the men targeted in the surveillance operation, were taken before the Special Criminal Court and charged with possession of firearms with intent to endanger life. Later associates of the captured men claimed that the surveillance squad was sitting outside Hogan's house when the drama began. Meanwhile Martin Cahill slipped back to one of the flats at Tom Kelly House off Charlemont Street where he sometimes stayed.

All Garda units in the city were given orders to arrest the General on sight for questioning in relation to the incident with Foy and Hogan. In jail the pair joined Eamon Daly who had been arrested and remanded in custody for failing to turn up for his trial on the receiving charge. He had been found by the Tango Squad the day before the drama at the Walkinstown roundabout. Gardaí later found Daly's fingerprint in one of the cars used by Foy and Hogan. He had been meant to be the fourth member of the robbery team that morning.

Cahill sanctioned a tyre-slashing spree to express his dissatisfaction with the Garda victory. He was a bad loser. His so-called 'B team', a collection of staunchly loyal young criminals, some of whom were relatives, went to work the night after the arrest of Hogan and Foy. On Friday, 26 February, 1988, a total of 197 cars were attacked, including ninety belonging to Cahill's neighbours in Cowper Downs. The ploy was intended to embarrass the Gardaí who were supposedly sitting there around the clock. Greens at St Anne's golf club in Dollymount, which had a large number of Garda members, were also dug up by vandals.

The following morning detectives raided the flat in Charlemont Street where Cahill was hiding. During a search they found wigs and false beards like those used in the Walkinstown incident. Cahill was arrested under the Offences Against The State Act and taken to the Bridewell Garda Station in the city centre. For the next forty-eight hours he treated the members of the Tango Squad to his mantra, 'I have nothing to say to youse men. BOOM.' The police provided a chorus and repeated the mantra with him. They repeated their request that the Beit paintings and the DPP files be returned. Cahill's clothes were confiscated for forensic examination. They bought him other clothes, including a jumper.

When Cahill left the Bridewell station on Monday morning a battery of press photographers was waiting for the new star of the Irish underworld. From now on he would have to cope not only with police, but with dozens of press photographers eager to get a glimpse behind the mask. 'It was like going out on stage,' he recalled. But the waiting pressmen and women were disappointed. Cahill had fashioned a balaclava from the torn sleeve of the jumper the Gardaí had bought for him. He walked through the waiting journalists humming a tune to himself. The next day a photograph appeared on the front page of the *Irish Independent* showing Cahill walking out of the Bridewell with Detective Sergeant Denis Donegan from the Tango Squad following. The caption read: *'The hooded Martin Cahill leaving the Bridewell in Dublin yesterday . . . but the law wasn't far behind.'*

Cahill was driven back by an associate to Cowper Downs where his wrecked car was sitting outside. Other cars attacked during the weekend incidents were still parked in the normally peaceful estate. It had all the appearance of the aftermath of a riot. Cahill went into the house. The Tango Squad pulled up in the front and other squad members took their seats on the back wall. The 'game' resumed.

The operation at the Walkinstown roundabout had gone ahead because Cahill reckoned that the large network of roads and back lanes which surround the area would make a getaway easy. But following the arrest of Hogan and Foy he was being more careful. When Eamon Daly was released on bail from Mountjoy he advised him not to go ahead with a planned armed robbery at the Atlantic Homecare store in Stillorgan in south Co Dublin. But Daly was hungry for cash.

On 18 March, 1988, the newspapers and TV had another excuse to flash Martin Cahill's name to a public anxious to read about the nation's new arch-fiend. The final chapter in the O'Connor's jewellery robbery unfolded in the Circuit Criminal Court with the trial of Michael Egan. Egan had been charged under the Accessories and Abettors Act for helping Cahill and his gang. After three days Egan was found guilty as charged. In the witness box Detective Inspector Michael Cannavan told Judge Gerard Buchanan: 'I am satisfied that this robbery was the work of Martin Cahill and his gang. They are notorious criminals in this city.'

Detective Sergeant Gerry O'Carroll described Egan as 'the most devious man I have ever met. He has the propensity for associating with evil men.' In sentencing Egan to seven years – a sentence considered particularly stiff in the circumstances – Judge Buchanan sent a message to the Dublin's criminal world which Cahill could not fail to interpret. 'The citizens of Dublin are heartily tired of crimes of this nature and they are abhorrent to them. The accused aided and abetted the perpetrators of this crime and as a result a hundred people lost their livelihoods. If the accused had been a member of the robbery gang I would find it difficult not to impose a life sentence, the maximum penalty in these cases.'

On the afternoon of Saturday, 26 March, Eamon Daly and three other armed men walked into the Atlantic Homecare store in Stillorgan. Daly had a nine-millimetre automatic pistol in his pocket and was wearing two sets of clothes, one of which would be discarded after the robbery, and a false beard. Unfortunately for him, however, two armed detectives walked into the store after him.

When Daly saw them he reached for his gun, but detectives William Craven and Patrick Campbell knocked him to the ground. A second armed man held a gun to the head of an employee who had

£12,000, the day's takings, in his hand. Campbell shouted at the man to put down his gun. The raider pointed it at the detective who fired a shot and the raider took flight. A third raider was seen trying to smash a glass door in a bid to save Daly. Detective Garda Campbell fired another shot through the door, hitting the raider in the shoulder. The robber dropped his gun and fled to a waiting getaway car.

Daly was arrested and taken to the Bridewell Garda Station for questioning. The rest of the gang got away. The injured man was subsequently treated by a veterinary surgeon for his wound. Daly was later charged with attempted robbery and possession of a firearm with intent to commit a robbery. He was remanded in custody until his trial.

At five o'clock that evening, a few hours after Daly's capture, Martin Cahill appeared on the roof of the pigeon loft at the back of his house near the wall where the Tango Squad were perched. He was wearing a balaclava and his customary anorak. The garden on the other side of the wall belonged to John Sisk and his wife, a retired couple. They had allowed the Tango Squad to use their garden.

Now Cahill was roaring abuse at them. 'Mr Sisk, don't be hiding behind the curtains. I can see you.' Tango One then turned his attention to the watching cops and told them: 'Ye'd have no problem gettin' a hole-in-one at the Garda golf club 'cause there's that many holes in it.' Cahill's son Christopher came out and joined him on the roof. Martin gave him a camera and began offering the watching detectives a bundle of twenty-pound notes saying: 'These are for guns.' The bizarre show lasted about forty minutes and then Cahill went inside.

The following evening at five o'clock Cahill again appeared on the pigeon loft accompanied this time by his associate, Martin Foley. A large video-camera lens was stuck out through a back window. Cahill shouted at his neighbour John Sisk that he was a 'builder of slums. Ya don't pay yer workers a decent wage.' Then he started roaring that Sisk had the Gardaí in his pocket. 'I hope you have them for the next ten years. A big bad wolf is out to get you, Sisk. I will get you.' The General also hurled sexual obscenities at Mrs Sisk, a woman in her seventies who was an invalid. One of the cops watching the extraordinary performance radioed to his astonished colleagues: 'It's Cahill. He's gone completely fucking mad.'

Cahill got down from the pigeon loft and Foley began throwing stones at him, shouting: 'We will get you, Cahill. We will burn you out.' Cahill turned around and shouted at Foley: 'Guard, get off my wall.' The baffling games continued the following morning when Christopher Cahill, then fifteen years old, appeared on the pigeon loft and began taking pictures of the Tango Squad on the wall. Cahill came out and climbed into the loft shouting out at the Sisk's house. 'Mrs Sisk, I'm going to get you. I can see you in the bushes. You won't be able to hide when I burn your home down. I know where all your children live. There is no place you can hide. You're an old woman.'

At that stage the Tango men reckoned they had heard enough. Detective Garda Colm Church shouted at Cahill that he would arrest him if he didn't cut it out. But Cahill turned and faced the rear of his own house and began to yell: 'Cahill, you're a robber, we're goin' to get you. We'll get him for you, Mrs Sisk.' Then the crime boss turned to one of the policemen and told them he had pictures of all of them and their home addresses. Back at Harcourt Square, the DMA headquarters, it was decided that the police would have enough evidence at least to seek a court order binding Cahill to the peace.

It was in keeping with the 'game' that the Tango Squad presented Cahill with a summons to appear in court on April Fool's Day. Later that day Cahill appeared in the front of the house with a megaphone shouting that the cops were 'tyre-slashers, perverts and rapists'. A number of friends arrived at the house with their kids. Cahill began playing a song through a loudspeaker: 'Don't Fence Me In.' Later the children were sent out to 'play'. They jumped up and down on the squad cars sitting outside. The surveillance was now entering its fourth month and neither Tango One nor his adversaries were showing any sign of fatigue. On the following Wednesday, 6 April, Cahill arrived at the District Court buildings beside the Bridewell in balaclava and anorak. The inevitable posse of photographers and reporters were waiting for him. In the court his solicitor, Garret

Sheehan, requested an adjournment on the grounds that 'certain Gardaí or masked people purporting to be Gardaí' had thrown stones at Cahill's house. In the court Cahill cupped his face in his hands and replied 'Yes' when he was asked to give an undertaking not to interfere with the Sisks.

As he was leaving the court complex after the brief hearing, Cahill put on an impromptu show for the gathered media. He began doing a striptease dance, throwing off his anorak. Then he twirled around and began unzipping his white jeans, dropping them to reveal a pair of multi-coloured boxer shorts. Then he whooped with a laugh: 'I'm Superman.' The show over, he dressed again and walked to a waiting car. Cahill had no problem showing his underwear to the Irish public – his face was the most private part of his body.

The following week Cahill was back in court for a hearing of the application to have him bound over to keep the peace. A man wearing the familiar anorak and balaclava arrived at the Bridewell and posed for the cameramen. The masked man walked into the toilets and wasn't seen again. Meanwhile, the real Martin Cahill, wearing his favourite apparel for armed robberies – a moustache, wig and gold-rimmed glasses – strolled in behind the excited media and Tango Squad who stood watching the toilets.

Inside, the courtroom was packed to capacity with Gardaí, media representatives and curious onlookers. Cahill was represented by Adrian Hardiman, one of the country's most eminent senior counsel. The hearing was before the president of the District Court, Judge Oliver Macklin. Cahill sat in the dock with his hands around his face, listening to the evidence from the Tango Squad men. At one stage, Hardiman claimed that his client was being 'fitted up'. He also said it was hard to believe that a man 'who neither drinks or smokes could have engaged in such gratuitous behaviour before so many Garda witnesses.' Judge Macklin looked down at Tango One and ordered him to take his hands down from his face, which Cahill did. After a while he covered his face in his hands again.

When Detective Garda Denis Palmer gave his account of the incident on 27 March, he was asked if he could identify Cahill. 'He is wearing a wig, false moustache and glasses and if he took his hands from his face I could identify him,' Palmer replied. Judge Macklin grew impatient with Cahill. 'This is a silly performance. Take your hands down,' he said, like a teacher reprimanding a bold boy. Cahill looked up at him and said: 'I'm just resting me head.' The Judge ordered him a second time to take his hands down. After a full day the hearing was adjourned for a week.

Outside Cahill was anxious not to send the photographers back to their darkrooms empty handed and gave another 'little show'. At the gates of the court he began to sing a song, 'I'm gonna sit right down and write myself a letter', a cheeky reference to three of the stolen Beit paintings which now resided behind an attic wall in Tallaght or in a damp bunker in the mountains. He handed out leaflets outlining 'What I think crime is', which included 'not giving pensioners enough money to live on', 'bosses causing strikes deliberately' and 'child abusers'. He continued to sing and gyrate his hips. Then he slipped off his anorak and dropped his jeans, revealing a pair of Mickey Mouse shorts and a tee-shirt. He sang out, 'It's Mickey Mouse' as detectives from the Tango Squad grabbed him and frog-marched him back into court.

There was bedlam as cops and photographers surrounded Tango One. One of the detectives tried to give the newsmen the picture opportunity they had been waiting for when he attempted to pull off Cahill's mask. 'I'm being assaulted by the police. I want to see my solicitor, Mr Sheehan,' the gang boss screamed. The following morning Cahill hit the headlines of every national newspaper. Martin Cahill, the sinister General of the underworld, was now the Joker of Irish crime.

However, three days later an incident occurred which caused anything but laughter in the General's gang. On the morning of 17 April, Martin Cahill and John Foy, now on bail for the Walkinstown incident, again slipped the net. Cahill waited in Ranelagh village while Foy went to pick up a number of guns which were to be used in a robbery. Foy, on a green lady's bike, cycled into Ranelagh Gardens Park. As he got off the bike and walked towards a green container, officers from the Tango Squad were watching. Foy began rummaging in the container and retrieved a plastic bag which contained four handguns.

Officers emerged from the bushes and shouted at Foy to freeze. Foy turned and told them to 'Fuck off' before running in the opposite direction. A detective fired a single shot in his direction but missed. Foy escaped. The detectives recovered the weapons, some of which had been stolen by Cahill from the old Technical Bureau in St John's Road. The following day Foy was arrested in Crumlin Garda Station when he walked in to sign on as part of his bail conditions. When he was later questioned he told detectives: 'Obviously I was set up.'

The arrest of Foy caused consternation and mistrust in the Cahill gang. Only four people knew where the guns were hidden – Shavo Hogan, John Foy, Eamon Daly and Cahill himself. With Daly on remand in jail, Cahill began to suspect that Hogan had turned informant. But he was slow to point a finger at anyone. He and Hogan had been close friends since their days in Daingean Industrial School. He later told associates that he suspected the whole thing could easily have been a ploy by the cops to create division and paranoia among them.

On the following Thursday, Cahill was back in court for the adjourned hearing. Once again he was the centre of attention as he winked at the female reporters. The Tango Squad played a tape of Cahill hurling abuse at the Sisks. They told the court that the Sisks had been too afraid to attend the hearing. They were now living in fear of Cahill.

Judge Macklin granted the state's application to have him bound over to keep the peace for a year on sureties totalling £1,500. Wearing his wig, false moustache and glasses over a Batman tee-shirt, Cahill was told by the judge that he had hidden his face 'like Little Bo-Peep' which was hardly the 'normal behaviour of a citizen'. He said that Cahill's demeanour in court was intended to avoid identification and instructed that he be on good behaviour towards his neighbours and the Gardaí. The Judge ordered him to pay £500 court costs and to produce the sureties before 8 May or face four months in prison.

After the case there was more pandemonium as Cahill rode off on a bicycle with three squad cars in hot pursuit. He cycled around the nearby fruit and vegetable markets and then joined friends in a nearby pub while the Tango men stood on the pavement outside waiting. Then he set off, walking his bike in the direction of Christchurch, while a detective walked after him pushing another bike.

The intense pressure was beginning to tell on Cahill, even though he stubbornly refused to believe that it was. He confided to friends that he needed a short spot of jail to recharge his batteries. He also reckoned that he would be going to Portlaoise maximum security prison where most of his men would be. 'I don't mind prison if it's not for long. I get a chance to catch up with my friends,' he said. He wrote to the Chief State Solicitor's office informing him that he was available for arrest.

On 16 May, 1988, Eamon Daly pleaded guilty in the Special Criminal Court to the attempted robbery at the Atlantic Homecare store. He was described as being 'a member of a notorious Dublin gang' who had never worked a day in his life but owned a £40,000 house he paid for with cash. A senior officer gave evidence of how, in the early eighties, Daly had been involved with INLA man, Thomas McCarton, who was murdered in an internal feud in 1986.

Daly said that he had nothing to do with the INLA and that he had been threatened by paramilitaries in Portlaoise. 'They have threatened me because they call me a "hood" and consider themselves POWs,' he claimed. Daly also claimed that he had got involved in the robbery to pay off a debt to moneylenders and that he had lost his nerve when he got to the store. Mr Justice Liam Hamilton did not believe him. 'This is one of a plague of armed robberies which are prevalent in this state and cannot be tolerated,' he said as he gave Daly twelve years. A week later Daly was back before Justice Hamilton. This time he got another five years on top of his twelve-year stretch when he pleaded guilty to the charge of receiving, along with Michael Cahill, the proceeds of the armed robbery at College Green in 1985.

Meanwhile the date for Cahill's imprisonment came and went. On 12 May the Gardaí sought a warrant for his arrest but did not act on it. Three of the original targets – Foy, Daly and Hogan – were now in jail or about to be sent down. Now the Tango Squad were watching Harry Melia and Eddie Cahill. Dutton and Lynch along with others had stopped calling to see the General. Cahill was a born loner and did not mind the isolation caused by the surveillance operation but he was disgusted that they had allowed the Gardaí to win the battle of wits.

On the afternoon of 3 June Shavo Hogan visited Cahill at Cowper Downs for a final farewell. He was up in the Special Criminal Court the following morning where he intended pleading guilty. Shooting at unarmed Gardaí was a serious offence and it would be a long time before he would see Cahill again – at least outside prison walls. Despite his suspicions, Cahill was glad to see his friend. Shavo spent most of the evening with Cahill.

The following day Cahill and his people expressed surprise when Hogan got an eight-year sentence, relatively light in the circumstances. The police did not remark on his few visible signs of income or the fact that he was part of a criminal gang. Eddie Cahill, the hot-tempered member of the family, left the court and went back to Cowper Downs to report to the General and accused Hogan of being a 'tout'. But Cahill still wasn't so sure. He said it was just a divisive plot on the part of the state. The following month – July – John Foy received seven years for the same incident. In October he got another two years on top for possession of firearms at Ranelagh Park. Also in July, Mark Fitzgerald, the young 'wheels man', got a total of 107 years for a total of sixteen armed robberies and car thefts between 1984 and 1988. As he was being led from court he threatened to kill the cop who caught him, Detective Inspector John McLaughlin.

On 5 June, the day after Shavo was dispatched to Portlaoise Prison and one month after Cahill was due to be arrested, the Gardaí raided the General's homes at Cowper Downs and Swan Grove. They were looking for firearms. Frances, who had been down in Swan Grove with her sister Tina, came back to Cowper Downs because she reckoned her husband was going to be taken away to begin his four-month holiday.

When she arrived she found Cahill, his face blacked up with his Al Jolson make-up and his balaclava at the ready. Upstairs the detectives found a Colt .45 pistol hidden in a cistern. Cahill became agitated and angry. The house was filled with members of the Tango Squad.

Cahill and his wife, Frances, and her sister, Tina, were arrested under the Offences Against The State Act. During questioning they were asked to make a statement outlining how the weapon came to be in the house or the names of recent visitors to the house who could have planted it there with a view to framing Cahill. On Sunday afternoon all three were released. As he was leaving the Bridewell, Tango One was arrested on foot of the warrant for not entering the bond to keep the peace.

He was brought to the high security wing of Mountjoy Prison. The atmosphere was tense as inmates eagerly awaited his arrival. But he spent only one night there. The following morning, an order was signed transferring him almost four hundred miles away to Spike Island prison in Cork Harbour. At first the General thought he was going to join his friends in Portlaoise as the prison van drove south. As it got near Portlaoise he heard on the radio that he was going to Spike, a former naval base and military stockade which had been converted to deliver a short sharp shock to youngsters convicted of joy-riding in Dublin.

For the next three months Martin Cahill was a prisoner on Spike. While he was away the Director of Public Prosecutions decided not to proceed with charges against the General arising out of the gun find in Cowper Downs. The decision caused anger and resentment among some of the men of the Tango Squad who claimed that it made them look like they had tried to frame their target. The Squad had been officially disbanded soon after the find. Members of the former unit later claimed that it would have been sheer folly to plant a gun at the end of such a highly-publicised surveillance operation.

The Tango Squad had been a new departure in the tactics of the Gardaí. At the end of it three of their primary targets were in jail serving long sentences, partly because of their own carelessness and partly as a result of the intense pressure they had been placed under. Others were facing serious charges before the courts. But Tango One was still smiling. The mind games played by the police had genuinely worried him. From now on he would be more cunning than ever before. He had proved a formidable opponent. Valuable intelligence and experience had been gained. Politically, it also restored confidence in the police that they were prepared to take on the big gangs. Now the officers were returning to their own districts with their new knowledge. The tactic of overt surveillance was over.

Journalist Michael O'Higgins and Frances Cahill made the long trek to Spike Island to visit the General after his first week away. They took the old motor launch from Cobh across to the island prison. It was a beautiful, hot summer's day. In the visitor's room the General was waiting, leaning his head on his hand, with that trademark smile on his face. He got up from his seat and shook hands with O'Higgins. He seemed glad to see him. He smiled shyly at his wife. Frances asked him had he read the previous day's *Sunday Tribune* article which was about himself, Daly, Foy and Hogan. He hadn't. He was more interested in whether she had bought him a new pair of Mickey Mouse shorts. The prison authorities had taken the others. He was perfectly happy, he told O'Higgins, with life on his 'treasure island'. The food was good, accommodation comfortable and the regime relatively lax. He was learning to be a plasterer.

But his mind was on being released. He was glad of the break but wanted to get back to Dublin soon. He mused about how he would return to the mainland. 'Maybe I'll dress up as Long John Silver with a wooden leg and stuffed parrot. I will tell them that my treasure is buried on the island golf course, but no matter how many holes they dig, they will not find it,' he joked to the journalist.

In the first week of September Martin Cahill was released. He returned to Dublin. On the day he arrived back his friends and associates had a celebration for him in the Furry Bog pub in Rathfarnham. They drank and cracked jokes while Cahill laughed and drank fizzy orange. Detectives sat at the next table. Cahill lifted his glass to them. They smiled back.

Two weeks later the cops won another victory against the General's organisation. His older brother, forty-one year-old John, and three other friends were caught red-handed following a £107,000 armed hold-up at an employment exchange on the Navan Road in Dublin. They had fired a number of shots as scores of squad cars chased them across the city. Eventually they were surrounded in a house in Ballyfermot. John Cahill had come out of prison in late 1986 after serving eight years for the Smurfit payroll robbery in 1978. He had set up his own gang and had not worked with Martin since getting his freedom. Cahill's oldest brother was sent down for sixteen years.

In Portlaoise Prison the tensions created among the General's gang continued for two years after the surveillance operation began. In September 1990 Shavo Hogan was segregated from the rest of the gang after another member accused him of being an informant, a claim which Hogan always strenuously denied and for which there was no proof.

On the morning of 8 October, while Shavo was exercising alone in the yard at the back of E 1, he was attacked a second time. Three criminals jumped on Hogan and tried to slice the tops of his ears off with a knife. It was a crude and brutal gangland ritual. The intention was to make Hogan's ears resemble those of a rat, the criminal's term for an informant. Hogan later underwent surgery to save the ears and his attackers were transferred to other prisons.

The Gardaí charged the three attackers. On 6 May, 1991, in the Dublin Circuit Criminal Court, the state decided not to proceed with the charges because of the high security implications. It was said in court that a battalion of troops, backed up by helicopters, would have been necessary to escort and guard the total of eighteen prisoners, among them some of the most notorious criminals in the country, who had been summoned to give evidence on behalf of the defence.

When he heard of the attack, Martin Cahill sent word to his men not to touch Hogan again. Cahill reminded them that Shavo was one of the few who knew where the Beit paintings had been stashed and that there was no evidence to suggest that he was an informer. Hogan was released from prison in 1992.

CHAPTER 11

The Jinx

The Beit paintings brought bad luck to Martin Cahill and his gang. Associates of the General have always claimed that after the spectacular art heist nothing went right for them. They never enjoyed the huge financial windfall they had expected the night they hit Russborough House. And after the narrow escape at Kilakee Wood in September 1987 Cahill realised how difficult it would be to off-load the collection. He told an associate that from then on whoever came to make an offer was likely to be a police informer. In the meantime he decided to keep the priceless paintings under wraps.

Cahill himself would admit before his death that the paintings had put a jinx on his operations. In reality he had made a major error of judgement and gone out of his depth – although he was loath to admit that. In the wake of the robbery, the General found himself facing down a much more determined enemy in the police. The surveillance operation had succeeded in unsettling the gang. The intense media attention gave a political incentive to putting them out of business. After the Tango Squad was disbanded a new, covert team of detectives from the Serious Crime Squad was put on Cahill's trail. The robbery had also brought Cahill into dangerous territory between both Loyalist and Republican paramilitaries.

Despite his lack of success as an art thief and the pressure from the police, Cahill began planning another art robbery in the winter of 1988. This time he was aiming nearer home at a £500,000 collection of paintings and jewellery belonging to the deceased former Supreme Court Judge, James Murnaghan. The late Judge's wife, Alice Murnaghan, had opened a public gallery at their impressive residence on Fitzwilliam Street. When Cahill announced his plan to other members of the gang he chuckled at the thought of stealing a dead judge's property. According to Cahill's warped logic, the theft would be another act of effrontery to the state.

This time, Cahill had a London-based criminal lined up to take possession of the collection. The Englishman was expecting to recover a substantial reward for the collection which he would split with Cahill. The General began planning the robbery when he came home from Spike Island and the overt surveillance stopped. Martin, his brother Eddie, his friend Harry Melia, and three other men were to be involved in the heist. But the cops were hovering in the background.

On the afternoon of 29 November, Eddie Cahill left his brother's house at Cowper Downs and drove by motorbike to a house in Lismore Road in Crumlin where Harry Melia regularly stayed. Cahill and Melia had ventured into the heroin trade as a sideline to their other criminal activities. Melia was a serious criminal with a reputation as a violent, armed robber. He was also a heroin addict. Melia had been released from prison in January 1988 at the start of the surveillance operation after serving time for firearms offences. Eddie got out in May after a seven-year stretch for kidnapping and aggravated burglary. They had taken the place of other members of the gang, Shavo Hogan, Eamon Daly and John Foy who had been jailed in the first half of 1988.

Cahill parked his motorbike outside the house on Lismore Road at 5.30 pm and went inside. He went upstairs to the front bedroom where Melia was sorting out a £50,000 consignment of heroin. For several days detectives from the Drug Squad had been watching the house and the movements of the two friends. At 6.10 pm the Drug Squad pounced. Detectives burst into the bedroom and caught the two criminals sitting on the bed with the drugs in their laps. In the follow-up searches at Lismore Road and Eddie Cahill's house on Lissadel Road in Crumlin, detectives seized over £10,000 in cash. Later the two men were charged under the Misuse of Drugs Act and remanded to Mountjoy Prison, a place they knew well.

The General was stunned by the arrests of his two lieutenants. He was fully aware of their involvement in the heroin trade but reckoned they were careful enough not to get caught. It had been a bad year.

Despite the set-back he decided to go ahead with the Murnaghan robbery. At ten o'clock on the evening of Wednesday, 7 December, Cahill and two other gang members climbed over a wall at the rear of the Murnaghan residence at Lad Lane. They broke a window in the basement and got in. Although the alarm system was on they had little difficulty by-passing it. The unarmed robbers confronted Mrs Murnaghan's housekeeper who lived in the basement.

They brought the housekeeper upstairs to where ninety-two year-old Alice Murnaghan was reading in her room. Cahill was not aggressive and did not ill-treat the women who were kept in a study on the first floor. He assured them that nothing would happen to them. Throughout the night, he made the two women several cups of tea and brought them biscuits. As in the Beit robbery, he knew what to take and what to leave behind. Cahill's men removed fifty paintings, a quantity of silverware and cutlery, goblets and candelabra, some pieces of furniture and jewellery. Included in the haul were works by German, Dutch and French artists. The loot was placed in a van parked on Lad Lane.

Unknown to Cahill the undercover team from the Serious Crime Squad had found out about his deal with the English criminal. They had, for a time, managed to place an informant in close to the General. They sat tight and waited for him to make a move. Two weeks after the Murnaghan robbery Eddie Cahill and Harry Melia were released on bail of £12,000 each. The next day Martin Cahill arranged for a video containing recently-filmed footage of the loot to be passed to an intermediary working on behalf of the London man. Then he waited for the deal to be done – so did the cops.

At the last minute the English criminal found out that the works of art were not insured. He pulled out of the deal and Cahill would never know why. The cops backed off and waited for their next opportunity. The General had no idea how close he had come to being caught. Now he was lumbered with two collections of paintings, and credible buyers were not exactly banging on the door to do a deal.

During October and November of 1988 Cahill had organised a number of 'tie-ups' in south Dublin. The long winter nights were the

General's favourite time of year. He had always enjoyed rich pickings in the upmarket south city districts. On the night of 6 October the gang struck at a residence in Clonskeagh. Stephen Benedict woke up to find two masked men sitting on top of him in his bed. One of the men pointed a pistol at his head. They tied up Mr Benedict and his wife Irene, and one of them said: 'I'm afraid we've taken some of your paintings.' Cahill and his men stole nineteen paintings and jewellery worth £80,000. They also took a rifle and a shotgun.

On 10 November they struck again, this time at the Killiney home of Roland Benner. The armed and masked men tied up Mr Benner's two daughters and son and several of their friends who had called during the robbery. They took over £14,000 worth of jewellery. In both cases detectives were given a clue that the burglaries had been the work of their old adversary. The occupants of the houses noticed that food had been taken from their fridges!

Cahill had hidden some of the loot from the two robberies in a hedge under a pole on a laneway off Roebuck Road. Detective Inspector Tony Hickey and Detective Sergeant Martin Callinan, who were in charge of the undercover squad, also got word of where Cahill had hidden his stash. In December they began staking out the spot. Cahill was bound to emerge at some stage from the shadows and reclaim the stuff. However, on the night of 22 January, 1989, Cahill's uncanny sixth sense was again in action. He had arranged to collect the guns and jewellery hidden in the lane himself and meet Eugene Scanlon and Harry Melia.

But at the last minute he changed plans and directed the two hoods to the hiding-place to pick up the stuff. He was to meet them nearby. Just as Melia and Scanlon retrieved the two bags armed undercover detectives appeared and told them to freeze. Scanlon shouted: 'Don't shoot. I've dropped the rods.' Melia exclaimed: 'The bastards set us up.' Scanlon told him to shut up. The two men were arrested, charged and remanded in custody. Within a few weeks they both got bail. This is one of the aspects of the Irish criminal justice system which annoys every cop in the country. They had already charged Melia with a serious drug offence and he had been on bail for two months when he was again caught red-handed. Many argue that Ireland's liberal bail laws only lead to further serious crime – for a criminal facing a long stretch is effectively given an incentive to rob a nest egg for his dependants to live off while he is away. And normally any further convictions are taken into consideration and run concurrently with the first sentence. Many of Cahill's men continued to carry out serious crimes while on bail.

Some months later the undercover squad again thought they were about to catch Tango One. Through the use of the mystery informant and high-tech bugging equipment they were aware that Martin and Eddie Cahill and another man were planning to abduct the owner of a busy city centre pub. The publican usually brought the takings back to his home in Tallaght where he kept them in a safe. The three robbers planned to rendezvous late on a Saturday night close to the pub-owner's house. They took separate routes. The seventeen detectives involved in the operation – there were twelve on surveillance with five back-ups – were all heavily armed and wearing bullet-proof vests. They expected a showdown.

In Templeogue one of the surveillance teams lost sight of Tango One. Later they found his car parked offside at Old Bawn. A team kept watch on it. Meanwhile the three men had met and were lying in wait for the publican to return to his home around one in the morning. The undercover teams took up positions from which they could move in quickly and surround the gang. But Cahill's luck held once again. A neighbour spotted the three men and promptly dialled '999'. In fact the worried neighbour made a total of three emergency calls. The patient undercover cops watched as the quiet *cul de sac* was lit up by the blue flashing beacons of squad cars that came from every direction. In the confusion Eddie Cahill and the third man were detained and found in possession of balaclavas. They were later released without charge. Martin Cahill had disappeared. He crept into a garden and hid in a tree, watching the cops below. At five o'clock in the morning the surveillance team could only watch in dismay as the empty-handed General came back for his car and drove away. Although he didn't know it, fate had again intervened on Cahill's behalf.

In the meantime Cahill, who was running low on money, continued his efforts to cash in his growing collection of stolen art. Around the time of the Murnaghan robbery he met salesman John Naughton from Terenure in Dublin. The forty-eight year-old family man had never been involved in crime and was experiencing financial difficulties. Cahill had burgled Naughton's house but later heard through the grapevine that his victim was a 'decent bloke on hard times'. Cahill returned the stolen valuables and offered Naughton a large amount of cash to act as his middleman.

In December 1988 Naughton phoned a fine arts consultant in London. Naughton told Trevor Hallword, an auctioneer with Christie's, he had a Gainsborough, one of the stolen Beit paintings, to sell. Nothing came of the contact.

In May 1989 Naughton again called the art expert and told him that he was working as a middleman for big-time art thieves. He said that they had threatened his life and would have no compunction about harming his family. Naughton was offering the eleven stolen Beit paintings for £12.5 million, of which Hallword would be paid £500,000. A special account would be set up in Geneva where over £10 million would be lodged, with the remainder going back to Cahill and his gang in Dublin. Naughton told the art expert that he could fly to Dublin where he would be able to view the paintings at various locations. Instead of calling his travel agent Hallword phoned Scotland Yard's arts and antiques squad.

The following day Naughton was arrested and charged with inciting another to handle the Beit collection dishonestly. In March 1990 he was jailed by Southwark Crown Court for two years. During his trial Naughton was described as a Walter Mitty-type character who had been manipulated by the gang behind the art heist. Back in Dublin Martin Cahill remained unscathed but still in need of cash. There were more difficulties on the way.

Wally McGregor from Clondalkin on the city's west side had been an associate and trusted friend of the General's for years. In his late fifties, McGregor had been a professional criminal since the sixties and was well-known to the police. Shortly after the Murnaghan robbery Cahill asked McGregor to store the paintings for him in a lock-up garage he had rented in Rathfarnham. The paintings were given to McGregor by Eugene Scanlon and he was told to sit tight until the General called. In August another English crime gang were interested in the collection and Cahill asked McGregor to move the pictures for him. McGregor agreed. He bought a car trailer to transport them to a pre-arranged location. The Serious Crime Squad had other ideas.

On the morning of 4 August, 1989, detectives arrived to search the garage rented by McGregor. Detective Sergeant Felix McKenna noticed the trailer in the corner. When he opened it he found thirty-six stolen paintings. Among the valuable art haul were two nondescript paintings, valued at £200, which had been stolen from a pub in Carlow a few weeks after Cahill was released from Spike Island. At the same time Cahill's old friend drove into the yard to collect his trailer. Instead he collected a two-year sentence for receiving stolen goods. When he was being questioned about the identities of the individuals who had asked him to store the Murnaghan paintings, McGregor told detectives that if he said anything he was a dead man. He revealed that he had agreed to 'try and do a deal' with an insurance company on behalf of the gang. The jinx had struck again.

Meanwhile Cahill and his two middlemen were not the only ones suffering from the bad luck which seemed to hover over the organisation. Harry Melia, who was in jail when the Beit robbery took place, was probably the most unlucky criminal of all. By September 1989 he was facing two serious charges with the prospect of a ten-year stint in Portlaoise maximum security prison. Melia decided that he had little incentive to spend his last remaining months of freedom as a model citizen. He continued to work with the General and his brother Eddie. He also continued his heroin dealing activities.

During the summer of 1989 Melia had been approached by members of the Republican movement and told that it was in the interests of his health to desist from selling drugs. Melia, not renowned for his diplomacy, told the Provos to 'Fuck off'. On the night of 16 September a representative of the organisation, carrying a sawn-off shotgun, came back to see Melia who was watching TV in his home at Tallaght. The gunman fired two shots through the front-room window. Melia was seriously injured in the arms and chest.

While Melia was recuperating in hospital, a petitioner called to see Martin Cahill on his behalf. Cahill was fully aware of the background to the shooting and reckoned that Melia had been asking for what he got. He smiled at the visitor in front of him. 'Tell Harry to watch the telly upstairs in future,' he said. But whatever about changing the rooms where he watched his soaps, Melia's zeal for criminal activity did not change.

A month after the shooting Detective Sergeant Mick Finn of the drug unit attached to Store Street Station walked into a café on Parnell Street where Melia was sitting drinking coffee. The criminal had one arm in a sling and had closed the fist of his other hand. Finn opened Melia's hand and a bag fell to the table. Inside were thirteen wrapped deals of heroin with a street value of £500. Over the next year Melia would be in the dock of the Special Criminal Court on three occasions. He received three jail sentences totalling seventeen years in prison. Eugene Scanlon, who was caught with him on Roebuck Road, got eight years. Eddie Cahill also got eight years on the drug charge. Within two years the General had lost ten of the toughest criminals in Ireland. His intermediaries had also been unlucky. And his attempts to make a profit out of art had so far failed miserably.

The jinx was to strike another blow against the General towards the end of 1989. The fence from Drogheda in Co Louth, who had been involved in the initial attempts to sell the Beit paintings, was still busy in negotiations. He had been central to five proposals to buy the collection, but all had fallen through. For a brief period he had also discussed the possibility of a deal with the IRA, who had considered converting into arms and ammunition the paintings they had once tried unsuccessfully to rob. The negotiations collapsed partly because of the lingering animosity between the organisation and the General. The fence was then approached by a representative of a UVF gang based in Portadown.

It was the first time that a Northern Loyalist terrorist group had considered doing business with an underworld outfit south of the border. All southerners, even apolitical criminals, were viewed with suspicion and contempt. The Beit paintings changed that attitude. When Cahill got word that the UVF were interested in doing a deal, he was happy to oblige. Over the last months of 1988 he held a number of meetings with the Portadown group which had been involved in some of the most brutal sectarian atrocities of the twenty-five year conflict. The group was led by a man whom the IRA had had in their sights for a long time. Cahill's anxiety to cash in on his art collection, coupled with his almost reckless disregard for organisations like the Provos, led him to do business with the Loyalists. It was not a politically-motivated decision. As someone who had never voted or even held a passport in his life Martin Cahill's concept of sovereignty did not extend beyond the southside of the River Liffey. It wasn't personal, just business.

Since the mid-eighties Loyalist terrorists had been anxious to boost their arsenals with the same kind of sophisticated hardware that the IRA had smuggled in huge quantities from Libya. The UVF, UDA and the Ulster Resistance had organised between them a major deal with South Africa, in which they would barter parts of a surface-to-air missiles system being manufactured in the Shorts armaments factory in Belfast. Hundreds of Kalashnikov rifles, handguns and grenades supplied by a South African agent were smuggled into Co Armagh by the Portadown group. Later three men acting on behalf of the Ulster Resistance were arrested in Paris while doing a deal for the missile system. One of the men directly involved in the deal with the South Africans met with the Drogheda fence. He and other members of his organisation also met with the General. The meetings, arranged by the Drogheda fence, took place in the Queen's Head pub in Portadown and in Drogheda and Dublin. Cahill agreed to hand over the least valuable painting in the collection, which the Loyalist middlemen could show a prospective buyer as proof that they had access to the paintings.

In February 1990 two men travelled with the Metsu painting to Turkey where they teamed up with three Turkish men who were helping them find a wealthy buyer. A series of meetings were held with a rich Turkish businessman who claimed that he had a sheikh who was interested in buying the lot. The Loyalists gave the Beit painting to the businessman who turned out to be an undercover Turkish policeman. Mysteriously, news of the sting operation was leaked in Ireland on 28 February while negotiations to buy the entire collection were at an advanced stage. On the same day one of the Portadown group received a phone call telling him that he should return to Ireland immediately because the people who had sent him had been in a traffic accident. The middleman understood the coded message and was arrested by Turkish police as he tried to catch a plane out of the country. All five men – the three Turks and the two Irishmen – were arrested and charged. Ironically, the same day that they appeared in an Istanbul court, John Naughton's trial began at Southwark Crown Court for his efforts on behalf of the General.

The recovery of the first of the stolen Beit paintings made big news back in Dublin. It was the kind of coverage Cahill could have done without. The Irish public's image of the amusing criminal joker disappeared. Getting into bed with terrorists, especially Loyalists, placed the General in a sinister light. The fun was going out of the game. Cahill had hoped that the deal would have been completed secretly and never be revealed. Now his old adversaries the Provos had a new, much more valid reason for watching the General.

CHAPTER 12

The Dole Man

An indirect result of the Tango Squad surveillance operation on Martin Cahill was the decision by the Department of Social Welfare to cut off his unemployment assistance. And, while he characteristically kept on smiling, beneath the balaclava he was seething with anger.

Ever since he walked out of his first and last job in 1969, the General had drawn the dole. Each week, without fail, he went to Werburgh Street employment exchange and signed for his unemployment assistance to support his wife Frances and their five children. He would queue at Hatch 10 and wait his turn.

The clerk on the other side of the protective grille would ask the compulsory question: Had he got any work in the past week? He would sign a declaration form that he had not, receive a docket and go to another counter for his cash. The clerks who dealt with him recall that he was courteous, pleasant and, unlike some other signatories, quiet-spoken.

Invariably when he arrived in Werburgh Street Cahill would wear a motorbike helmet or balaclava or hold his hand over his face. It was well-known that the police brought witnesses to the exchange for the purposes of informally identifying criminals. He revealed himself only at the hatch. One week in the mid-1970s he turned up twice wearing a helmet – the first time to collect his dole and the second to rob £100,000 in cash. In fact he planned his jobs around his designated days for joining the dole queue. It was a cast-iron alibi. And if he dropped out of sight the cops simply had to wait for him to turn up to collect the 'labour' – then the problem was keeping him in their sights.

In the Dublin underworld most criminals ensure that they collect their social welfare assistance no matter how lucrative 'business' is.

Their attitude is that if a criminal with 'no visible means of income' shirks the indignity of signing on he is showing the authorities the two fingers and giving the police ammunition to sink him further in the eyes of a judge.

But the *Today Tonight* exposé of the General had revealed he was abusing the social welfare system. There was a public furore and uproar in the Dáil. The government were embarrassed that a man suspected of being the country's most successful criminal was, effectively, on their payroll. The then Social Welfare Minister Michael Woods announced that Cahill's payments were to be suspended immediately and a departmental investigation begun. Cahill had made himself available for a number of 'job search' interviews arranged by the Department although he had not been fortunate enough to find 'suitable' employment.

Mary Harney, then a Progressive Democrat deputy, was one of the most vociferous in the debate. She wanted Cahill investigated in the same way Elliot Ness had nailed Al Capone. The image conjured up was of a Chicago-style swaggering mobster. Harney also wanted Cahill evicted from the Corporation house at Swan Grove. If the law didn't exist to do it then the law should be changed to make it possible. But the politicians merely tossed the balls. Outside the sanctuary of the Dáil it was left to the civil servants to do battle with the major-league criminal.

A few days after the Dáil debate, investigators from the Department of Social Welfare arrived at the door of Cahill's house in Swan Grove. Faced with the awesome reputation of the sinister figure in the balaclava, they were expecting at least a hostile reaction. Instead they were greeted by a portly, balding man with a big grin on his round face, who welcomed them into his home. Cahill enjoyed doing the opposite to what people expected. A source later told the *Sunday World*: 'Mr Cahill was most pleasant – he seemed like a nice man.'

But Mr Cahill politely refused to answer any questions about his comments on the *Today Tonight* programme or about any other income he may have had. The cars and motorbikes he had were left to him in a will and neither of the two houses he resided in were in his name, he told the investigators. The matter could have been sorted out straight away if he had simply denied that he had any other source of income, but Cahill had his own way of doing things. To give any details to the investigators would be an acknowledgement of their authority and he was loath to do that. He hated what he called the 'faceless men behind the misery of the dole queues' or the 'red tape men'. They had thrown down the gauntlet to him and he was determined they were not going to beat him.

There was no love lost between Cahill and the Revenue Commissioners either. Some time after his TV debut a tax inspector arrived at Cowper Downs for a 'chat' with Martin. The General had purposely agreed to meet in the £85,000 private house because he knew it irritated the tax people no end. The house, which had been bought with cash, was not in his name and there was nothing they could do about it. Again he was courteous and invited the taxman into his sitting-room.

At one stage he excused himself from the room saying that he had to make a phone call. He returned a few minutes later and diverted attention away from the matter of his 'taxable earnings' to the subject of crime. With his hands stuffed down in the pockets of his jeans, Cahill frowned as he reflected on the woeful state of modern Ireland with its rampant drug abuse and vandalism. The nervous tax inspector agreed. Then something caught Cahill's eye. 'Now, d'ya see what I mean, just look out that window and look what those bloody vandals have done now,' he said, pointing out the front window. The tax inspector was horrified by what he saw – his nice car was engulfed in flames. The General had made his point.

Meanwhile Cahill's new-found stardom was causing a stir each week down at Werburgh Street employment exchange. He turned up as normal to sign on despite the fact that his payments had been stopped. Everyone on the queues now watched for the enigmatic character in the anorak and balaclava. It added a little diversion and excitement in otherwise monotonous lives. Behind the hatch windows there was concern among the staff about who would break the unpalatable news to the godfather – that he was permanently losing his social welfare money. The decision had been reached towards the end of 1988 but no one had informed Cahill who still smiled and thanked the clerks when they handed him his worthless docket.

On 9 January, 1989, Martin Cahill finally received a letter from the Department of Social Welfare's employment branch informing him that his dole money would not be restored. It was signed by Brian Purcell, a Higher Executive Officer (HEO) at the Department's HQ in Townsend Street.

In his worst nightmare Brian Purcell could not have imagined what he was letting himself in for when he signed the letter addressed to Cahill. After all, the civil servant was just doing his job. He was another cog in the machinery which caters for the financial welfare of over 300,000 people each week. At thirty-one years of age with an arts degree, Purcell had a promising career in the civil service. He was married and had two little boys. The couple were expecting their third child and had moved into their first home in Santry a few weeks before Purcell's letter dropped through the letter box at Swan Grove in Rathmines.

Cahill, through his solicitor, Garret Sheehan, appealed the Department's decision to cut his dole payments. On 9 March, 1989, an oral hearing of the case took place in the offices of the North Cumberland Street employment exchange. Martin and Frances Cahill were accompanied by Garret Sheehan. It was the first time Purcell had ever set eyes on the General. During the hour and a half long hearing Brian Purcell outlined to the appeals board the reasons why Cahill's payments were terminated and the relevant laws under which he was obliged to arrive at that decision.

Cahill stared intently at the hitherto anonymous 'red tape man'. He later described to associates how he sat in front of a big boardroom table as the members of the appeal board looked sternly at him. Cahill hated them for putting him in such a humiliating position. Brian Purcell became the focus for that hatred. Civil servants were about as popular with Cahill as the police. At Garret Sheehan's request the hearing was adjourned until 29 May. On 9 May Brian Purcell again came in contact with Cahill and his family. This time he appeared on behalf of the Department at an appeal hearing by Cahill's sister-in-law Patricia Lawless whose dole had also been cut. The hearing was adjourned at her request.

Brian Purcell's routine was predictable. He cycled from Santry to his offices on Townsend Street at the same time each morning and took the same route home each evening. Within a few days of the hearing Cahill was hovering in the shadows watching him as he left work. Brian Purcell was followed on several occasions. Cahill's men watched his house and built up a detailed picture of the movements of the Purcell family. Cahill was planning a terrifying ordeal for the innocent civil servant.

Shortly after midnight on Monday, 29 May, Brian Purcell was sitting in his living-room watching TV and reading the Sunday newspapers. His wife, Sandra, had gone to bed and his little boys, Karl and Andrew, had been asleep since nine o'clock. Around ten minutes past midnight the front door bell rang. When Purcell opened it a masked man put an automatic pistol to his neck and bundled him back into his hallway. Three other hooded men pushed in behind him.

The first gunman shoved the civil servant into his kitchen and forced him to lie face down on the floor. A hood was placed over his head and his hands were tied behind his back. His upper arms and chest were also bound with cords. A gun was held against him as he lay on the floor. When he asked what the gunmen wanted he was told to shut up. He could hear the other men racing up the stairs.

Sandra Purcell had been woken by the noise of the door bell. She got out of bed and met three masked men running up the stairs. The pregnant mother was terrified and screamed. Cahill's men told her to shut up. One of the hoods stood beside her on the stairs and made her sit looking downwards. The other two began searching the rooms. She told the man beside her that they would wake her two sons. He replied that the children would not be harmed.

After a few minutes one of the gang caught Sandra by the hair and walked her into the kitchen where she saw her husband lying on the floor. She was crying and told them that she was pregnant. They made her sit on a couch and one of them snapped at her: 'Shut fucking up.'

When the couple tried to speak to each other they were told 'No talking.' The gang spent almost an hour in the house. They rummaged for documents connected with Cahill's adjourned hearing which would take place within a matter of hours.

Brian Purcell was pulled to his feet and put lying on the floor in the back of his own car with pillowcases over his head. Inside the house the gang members moved Sandra to a chair and tied her legs and arms. One of them gave her a drink of water and told her the sleeping children were OK. They tied a gag around her mouth before they left. Sandra had told them that she would not be able to get to her kids. The men said they would call the police and leave the door open for them. A few minutes later she heard the door closing and the family car driving away.

Two members of the abduction gang drove the social welfare officer to Ailesbury Gardens in Sandymount on the city's southside. Purcell was taken from the car and walked a short distance and made sit in a hedgerow a few yards from two railway lines. He was kept in that position for around twenty minutes and heard two Dart trains pass. At one stage he feared that he was to be tied to one of the rail lines. The two men holding Purcell said nothing. Purcell couldn't figure out what was going on. It worried him that he had not been questioned about anything and there appeared to be no explanation about what was happening.

At that stage he had no idea that it had to do with his investigation of Martin Cahill's claims for unemployment assistance. He wasn't to know that the two criminals were waiting for the General to arrive at the pre-arranged location to take care of some personal business.

Shortly before 1.50 am the men lifted Brian Purcell, walked him a further twenty yards and put him sitting against the wall of an ESB pumping station with his legs straight out in front of him. The General emerged from the shadows with a .38 revolver in his hand. It was from the cache of firearms Cahill had stolen from the old Garda Technical Bureau.

Cahill's associates say that they never once saw him taking someone on by using his fists. He wasn't one for head-on confrontation.

His favoured way of 'dealing' with such situations was from behind a gun in the depths of night, when his opponent had no way of retaliating. Cahill pointed the gun at Purcell's legs. He never said a word. A single shot pierced the night air. Purcell felt a thud in his right leg and the stinging pain as the bullet went through his thigh. Cahill changed his aim. Another shot rang out. This time his victim was shot in the left leg. The General wrapped his gun up in a balaclava and ran off with his men. At the same time two other gang members set fire to the victim's car and also made their escape.

Purcell was left lying on the ground, tied and hooded, as blood oozed from his wounds. He was afraid to cry out for help in case his abductors were still present. He fell to his side and began worked the pillowcases from his head. Only then, he began calling out and local people came to his aid.

At the same time back in Santry, Sandra Purcell had managed to wriggle out of the cords tied around her arms and legs. She climbed across a back wall and into a neighbour's garden. Within minutes Garda units across the city were aware of the abduction. Detectives later believed that Sandra's quick escape had not been anticipated by the gang and that Cahill may have intended a worse fate for his victim.

A week later children out playing in Tranquilla Park two hundred yards away from Cahill's home found the loaded revolver used to shoot the civil servant. They also uncovered a replica gun which had been traded for heroin with a member of the General's gang some time earlier. The revolver could have claimed an even higher body count – for a short while the kids played cowboys with the piece. They later brought the gun to Rathmines Garda Station.

Brian Purcell was rushed to St James's Hospital where he underwent an operation to the two bullet wounds in his thighs. The bullets had narrowly missed major arteries and no bones were broken. It is unlikely that Cahill was overly concerned with his marksmanship as long as he hit his target. Purcell was hospitalised for two weeks and was under medical supervision for a number of months. During his stay in hospital he received an anonymous 'get well' card which simply read: 'The General prognosis is good.'

The shooting provoked an inevitable outcry. The following morning Social Welfare Minister Michael Woods requested Garda protection for other department officials involved in the Cahill case. He described it as a 'new and sinister departure in intimidation'. Not since the bomb attack on Dr James Donovan had a civil servant been the target of a criminal. For a second time in seven years Martin Cahill was sending a brutal message to the state he despised. He had consolidated his position as a gangster to be reckoned with – a godfather who would go to savage extremes to get his way.

As Brian Purcell lay in a hospital bed recuperating from his ordeal the following afternoon, Martin Cahill was attending the re-convened appeal hearing in the Department of Social Welfare. The appeal board concluded that Cahill would no longer receive social welfare.

In the follow-up investigation detectives arrested five men, including Harry Melia, for questioning but no-one was charged. Two of Cahill's other relations, on bail for serious crimes, were also suspected of involvement. The investigation team deemed it a waste of time lifting Cahill because of the lack of evidence and his reluctance to indulge in conversation with the police. It is a decision that was the subject of controversy up to the time of Cahill's death. Many detectives believe that the General should have been brought in every time he was a suspect in a serious crime, if only to disrupt two days of his life.

In the months before the attack on the civil servant Cahill had been in the circuit court appealing a seven-day jail sentence for non-payment of a £750 gas bill. He claimed that he could not pay the bill because his dole had been stopped. His solicitor Garrett Sheehan said that his client would probably be able to pay the bill in instalments if his unemployment benefit was restored. A few weeks after the incident with Brian Purcell Cahill quietly paid the gas bill and the sentence was quashed.

Under the laws concerning the payment of social welfare Martin Cahill was entitled to a basic minimum weekly allowance – of just tenpence. For several weeks he queued at Hatch 10 and collected his docket for that amount. He would collect the coin from the cashier's desk and throw it down the length of the employment exchange, shouting: 'Youse need this more than I do.' He would shrug his broad shoulders and swagger out. It became a weekly spectacle. A source of entertainment for the other recipients. For the clerks it was an unwanted addition to the tension of the job.

Shortly before Christmas 1989, seven months after the Purcell shooting, Cahill queued as normal at Hatch 10. When he got to the top he reached up to the top of the protective screen and handed the nervous clerk a package, wrapped in gift paper, saying, 'This is for you.' The young man wasn't sure whether he should accept the gift or call the bomb squad. Later he plucked up the courage to open it. Inside was a silver Shaeffer pen worth about £15 or the equivalent of 150 weeks' dole money. An accompanying note read:

> 'For all your kindness throughout the year,
> You've made it worthwhile to come in here.'

CHAPTER 13

Year of the Gun

The year 1990 was a year of violence and bloodshed. The crime war spilled onto the streets and a shocked Irish public was confronted with a real life cops and robbers drama. To the opposing sides it would be remembered as the year of the gun. Shoot-outs between the criminals and the police were no longer a terrifying exception. The cops were taking on the bad guys and winning, but the victories were calculated with the blood of dead and wounded robbers who decided to fight rather than put their hands up.

In the first six months of the year three Dublin criminals were shot dead and several more wounded by Garda bullets. Three gangs were captured and put behind bars. But the Gardaí narrowly missed their greatest prize, Martin Cahill, who fired the first angry shot in the year of the gun.

Porter Willie Blake arrived at the Allied Irish Bank branch in Ranelagh village on the city's southside to open up at 7.35 am on Monday, 8 January. It was a wintry morning and traffic on the inbound route to the city centre was building up for rush hour. Inside, Blake switched off the alarm system. Everything appeared in order.

He admitted the cleaner, Beatrice Hand, who went upstairs to make the morning tea. Blake lifted blinds on the front windows, a signal for arriving staff that all was well inside. He also raised the shutters on the back windows which faced into the branch car park. He walked outside to unlock the sliding gate which adjoined Ranelagh Avenue. Just as he was about to open the gate he was hit from behind.

He looked around and found two masked men with guns standing behind him. One of them told him, 'Do as ye'r told.' The gunmen pushed the porter back into the building. They tied up the cleaner and blindfolded her. The gangsters demanded to know who held the keys to the various safes. Around 7.55 am one of the masked raiders responded to a knock on the back door. Martin Cahill entered the bank armed with two handguns and a grenade.

The General immediately took over the interrogation of the porter. Cahill was more aggressive than the others and left no doubt that he was the man in charge. He held the grenade – one of his favourite weapons – to Willie Blake's face. It had black tape where the pin should have been. He said to the terrified porter: 'See this? You know what it is, it's a grenade, any messin' and I will take the tape off and you're gone.'

Unlike the other raiders, Cahill was interested only in the keys to the night safes. Typically he had done his homework. He had been watching the bank for several weeks. After all it was only a short walk from his Corporation house in Swan Grove. On Friday nights the bank's cash deposits were cleared out and brought to a cash-holding facility. But there could be anything up to a few hundred thousand pounds in the bank's night safes. The cash in used notes was the weekend lodgements from the scores of restaurants, fast-food joints, bars, discos and twenty-four-hour shops concentrated in the bustling flatland.

He had selected a close-knit team for the job. Two of the gang were on bail awaiting trials for serious charges. Cahill took Willie Blake and stood inside the front door waiting for the staff to arrive. He placed a noose around the porter's neck and shoved a gun into his back. He instructed his victim to admit each individual 'quick as hell'. As the bank staff arrived they were frisked and ordered to lie on the floor. At 8.35 am, almost an hour since the raid had begun, assistant manager Oliver Williams arrived and was questioned about the keys to the night safes. He was kicked to the ground and a gun cocked beside his ear, but he didn't have the keys.

At 8.45 am a fourth member of the gang outside banged hard on the rear window of the building to relay some kind of signal. For all his planning, the General was unaware that the windows were connected to a silent panic alarm. Within minutes the Gardaí were on their way.

Uniformed officers John Moore and William Joynt from Donny-brook Garda Station were on patrol in their squad car in the Ranelagh area. They had been on duty since 6 am and now at a few minutes to 8.50 am they were stuck in the inbound bumper-to-bumper traffic. They welcomed the emergency call. They put on the blue lights and siren and Joynt somehow managed to squeeze through the throng of cars. As the car approached the bank Cahill heard the siren blaring. He listened intently for a moment, trying to work out whether it was police or just an ambulance or fire engine.

Cahill peered out through the holes in his balaclava and spotted the squad car coming off the Ranelagh Road towards the building. He ran back into the main part of the bank and calmly told his gang: 'There's sirens all over the place, they're out the front.' Without another word the three men scattered out the back door of the bank, leaving behind a hold-all containing two guns and assorted ammunition.

Meanwhile Garda John Moore was already ringing the door bell at the front of the bank. His partner remained in the squad car. Visibly shaken, Willie Blake opened the door with Cahill's noose still around his neck. 'Go to the back, go to the back, they're gone to the back. We've been raided,' he blurted out. Moore ran around the corner onto Ranelagh Avenue. As he did so two of Cahill's men also stepped out into the avenue from the bank car park. When they saw the uniform they turned and fled down the laneway that runs along the rear of the bank and the adjoining Richard Crosbie's Tavern car park. For a moment Moore lost sight of Cahill and his team.

As he ran further down the laneway Moore spotted a third man also running into nearby Ranelagh Park. He took off in pursuit. The fourth man had already split from his companions and skipped out of the park through the Northbrook Avenue entrance. The other three headed for the Chelmsford Avenue exit.

Soon the General started to lag behind the other, fitter men. The years of washing down sweets and cakes with litres of orange pop had taken their toll. Like other 'generals' he would probably have been better suited to guiding operations from the comfort of one of his homes. The policeman began to close in. Later, Cahill told associates that he swore to himself: 'I'm packin' in this fuckin' game. If I get away I'll never rob a fuckin' bank again.'

Moore got within four feet of the General and prepared to topple him with a rugby tackle. But Cahill, now gasping for breath, had other ideas. He pleaded in a croaking voice to the men ahead: 'Lads, come back, come back.' As he did so he turned around and faced Moore, pulling a gun from his pocket. Cahill fired two shots from point-blank range.

In the rush of adrenalin the young officer did not feel one of the bullets ripping into his right arm. Cahill turned and continued running. The cop kept on his heels. At the same time one of the two men, who had been running on ahead, circled around and behind John Moore and fired a shot from a .45 revolver. The officer heard the shot and felt a burning sensation in his right leg. Another shot was fired, this time by the General, bringing to four the total number fired at the unarmed cop.

But Moore kept going. As he came to the gates at Chelmsford Avenue he stumbled and fell face down on the footpath. He tried to get up and continue the chase. Another burning pain shot through his right arm. He fell down again. Blood oozed from the wound. A young woman on her way to work came running to his aid. She placed her coat over him and her handbag under his head. The injured officer was conscious enough to radio his station for help.

As he lay there, Moore could hear the wail of sirens as colleagues raced to help a 'member down'. Within minutes two detectives were at his side. They picked him up and placed him in their squad car. Other police on motorbikes escorted them to St Vincent's Hospital.

Meanwhile the three gang members were still making a getaway. They ran down Chelmsford Avenue towards Chelmsford Road. Another young woman who had watched the incident threw her bicycle in front of the General and his men. Two of them tripped and fell over it. They picked themselves up quickly and continued running, one limping.

At the junction between Chelmsford Road and Appian Way they surrounded the driver of a Jaguar car. One of them shoved a handgun through a partially opened sun roof and ordered him to 'open the fucking door'. The driver managed to take off, leaving the men on the road. The three then split up, the General and one of his men up Sallymount Avenue where they turned off and disappeared down a laneway. The third man hi-jacked a car a hundred yards down the road. He ordered the driver out at gun-point and sped away towards Leeson Street.

The General and his fellow gangster scaled a wall and went through the grounds of the Royal Hospital in Donnybrook. By this stage Cahill was puffing and panting and holding his stomach. The pair split up and faded into the background as squad cars searched the streets frantically. The criminal who had hi-jacked the car abandoned it off Pembroke Lane in Ballsbridge. He too vanished. Two weeks later a plastic bag containing the .45 used against Garda Moore was found stuffed in a hedge nearby.

Less than an hour after the robbery Cahill was seen walking into the Tom Kelly House flats complex off Charlemont Street to his hide-out. Now he had no need to worry about being arrested. There was a ready collection of people he could rely on for a convincing alibi. He listened intently to the radio reports about the morning's events and the condition of the wounded Garda.

John Moore underwent emergency surgery in hospital where a bullet was removed from his right arm. He was also treated for a flesh wound to his right leg. He was remarkably lucky to be alive – two of the shots fired by the General at point-blank range had missed their target. Moore told reporters who interviewed him about the incident: 'I would do the same thing again.' But according to the General himself, John Moore did not realise how near he came to never doing anything again. Cahill later claimed to associates that the trigger of the gun broke as he aimed the final shot at the officer's chest. Yet again, the weapon, a .25 calibre pistol, and some of the other guns recovered in the bank had been stolen from the old Garda Technical Bureau in the early eighties.

But Cahill lost no sleep pondering the moral implications or otherwise of what he had done. To him anyone, especially a policeman, deserved to be shot if they 'had a go'. His only concern was that if Moore was 'brown bread' (dead) then the police would come looking for retribution. As it was he was preparing himself for the heat.

The descriptions detectives received from witnesses to the drama soon pointed the finger of suspicion at Cahill and his men. However, there was no forensic evidence on which to build a case. All the Gardaí had were the sightings of the various individuals involved, in themselves inconclusive. For the General was meticulous when it came to leaving no evidence. Each man wore two sets of clothes on a job. One of these was discarded soon after the crime. Members of the gang habitually covered up their faces to prevent identification. In fact, on the days that they collected their unemployment assistance from Werburgh Street exchange, Cahill's men were easily picked out – they were the only ones in the crowd with hands over their faces or anorak hoods pulled tightly around their heads.

At the investigation headquarters in Donnybrook Station Superintendent Jim McHugh, who was heading the case, eventually decided to lift Eddie Cahill, the General's brother, and Eugene Scanlon, his brother-in-law. With both men on bail they might have an incentive to assist with enquiries in the hope of beating the rap. However, it was considered a waste of time bringing Tango One in if they hadn't something concrete to charge him with. Without a positive identification and with no forensic evidence the police could look forward to a marathon of mantra-chanting with nothing to show for it.

On 15 February, teams of armed detectives surrounded the homes of Eddie Cahill in Crumlin and Scanlon in Clondalkin and arrested both of them. Scanlon refused to co-operate. When the police arrested him under the Offences Against The State Act, he told them: 'I am saying nothing to youse men. I have done nothing.' He also called them 'stitch-up bastards'. Before he was taken away he had asked his wife to tie his shoe-laces so that he didn't have to take his hands down from his face. For the duration of his stay in custody Scanlon held his hands over his face and repeated his mantra.

When the police came to arrest Eddie Cahill, he smeared black shoe-polish over his face and refused to say anything. When he was taken to Donnybrook Station he was led to an interview room for questioning. He sat on the floor facing into the wall with both hands covering his face. Then he put his head between his knees. An eyewitness who had seen him making his getaway in the hi-jacked car had been invited to the station for an informal identity parade. The members of the gang had been well-trained by their General in the methods of frustrating identification. He opened out his pony-tail and pulled it over his already blackened face.

The detectives were forced to handcuff Eddie while they pulled back his hair and tied it. Then they washed the polish off his face. He began screaming and calling them 'fucking bastards' and demanding to see his solicitor. As he was marched from the station for the informal identity parade Eddie Cahill struggled, made faces and stuck his tongue out. A positive identification was made. But there still wasn't enough evidence to link either man with the robbery. They were released without charge. Once again Martin Cahill and his gang narrowly slipped the net.

But his confrontation with the law was the only one where the Gardaí were the losers in the year of the gun. On the morning that the General and his men were on their way to the AIB in Ranelagh the Gardaí were limbering up for an unprecedented showdown with a notorious gang of armed robbers which had become one of the most active and dangerous gangs in the country during 1989.

Its leader, P J Loughran, a former paramilitary, was a meticulous planner and well-trained in the use of firearms. From Dungannon in Co Tyrone he had moved to live on the northside of Dublin in 1987 in the sprawling working-class suburb of Coolock. There he got involved in armed crime and worked for a time with Martin's older brother, John Cahill. Loughran was also a good friend of the General.

He had organised his own highly-efficient team of hoods. They included Austin Higgins from Donaghmede on the city's northside and William Gardiner from Cabra, both of whom had a record of petty crime but not armed robbery. The other two were Martin Cahill's protégés, Thomas Tynan from the South Circular Road and Brendan

'Wetty' Walshe from Charlemont Gardens. Both men had a string of serious convictions, particularly Walshe, who had served time for serious offences including armed robbery. Walshe was also facing armed robbery charges along with Eugene Scanlon for a raid on a bank in Rathmines in the summer of 1989.

Their *modus operandi* was always the same. They hit banks in country towns where the risk of running into armed Gardaí was substantially less than in the larger cities and towns. Each job was carefully planned and executed – the heavily-armed raiders could be in and out of a bank within four minutes. Their mode of transport was invariably high-performance cars driven by Loughran.

In October 1989, Austin Higgins was arrested following an armed robbery on a bank in Roscrea in Co Tipperary but was released on bail. During that heist, in which the gang took over £13,000, shots were fired. Around the time of the Roscrea robbery and Higgins's arrest, senior officers in Dublin decided that the gang had to be stopped and a major undercover surveillance operation was ordered by Assistant Commissioner Ned O'Dea, the chief at the Crime and Security Branch (C3) in Garda HQ. There was concern that with each robbery the gang was becoming more violent. They were armed to the teeth with heavy calibre weapons, including assault rifles of the type used by paramilitaries, and they were prepared to take on the cops in any confrontation.

A little-known elite anti-terrorist squad had been formed from within the Special Detective Unit, (Special Branch). The force had never seen the likes of the Emergency Response Unit (ERU) before. In fact, many members didn't know it existed in the first week of 1990. Armed with powerful Heckler and Koch assault rifles, automatic shotguns and pistols, this thirty-two man unit was designed for siege situations, hi-jacking – and taking on gangs like Loughran's.

Just after Christmas, Detective Inspector Tony Hickey, the officer in charge of the surveillance unit in the Serious Crime Squad, got information that the gang was planning to hit the Bank of Ireland in Emily Square, Athy, on a Friday in January. They were suspected of hitting the same bank on 16 September – three months earlier – when they got £40,000. Operation Gemini was launched to catch them.

From the outset the plan to intercept and arrest the gang was fraught with difficulties and extreme danger. The gang drove to Athy on a number of occasions on dry runs. Each time the ERU and their colleagues were watching but nothing happened. If the police decided to move in they might find that the gang were unarmed and so only be able to charge them with driving a stolen car. The decision was made to wait and move in just as the gang was running into the bank. It was a major risk, but in the circumstances, the police felt that it was one of the few options open to them.

On Wednesday, 10 January, the surveillance squad watched the gang steal a BMW and another car in Dublin in preparation for the robbery. On Friday morning the ERU and Serious Crime Squad took up positions around Emily Square. One team hid in the nearby fire station while the other waited around the corner in Leinster Street. An undercover man sat in a car in the car park directly facing the bank.

At 12.20 pm the gang drove into Emily Square. Their method, based on the dry runs, was to circle the Square first to find a parking place in front of the building. This time their luck was in, a space was available outside the door.

Tynan, Walshe, Higgins and Gardiner were out of the car and racing through the door as the undercover man radioed 'The eagle has landed, the eagle has landed.' Two of the gang had handguns and the other two a sawn-off shotgun and an M1 Carbine assault rifle. They all wore false beards and wigs. There was panic inside as the men ordered the customers, including a pregnant woman and her child, and staff to lie on the floor. One member of the gang covered them while the other three vaulted the counters. Loughran remained outside in the getaway car.

At the same moment the ERU moved in. Detectives in two Granadas hemmed in the getaway BMW and officers took up positions around the bank door. The plan was to get Loughran to surrender and then wait for the rest of the gang to come out. But Loughran tried to ram the two cars out of his way to escape. Officers began firing at the wheels of the BMW to immobilise it. As detectives approached,

Loughran lifted his automatic pistol to aim at one of the Granada drivers. Other officers opened fire and hit Loughran in the neck. He slumped paralysed across the front seats.

Meanwhile, the gang in the bank heard the shots. Higgins and Walshe ran to the window to see what was going on. They ran back to the others, shouting, 'We're set up, we're set up, the cops are everywhere.' They began roaring and swearing at each other. One of them kept saying: 'It's over, it's over, we're fucked. I don't want to die anyway. They're shooting on the street. I don't want to die.'

The trapped raiders had no intention of giving up. Austin Higgins said: 'We are going to take hostages and we will have to negotiate this.' He grabbed bank official John Condron. Tynan and Walshe took hold of other hostages and walked to the door using them as shields from the police outside.

The raiders were edging towards one of the police cars jammed against the BMW. The keys were in the ignition and the four made to get into it. Detectives opened fire at the wheels to prevent a getaway. 'I'll blow his fucking head off,' Higgins screamed, pointing the shotgun at the back of the bank official's neck. Detectives saw him move his finger to the trigger and fired a number of shots, hitting the robber in the head. Higgins slumped back onto the footpath. The bank official also fell on the ground.

Thomas Tynan, who was holding a handgun to the head of his hostage, swung round to aim at one of the detectives who fired first with an automatic shotgun, hitting the raider in the thigh and lower abdomen. The hostage, another bank official, was injured in the legs. At the same time other shots were fired in the confusion and the bank official, John Condron, was hit in the back. The gunfight was over.

Meanwhile, Walshe and Gardiner had retreated into the bank. They were flustered and confused. They were sweating so much that their false beards fell off. Neither of them seemed to notice. Gardiner kept repeating, 'We're done, we're done.' Detective Inspector Hickey phoned the bank and talked to Walshe, the calmer of the two and offered to negotiate with them. Walshe agreed to surrender and released the pregnant woman and her child. He asked that a local priest be sent in to them to ensure they weren't shot when they walked out front. Fr Patrick Mangan, the town curate, volunteered to go into the bank. When he did the two raiders were remarkably calm.

Gardiner started laughing and remarking that they were reliving the scene in the film *Dog Day Afternoon* and that there would be batteries of TV cameras waiting outside. He borrowed a comb from one of the remaining hostages to fix his hair. Walshe took a bullet from one of the pistols they had discarded and handed it as a souvenir to the prettiest girl in the bank. They both lit cigarettes and walked out into the afternoon sunlight with the priest behind them.

Austin Higgins died before he was taken from the pavement. Tynan underwent emergency surgery. When he recovered he joined Walshe and Gardiner in Portlaoise where they had been sentenced to twelve years. P J Loughran was paralysed from the neck down.

But the Garda victory soon turned to controversy when it was revealed later that, while the gang had fully-loaded and cocked weapons, the only shooting came from the police. Six other people were injured, including the two bank officials, three detectives and a passer-by. The most serious of these was John Condron, who had been shot in the spine, and a detective who suffered a leg wound. The rest of the injuries were not serious and some were treated at the scene. The astonishing scenes in Athy, while controversial, had sent a message which chilled men like Martin Cahill to the bone. Never before had such heavily-armed police been seen on the streets. It confirmed Cahill's paranoid conviction that they would 'do him on the street'.

Officers involved in the shoot-out later admitted that mistakes had been made. But, it was argued, in such situations even the best-laid plans and training could not predict the outcome. In the Dáil there were protests to the Minister for Justice, Ray Burke, from the Opposition benches about what had happened in Athy. But, in the days that followed, the controversy fizzled out. There appeared to be widespread public backing for the action taken by the police. As Irish society moved into a new decade the opinion polls showed universal concern and anger at the growth in armed crime. There was little sympathy for the criminal caught with a gun in his hand. The politicians said no more.

In May, a seven-member IRA gang hit the Allied Irish Bank in Enniscorthy, Co Wexford. The inexperienced gang had spent more time than they should have in the bank and four local uniformed officers, armed with pistols and sub-machineguns, were waiting for them as they left. One member of the gang was seriously injured, others less so. The entire gang was arrested.

Then on Friday, 6 July, two Dublin bank robbers, Thomas Wilson and William 'Blinky' Doyle, were shot dead following a high-speed chase across the city. Wilson, a thirty-nine year-old former IRA man from Antrim, and Doyle, a thirty-four year-old from Ballyfermot, had earlier robbed a bank in the Dublin satellite town of Leixlip. They were quickly intercepted by a convoy of police cars. During the forty-minute chase the two desperadoes caused traffic chaos, with Wilson hanging out of the window, a gun in either hand, firing at the pursuing squad cars. The pair were cornered and rammed by squad cars in a quiet street in Artane in north Dublin.

In the ensuing gun fight, Doyle and Wilson died in a hail of bullets from a policeman's Uzi sub-machine-gun. Later, detectives recovered a total of four guns – .38, .45 and 9mm automatic pistols and a sawn-off shotgun. At the funeral of 'Blinky' Doyle, Martin Cahill's bald pate was just discernible amid the underworld fraternity who stood in silence at the graveside. 'Blinky' was not a hugely popular man but they still turned out in large numbers to pay their respects to a fallen colleague. Many of them were stunned, if not frightened, at the way the cops were fighting back. Cahill knew the war was merely moving onto a different plane. It would mean being more careful and circumspect than ever. Following his near miss in January he had decided to let the younger men do the running, but he had no intentions of retiring. The shoot-outs were not going to be a deterrent. Martin Cahill hated being a loser.

CHAPTER 14

The Hot-dog War

Almost every big-time gangster, at some stage in his career, considers going straight. Seeking legitimacy is the middle-aged criminal's version of a mid-life crisis. But Martin Cahill never wanted to be anything other than a respected criminal. Social status and a bourgeois lifestyle were repugnant to him. Cahill never suffered from delusions of grandeur. He was happy in the underworld where he was the boss.

Nevertheless, in 1992, he began considering semi-retirement. In the four years since the Tango Squad's surveillance operation, Cahill had kept relatively quiet. With most of his lieutenants behind bars or gone their separate ways, there had been no spectacular heists. Just like the fictional character, Michael Corleone in the movie *Godfather III*, Cahill had been diagnosed as suffering from diabetes as a result of his sweet tooth – a condition not helped by his high-pressure lifestyle. He was too stubborn to admit it, but at forty-three years of age Martin Cahill was not as fit for the rigours of a crime as he used to be.

Although he had no intention of opting out of crime altogether, Cahill began looking for a legitimate business which would bring in a steady flow of cash. And as a father, he wanted to see his children set up with a means of making a decent living. Through the years Cahill had invested some of his money in modest business enterprises. At various times he owned, or had shares in, a pub, a corner shop, a pigeon food shop, a coal yard and a launderette, none of which, perhaps, symbolised a highly-successful career of crime

The seedy twilight world of nightclubs and gambling joints is considered by many criminals to be a suitable compromise between crime and respectability. The Krays in London used their chain of swinging night spots as a cover for their criminal empire. In the States the mafia have dominated Las Vegas. The Leeson Street Strip is Dublin's famous nightclub zone. Its poky, smoke-filled clubs inhabit the basements of splendid Georgian houses in the city's up-market business district. They are open until early morning, selling cheap wine at exorbitant prices to the punters who stumble down the steps at pub closing time. Hookers, cops, bouncers, lovers, drunks and cheating spouses are among the inhabitants of the surreal nocturnal world of the Strip.

For a night creature like the General, Leeson Street was the most suitable location for a new business. But he had little interest in raking in the cash as a trendy nightclub owner. Instead, Cahill chose to apply his entrepreneurial skills to selling hot dogs on the pavement of the Strip. He planned to take over the entire operation. And being an unorthodox capitalist, Cahill had his own methods of beating the opposition. When the General hit the nightclub zone, fear, intimidation, violence – and the Serious Crime Squad – followed not far behind. Cahill would turn the Strip into a veritable war zone in his desire to make an honest pound.

Since his close shave with Garda John Moore following the aborted bank raid in Ranelagh in 1990, the General had decided to let his younger hoods do his dirty work. Cahill was happy with one or two well-planned heists a year. He wasn't greedy. And to keep himself amused in between times he went out burgling. He hadn't lost his propensity for the audacious stroke either.

At eleven o'clock on the morning of Tuesday, 25 February, 1992, Martin Cahill walked into the Allied Irish Bank branch on Morehampton Road. Instead of arming himself with an automatic pistol he was packing £19,500 in cash. He wore no balaclava, no false beard, no sunglasses. He looked like a down-on-his-luck second-hand car salesman in a tight-fitting polyester jacket and slacks. The money was in used fifty-pound notes which Cahill converted into a bank draft to buy property. The bank's security camera filmed the General as he walked out the door.

A half hour had passed when two men wearing motorbike helmets and brandishing handguns came through the same door. They vaulted across the counter at which Cahill had earlier lodged the money. They ordered a bank clerk to put the cash into a bag. In the minutes before the arrival of the raiders, £8,000 of Cahill's earlier lodgement had been moved to a safe upstairs. The men knew exactly what they were looking for. 'Where's the rest of the fuckin' fifty-pound notes? There should be more here,' one of them exclaimed. The pair left within two minutes more than £11,000 richer. Cahill met the two raiders later. It had been a good day's work. He had lodged almost £20,000 of stolen money, turned it into the price of a house and still got back over half of it. No wonder he was grinning from ear to ear.

Over the many years of rummaging around people's homes, the General had noticed that, without exception, every kitchen had a refuse sack. When Cahill told his associates of his 'amazing discovery' they looked at their leader perplexedly and replied, 'So?' As usual, when the General got an idea it became an obsession. He reckoned that, based on his rather unusual market research, there was a ready market for selling black refuse sacks door-to-door around Dublin. He went out and bought a container load of the sacks to get started. He also bought a black Renault 5 vanette equipped with a mobile phone.

At the same time he got the notion of selling hot dogs. Up to £1,000 a night could be made on a stall on a good weekend. It wouldn't bring millionaire status but it could buy a lot of sweets and cake. In April Cahill decided to combine both business ideas. He leased the ground floor of No 74, Leeson Street in the name of a company, Irish Sack Suppliers, with an address in Dolphin's Barn. The upper storeys of the fine Georgian house were in apartments and the basement was rented by twenty-eight year-old Wolfgang Eulitz, who ran a restaurant called the Hungry Wolf. Irish-born of German parents, 'Wolfie', as he was known, had set up the first hot-dog stall on the Strip six years earlier. The go-ahead entrepreneur had been running the restaurant for five months and business was good. But not for long.

In May an associate of Martin Cahill's appeared on the Strip equipped with a van and hot-dog stall and set up for business outside No 72. The General, who had paid for the equipment, also appeared with four of his men. He warned Wolfie and some of the other stall-holders that they would all suffer if the police seized or moved his stall. After that he hovered in the shadows. It wasn't long before detectives in the Serious Crime Squad got wind of Cahill's latest venture. Increased Garda attention was the last thing the Strip needed. The hot-dog war was about to begin.

The hot-dog stalls on the pavement of Leeson Street were in violation of the Casual Trading Act. Before Cahill's arrival the police had turned a blind eye to the practice. Within weeks there was a noticeable increase in patrols by uniformed police, while detectives kept an eye on developments from a discreet distance. Stalls belonging to the hot-dog men were impounded under the provisions of the Casual Trading Act, including the stalls belonging to Wolfgang Eulitz and the General. One night while Cahill's stall was impounded by the Gardaí, the General's men set Wolfie's stall on fire, causing extensive damage. Wolfie was, for a time, forced out of business.

The next three months was a period of relative peace while Cahill, who closed his stall temporarily, worked out his strategy for a full take-over of the hot-dog market. He used the 'marketing' techniques he knew best – intimidation and fear. His aim was to force each stall-holder to 'rent' a stand from him and split their profits. If they wouldn't play ball then he was 'forced' to put them out of business. It was a classic protection racket. In particular, Cahill had plans for his nearest rival.

Wolfie had continued his restaurant business in the basement of No 74. In August a continuous noise could be heard through the ceiling in the Hungry Wolf restaurant each night after it opened for business. The racket came from the ground-floor office. Cahill had sent his people into the empty apartment at night to jump and drop heavy objects on the floor. He wanted to create enough disturbance to force Wolfie to close down, leaving the basement free for him to lease. Wolfie had regular rows with one of Cahill's representatives in protest at the interference. But he was left in no doubt who he was dealing with and was understandably nervous at the way the situation was developing.

In late August, another stall-holder set up on the steps above String's nightclub which is situated in the basement of No 24. Because his stall was on private property, he was not in breach of any law. One night, shortly after, Cahill appeared on the scene and made it obvious that he was watching the newcomer. He said nothing and stood a short distance away for about half an hour. At four o'clock on the morning of 18 September, the stall and pick-up truck were burned out beside the owner's house in Dundrum. Two weeks later he received an anonymous letter with a proposal that he could resume business by 'renting' a stall. He turned down the 'offer'.

Two nights after the Dundrum arson attack, Cahill was spotted prowling around a laneway at the back of some houses in Donnybrook where Wolfgang Eulitz lived. A man returning from a party at four o'clock spotted the General standing at the door to a rear garage. When the man challenged Cahill he replied that he was 'having a piss'. The man did not argue any further and went into his house to call the police. He came back out with a torch, shone it into a garden and spotted Cahill crouching in the bushes. The police were called but on arrival found no-one. The elusive General had disappeared. Later that morning the man's car was burnt out. Cahill had sent his men back to burn Wolfie's car but they got the wrong one.

Cahill had also burgled Wolfie's house. He found the restaurateur's bedroom and took £300 in loose change. He made sure not to touch anything else in the house – he wanted to leave a message for his victim. Cahill's plan was to soften up his target by making life so intolerable that he would eventually come looking to make a deal.

Early in October Wolfie approached one of Cahill's associates who was a regular visitor to the empty office over his restaurant at the times when the mystery noises occurred. Wolfie wanted to end the disturbances and be allowed to set up his hot-dog stand without hassle. By this stage all the hot-dog men had vanished from the Strip. The name of the General was enough to make them decide to move on. The associate told Eulitz that Cahill was setting up a stall on the steps of No 74. He and his people were using a power line from the ground-floor office. Cahill's man referred to the burglary at Wolfie's home.

'We did that,' he said smiling. He would have to consult with the General to see what could be done.

Cahill worked out his business proposal for the restaurateur from his armchair in Cowper Downs. His lackey was sent back to the Strip with the deal. Wolfie would run a stall next to one run by Cahill's associate on the steps of No 74 over the Hungry Wolf restaurant. Eulitz, Cahill decided, would keep one-fifth of the total turnover on the stall to pay for his stock. Then he would pay Cahill £100 per week to cover the rent of the ground-floor office. From the rest of the money Wolfie made, Cahill was to receive a further two-thirds, with just one-third going to Wolfie. Eulitz agreed to work under the General's extortionist scheme. After operating for one night he gave up in despair.

On the night of Friday, 9 October, Wolfie began selling sandwiches from the top of the basement steps over his restaurant. Within a few minutes the General appeared. 'Any more of this bullshit and you are dead,' he threatened. He said no more and held up both hands to indicate that Wolfie had ten minutes to clear off. Wolfie obeyed. Cahill stayed around to make sure Wolfie didn't change his mind again. Later the General approached Wolfie and told him that, if he wanted the noise from the ground-floor office to stop, he would have to give him a cut of the profits. But by now, exasperated by the constant bullying and intimidation, the restaurateur told Cahill that he was not in a position to pay. Cahill grinned and walked away. That was always a bad sign.

At the same time the landlady of No 74 became aware that Irish Sack Suppliers was breaking the terms of the lease agreement by allowing the stall to be set up on the steps of the building and running a power line to it. The owner was also concerned about the continuous noise which disrupted trade in the Hungry Wolf restaurant and the fact that the Irish Sack Suppliers was late with rent. But she was also aware of the awesome reputation of the General and became anxious when she heard what he had said about her to Wolfie on 9 October: 'That old lady better do nothing about it for her own sake.' She began legal proceedings to seek an injunction preventing the hot-dog stall operating and to have the company evicted. She automatically became a focus of the General's attention.

At any one time Martin Cahill had a top ten list of people he disliked most. The names on the list changed position from time to time. Some names disappeared – usually after the unpopular individual was shot, robbed or had made some gesture to ameliorate the General. Names on the list over the years included, among others, the state forensic scientist James Donovan, social welfare officer Brian Purcell, the associate he sent to England with his haul from the O'Connor's robbery and Detective Superintendent Ned Ryan. Now the landlady joined the list. Cahill began watching the house where she lived with her husband and family. One associate recalls how Cahill had contemplated breaking into her home and forcing her at gun-point to sign No 74 over to him. The wider implications of such blatant coercion did not occur to him.

The head of the Serious Crime Squad, Detective Superintendent Tom Butler, was aware of the problems of both Wolfie and the landlady. His men had been watching developments on the Strip where Cahill's men made no effort to keep a low profile. Cahill was not concerned about the police and wanted everyone to know that he was back in business. On 12 October, a team of detectives was assigned to investigate reports that club managers were being hit by criminals for protection money. During the investigation detectives compiled extensive intelligence on the underworld's associations with the Strip but were unable to uncover any evidence of intimidation or extortion. In fact, Gardaí have never been able to prove that protection rackets are in operation in certain parts of Dublin although there are a number of gangs who specialise in protection racketeering. The main reason for this is fear of intimidation.

In the meantime, Martin Cahill was making in the region of £300 a night on a good weekend on Leeson Street. But his campaign of intimidation was not over yet. On 23 October, his men set fire to the ground-floor of No 24, Leeson Street, in the basement of which String's nightclub had operated. Shortly after that, Cahill again sanctioned an arson attack. This time his gangsters set fire to Wolfie's restaurant, the Hungry Wolf, in retaliation for not paying protection, and put him out of business. In November the landlady of No 74 succeeded in obtaining an injunction preventing Cahill's company from allowing the sale of hot dogs on the steps of the property.

Despite the court injunction Cahill instructed his people to continue operating the hot-dog stall. At the same time the son of a district court judge, who was in business on the Strip, complained to the Gardaí about the hot-dog stand because of the rough underworld element it had brought to the clubs. Shortly before Christmas Cahill actually phoned the judge in person. He casually told him who he was and that he was looking for his son's telephone number. The judge, having a good working knowledge of the Dublin underworld, immediately called the Serious Crime Squad which gave him and his son protection.

On 30 December, a director of Irish Sack Suppliers was sent to prison for one night for contempt of court for ignoring the injunction. That same night Cahill's fire-bugs were again busy. This time they succeeded in burning out the entire building at No 74. But the most serious incident was to occur a month later when Eulitz, determined not to be put down by the General, indicated that he was going to get back into the hot-dog business. Martin Cahill had other ideas.

On the evening of Thursday, 28 January, 1993, Wolfgang Eulitz was at home with his girlfriend, Katza Schuller, a German. They had watched TV and eaten a meal when Wolfie decided to go out for a video. Katza put the dishes in the sink and was relaxing in front of the TV in the sitting-room when two masked men suddenly burst in. Both of them carried handguns. One of them told her: 'Be quiet and lie on the couch.' They took a cigarette out of her hand and tied her arms and legs. They covered her head with a jumper and waited for Wolfgang to return.

Martin Cahill referred to the two hooded thugs affectionately as his 'Rottweilers'. They were both loyal henchmen and worshipped their General. The men have long been suspected of involvement in serious crime and are considered to be dangerous armed criminals. The pair often bought Cahill presents with their cut from armed robberies. They considered it an honour and privilege to do his dirty work.

The 'Rottweilers' questioned the terrified German student at length about Wolfie. Shortly afterwards, at 11.15 pm, he returned. The men jumped on him and dragged him into the sitting-room. They tied his hands and legs with electric cable. The two gunmen demanded to know Wolfie's identity, holding a gun against his skull, as they asked him the same question several times. They demanded money and took £100 from the victim's pockets. A half-hour later Martin Cahill arrived to check that his operation was going as planned. Happy that everything was in order he left and headed straight for Rathmines Garda Station.

One of the gangsters asked the other the time. It was just past midnight. At this stage Wolfie thought that he was going to be murdered. He had been living in fear since the night Martin Cahill and his men had arrived on the Strip to sell hot dogs. One of the men asked him was he all right. When he told them that the cable around his hands was hurting him, they laughed and told him 'Don't worry about it.' Then they dimmed the lights in the room and turned up the volume on the TV.

One of Cahill's men placed a pillow over the calf of Wolfie's left leg. He pushed the gun into the pillow and fired a single shot. The restaurateur screamed in agony as the bullet ripped through his leg. The smell of cordite burned in his nostrils. A second shot was fired into the same leg. The gunmen got up and calmly left the house. Wolfie lay writhing in agony on the floor while his girlfriend managed to break free and activate a panic alarm.

As the 'Rottweilers' were shooting his business rival the General was standing at the counter of the front office of his local police station. He presented his driver's licence and insurance certificate to the desk sergeant who eyed him suspiciously. A few minutes later the policeman's suspicions were justified. As he was being taken out to an ambulance a Garda asked Wolfie who shot him. He screamed back: 'I am not talking to nobody, you know who did it, you know.' He later underwent surgery and doctors saved the leg.

Wolfie was right. The Gardaí knew well who was responsible for his shooting. The General had more or less told them when he walked into Rathmines Station at midnight. But knowing it and proving it were two very different things. Martin Cahill had won another battle.

CHAPTER 15

Incest Case

In the brutal world of Martin Cahill, two criminal types were hated and despised by their peers. The first was the informer or tout who was beyond redemption as far as Cahill was concerned. Cahill was paranoid about informants. In the cult gangster movie *Goodfellas* Robert De Niro offered a piece of advice the General often gave his own trainee thieves: 'Never rat on your friends and always keep your mouth shut.'

The other loathsome deviant in Cahill's eyes was the child sex abuser. And he wasn't alone among the criminal confraternity in hating abusers. In Irish jails it is common practice to segregate sex offenders from the rest of the prison population for their own safety.

Once, in 1988, when I attempted to interview Cahill on a Dublin street, I asked him what he actually thought a criminal was. 'The only real criminal is a man who abuses kids,' he told me from behind the hand covering his face. Four years later, in 1993, Cahill would contradict that strongly-held view when one of his criminal associates was arrested and charged with raping and buggering his own fourteen-year-old daughter.

Cahill found himself in a desperate dilemma. His main concern had nothing to do with the fact that a member of his circle had violated one of the strict moral codes of the underworld. Cahill's fear was that his friend's trouble could also cause him problems. He told associates that he had to consider the fact that a man who could rape his own child also had it in him to turn tout. Cahill's worst nightmare was that his friend might even cut a deal with the police to have the incest charges dropped in return for Cahill's head on the dock of the Special Criminal Court. He had two choices if he was to stay in control of the situation: stand by his friend or have him killed. He chose to support the criminal and do everything in his power to prevent the case ever going to court.

For there was another aspect to this case which illustrated Cahill's absolute abhorrence of the authorities. In his world the police had no role whatsoever in the administration of justice. No matter what a criminal did, no-one had a right to call the cops. If anyone was to be punished then it would be done gangland style. The General was to embark on a sinister campaign of intimidation against the terrified victim in a bid to stop her co-operating with the Gardaí.

The girl had helped to care for the family since her mother's death. The dead woman had been a devoted spouse and doted on her children. In the years before the mother died, Martin Cahill often visited their home – he would call in while out 'creeping' or burgling during the middle of the night. Cahill would sneak into his friend's house through the window at the back in case the Gardaí were keeping an eye on the place. The criminal was always glad to see Cahill and would get his wife out of bed to cook for him.

A short time after her death he moved a pregnant girlfriend into the house. When the baby was born the daughter was also expected to look after it. After a few years the relationship between the man and his lover broke up when she could no longer endure his beatings.

Tension began to build up between the eldest daughter and her father over his behaviour. She still grieved for her mother and was deeply hurt by how little her father was affected by the death of his wife, and by his foisting girlfriends on his neglected children. The tension in the home grew and soon she was having rows with him about going out with her friends. She eventually moved out to live with her maternal grandmother.

On Thursday, 5 November, 1992, the youngest children went to see their teenage sister and their grandmother although their father had strictly forbidden them to do so. Their obvious state of neglect shocked and disturbed the teenager. That evening she returned home to care for them. Her father appeared glad to see her. The next night, Friday, the criminal brought her out for the evening. He bought her three glasses of Harp in a local pub. Later that night when she was in bed her father came into her bedroom and asked if she would move over and let him in beside her. When she refused he left the room.

On Saturday night he came in from the pub and got into bed beside his daughter. She jumped out and went to sleep in her younger sister's room. Around six o'clock the next morning the criminal got into bed beside his two sleeping daughters. When her younger sister got up around 7.30 am the criminal began to fondle and molest the teenage girl. She jumped out of bed and screamed 'No'. He told her: 'I'm only doing this because I love you and I miss you. Don't tell anyone.' She walked out of the room.

On Sunday he spent the day drinking with his friends, members of Cahill's gang. That night he went to bed at eleven o'clock. His daughter slept with her younger sister again. Around midnight he came into the room and ordered the younger child into another room. When he started to fondle his teenage daughter, she began to cry and told him to stop. He ignored her plea, replying: 'Don't tell anyone. I'll buy you anything, just don't tell anyone.' Then he raped and buggered her and forced her to have oral sex with him. When it was over he returned to his own room.

The following morning the distraught teenager ran to her grand-mother's home and told her what had happened. Incensed by what she heard the grandmother phoned the man. She told him that she was taking her granddaughter to hospital and that if there was anything wrong with her she would kill him. The gangster pleaded with her not to report the incident. 'Don't take her to the hospital, you'll have the police down on me and I'll be charged,' he told his mother-in-law. She put down the phone, grabbed her coat and brought the teenager to hospital.

The man was now frantic. He knew that he could not call Cahill and tell him what happened. He sent an associate to the home of the girlfriend he had severely battered just weeks before. 'He's in a bit of trouble, it's heavy and he wants to see ya,' the girlfriend was told. She went to meet him in a city-centre pub. He looked flustered and anxious. He told her that his daughter was making false allegations against him and begged her to 'do a runner' with him. He went to the bank and withdrew a large amount of cash.

Later he went with his girlfriend to his brother's home and spent the night trying to figure out what to do next. The following morning, Tuesday, 10 November, he went to a hospital and spoke to a doctor who at first refused to admit him. The doctor was convinced that there was nothing wrong with him which merited hospitalisation and told him that he could be treated as an outpatient. The criminal's brother – another notorious crook – took the doctor aside for a few moments. The criminal was called back and was allowed to stay in the hospital for a week.

Detective Inspector Michael Cannavan, who had been involved in the enquiries into the O'Connor's jewellery robbery and the killing of John Copeland, was put in charge of the case. Cahill considered Cannavan to be a dangerous adversary. On the morning of 9 November, Cannavan was in his office when he was interrupted by Detective Sergeant John McDermott, a former Tango Squad member whose name featured on Cahill's list of 'least-liked cops'. McDermott told Cannavan of the accusation the criminal faced. That such a hard man of the underworld, who knew all the tricks, would actually get himself into serious trouble in such a way astonished both of them. Cannavan and McDermott set up an investigation team and despatched Garda Noreen McBrien to the hospital to interview the teenager and her grandmother.

Later that day Cannavan ordered his men to begin a search for the criminal. They soon discovered that he too was in hospital. On the morning of his release, 16 November, Garda McBrien, accompanied by Detective Sergeant McDermott and a team of detectives and uniformed officers, arrested him as he was leaving the hospital. He was taken to Sundrive Road Garda Station where he was detained for questioning under Section 4 of the Criminal Justice Act. He was taken to an interview room by Detective Sergeant McDermott and Detective Gardaí John Duignan and Michael McMahon.

McDermott informed the criminal that his daughter had already given a written statement outlining the allegations against him. As McDermott read them out the criminal became agitated and began to pace nervously around the room. Suddenly he became violent and drove his fist through the window, smashing three panes of glass. Then he tried to break another pane by hitting it with his head. A violent struggle followed as McDermott, Duignan and McMahon tried to overpower the criminal. During the scuffle he bit Duignan on the hands. After a few minutes the detectives managed to put handcuffs on the criminal and hauled him down to the cells.

When Detective Inspector Cannavan went to the cell, the criminal had begun to calm down. 'Take these fucking cuffs off, Mick. I won't mess anymore,' he pleaded with his old adversary. Cannavan asked why he had cut up rough in the interview room. 'They were accusing me of raping my daughter. I lost the head. Take these off. I give you my word, I won't mess anymore.' Cannavan agreed to take the cuffs off. He lit a cigarette and handed it to the criminal. Later that afternoon he was again brought to the interview room. Present were Cannavan, McDermott and Detective Sergeant Gerry O'Carroll. Cannavan read his daughter's statement over to him. The criminal then shook his head and replied: 'I don't know, if I'm guilty of that I'll kill myself. I would kill anybody if they did that to any of my brother's daughters. I've been drinking very heavily for the last four years.' He refused to say any more. He also declined to give a police doctor a blood sample for the purposes of DNA testing. Later that afternoon the man was formally charged before the Dublin District Court on five counts of rape, incest and sexual assault. He was remanded to Mountjoy Prison for a week with a recommendation that he be admitted to the Central Mental Hospital.

When Martin Cahill got word about what had happened he was furious. The two had been in the process of planning a major kidnapping. The target was a Dublin businessman and the pair were going to abduct his entire family. They were going to hold the family for a week during which time the businessman would be forced to withdraw £50,000 in cash from his bank each day. By doing so they could avoid arousing suspicion. As an anti-ransom security measure banks report suspicious cash withdrawals of over £50,000 to the police. Since most of his old gang were now either locked up or had distanced themselves from him because of the police attention he was attracting, Cahill had been relying on his long association with the rapist.

The planned abduction and ransom were now in serious jeopardy and Cahill decided immediately to abort the crime. When the criminal was released on bail Cahill sent for him. He sat back in silence and ate a bowl of stew as he listened to the criminal's account of what had happened. He reassured him that the case would never go to court and that he would see to it personally that the teenager did not get into the witness box. Later he would tell another criminal associate why he stood by the rapist. 'I had to convince him that I believed him. If I didn't then he would crack up and we all know what kind of shite that was goin' to raise.' The fact that the Gardaí were now involved greatly troubled Cahill and he condemned the terrified teenage girl as a 'tout'. The trauma she had endured made no difference to Cahill's twisted logic.

The girl meanwhile was diagnosed as displaying the symptoms of post-traumatic stress disorder. She experienced conflicting emotions ranging from anger and resentment to guilt and fear. From the moment she made the statement to Garda McBrien, the girl knew what she was up against. She was terrified that her father would send his friends after her now. In her father's eyes she was a tout. Her heart said she was not.

Three weeks after her father was charged, on a cold, dark evening in late November 1992, the teenager was walking to the shops near her grandmother's home. As she passed a school building Martin Cahill emerged from the shadows. He had his characteristic grin spread across his chubby face. Before she could blink he was standing looking into her face.

She knew who it was and why he was there. She froze. 'How'ya, love,' smiled Cahill, waving his balaclava in the air. 'As you know, love, I'm like a bat – I only come out at night. But for you I've made an exception and come out a bit early this evening.' Cahill went on to offer the girl a new life. He promised her £20,000 and a new home where she could live in peace with her siblings. He also suggested that, if she wished, she could be sent to England. He said that he would have her father punished for what he had done to her.

But he told her it was wrong to involve the Gardaí, the enemy, in something that could be sorted out by the criminal fraternity. The girl would later recall that, while he spoke politely, Cahill's tone was sinister and threatening. Before disappearing back into the shadows he arranged to meet her and her younger brother and sister in the same place on the following Sunday. 'I'll bring youse all to McDonald's in town for a treat and you can tell me what you have decided.' The terrified teenager never turned up for the meeting with Cahill. In the months leading up to her father's trial in the Central Criminal Court Cahill upped his offer to £35,000. She refused to accept.

In the weeks before Christmas strange incidents began happening around the grandmother's house where the teenager was staying. Flashlights were shone in through the windows in the early hours of the morning and noises would wake the girl and her grandmother. One of the girl's uncles brought her to live with him and his family in another area of the city. The girl's uncle had had a few scrapes with the law and had a record for petty crime. He had known Cahill since they were children. On a number of occasions he had been arrested for questioning in relation to crimes which Cahill had organised, although he had never been charged.

One night as the uncle was walking from the pub he was stopped and 'asked' to take a trip in a van with Cahill and a number of associates, including the girl's father. He was offered £10,000 as an incentive to encourage the girl to keep her mouth shut. He told them to 'fuck off with yer blood money' and got out of the van. Early in 1993 Cahill again approached the girl's uncle through an associate and a meeting was arranged at the Tallaght bowling centre. When the uncle arrived for the meeting Cahill was sitting with two associates slurping from a paper cup full of orange pop. The girl's uncle was being covered by a friend who sat watching the meeting from a distance. Under his jacket he carried a 9mm automatic pistol, just in case the General caused problems.

Cahill looked into the uncle's eyes and began to grin. He suggested that the uncle and his brothers could punish the rapist for his crime and there would be no interference from Cahill or any of his people. The girl would be paid a large sum of money and the cops would be told to 'piss off'. When the uncle declined the offer Cahill began to lose his cool.

He leaned further across the table and spoke in a low voice. 'Then what are you going to do about the fucking tout in your house?' The girl's uncle replied: 'What tout?' 'That little bitch who is going to give evidence against [criminal's name]. You shouldn't have a fuckin' tout in yer house. That's very dangerous ya know.' The girl's uncle told Cahill that he did not consider his niece to be an informer and that he would back her all the way to the steps of the court. Cahill's lip began to curl in anger and he told the uncle that he would have him, his wife and his niece killed if he continued to 'act the bollix' and refuse to co-operate.

Then he stood up with his two associates and told the uncle to 'get the fuck out' and left. For several weeks shadowy figures were seen prowling around the uncle's house at night, shining lights into the house. Detective Inspector Cannavan ordered close protection for the girl and her uncle's family. He was concerned about the threats being made by Cahill. Squad cars began paying close attention to the uncle's house.

The reaction from Cahill's people was to daub slogans on walls around the area calling the uncle and the niece 'rats' and 'touts'. The uncle decided to do something about the problem himself. He asked the Gardaí to stop their patrols around the house. He went to see some associates in the INLA – although not a member of it himself. As a result, a message from the group was sent to Cahill: the teenager was not to be harassed any more or Cahill would be shot. When he was told of the threat Cahill shrugged it off with his usual grin. 'Fuck them,' was his only comment. Cahill's fatal flaw was never to believe that anyone could get the better of him. But despite his apparent indifference, the General ceased his efforts to intimidate the girl into silence. He had another plan.

The criminal's trial was adjourned on a number of occasions in late 1993 and finally a date was set for 19 January, 1994. The criminal agreed with Cahill that the best way to avoid standing trial was to be shot in a 'gun attack'. The General assured his friend that the wound would not be fatal, just serious enough to keep him out of court for long enough to convince his daughter of the error of her ways. Four days before the trial date, Cahill and one of his men visited the girl's father at his home to warn him to be in the next night for his appointment with the gunmen. The criminal agreed but insisted that he would be drunk for the shooting so as to kill the pain of the wound.

Cahill would not carry out the shooting himself. Instead he sent the loyal 'Rottweilers' who had helped in Cahill's hot-dog war to do his dirty work. He assured his friend that they knew exactly what to do and to trust them. On the morning of 16 January, the two masked men broke into the man's home and shot him once in the leg. Detective Inspector Cannavan and his men would later inform the courts that the criminal had arranged for the shooting himself so that he would not have to stand trial. The criminal was treated for his injury and kept in hospital for five days. On the morning of 19 January, Mr Justice Fergus Flood issued a bench warrant for the criminal's arrest for failing to appear in court. He was arrested on foot of that warrant on 21 January as he was leaving hospital. He was remanded in custody until his new trial date, 2 February.

On the morning of the trial the criminal and his family were visibly shocked when it became clear that the teenager had decided to go ahead and give her evidence. A jury of five women and seven men were empanelled for the trial before Mr Justice Ronan Keane. The criminal pleaded not guilty to all five charges.

In a video link with the courtroom (this was the first time such a device had been used in an Irish court) the girl recalled in tears her ordeal at the hands of her father. During cross-examination his counsel, acting on instructions, put it to her that her allegations were 'a tissue of lies', which she denied. Medical evidence was given of semen stains found on an external swab taken from the girl on the morning after the attack. Dr Roisín Healy also told how there were indications of trauma in the girl's vaginal and anal areas.

In his evidence the criminal claimed that his daughter was telling lies and that the allegations had been made up by her grandmother. He said that the family were jealous of his new girlfriend. The trial lasted three days. On 9 February, 1994, the criminal was found guilty on all counts when the jury returned a unanimous verdict after two hours of deliberation. On 25 March, the criminal was given a total of ten years for the five charges.

Before sentence was passed Detective Sergeant McDermott told the court that the accused man was well-known to the Gardaí and had lived a lavish lifestyle although he had become unemployed. Garda Noreen McBrien said that the teenager had been 'extremely upset and suffered mood swings for a long time after the attack'. The girl had completely lost her confidence. Child psychologist Dr Paul McCarthy said that she demonstrated the symptoms of post-traumatic stress disorder. She regularly got flashbacks to the rape incident in which she 're-experienced the actual frightening feeling of the attack'.

During his summing-up Mr Justice Keane said that he was taking into account the fact that the criminal had denied the charges, thereby putting his daughter through the stress of cross-examination. He said that the man was guilty of the rape of his own daughter, 'a person who above all should have been able to regard him as somebody of trust. The courts have to take a very serious view of this. This case does not present very many redeeming features.' But he said, in the interests of fairness, that he would disregard the Garda evidence about the man's criminal background. The man's defence counsel had submitted that the Garda evidence was being used 'as innuendo that there is more behind the matter'. There had been a 'deliberate attempt by the Gardaí to paint the man in a bad light'.

The criminal stood impassively as the judge made his remarks and passed sentence. An associate had been waiting in the back of the court. When he heard the sentence he immediately left and went to Cahill's home at Swan Grove to tell him the news. Cahill showed no emotion *'Que sera sera*, whatever will be, will be,' he sighed, repeating his favourite phrase. The General would later send a message to his friend in jail wishing him the best and promising that he would be looked after when he got out.

Two prison warders escorted the criminal in handcuffs from the court, down the long corridor leading to the street that runs alongside the Four Courts and into a waiting prison van. It was a wet Friday afternoon and traffic was heavy. As the van drove towards the Naas Road the criminal drew some consolation from the thought that he was destined for Portlaoise high security prison where all his old friends in Cahill's gang were ensconced. But at Newland's Cross the prison van suddenly turned off and headed for Wheatfield Prison in Clondalkin – and a segregation unit for sex offenders. The hard man, tough criminal, feared gangster, would serve his sentence away from his old friends in the rest of the prison population – for his own protection.

CHAPTER 16

The Lacey Kidnap

After the Tango Squad broke up his gang in the late 1980s, Martin Cahill found life dull. He missed the exhilaration of a well-planned robbery and the publicity it would attract. He was still smarting from his foray into the art world and the bad luck it had brought him. He found it harder to gather a team for a job. And he was short of cash. Following a near miss in 1990, when he shot Garda John Moore and was almost caught, he had learned that armed robbery was now too dangerous. He needed another big heist to enable him to retire and enjoy his food, his racing pigeons and his growing family.

He turned his agile mind to plotting a last big job. This time it would be the much more serious crime of kidnapping. He reckoned it was a relatively easy way to extract a large amount of money from some of the business world's fat cats who could live with the loss. The idea came from a magazine article that named some of the country's richest and most influential businessmen and described their lifestyles. Such features are regularly published, to the annoyance of the Gardaí, who feel too much intelligence is provided for potential abductors.

In April 1993 one of Cahill's closest associates, who had provided the inside information which led to the O'Connors' jewel heist, came up with an interesting possibility. He had learned a good deal about the internal workings of the National Irish Bank. Cahill was particularly excited by the news that NIB's biggest branch at College Green in Dublin regularly held anything up to £10 million in cash. The building was in the heart of the business district and a well-planned operation could use the hustle and bustle of centre-city traffic to facilitate a get-away.

Cahill talked to one of his closest partners in crime. Joseph 'Jo-Jo'

Kavanagh was a thirty-six-year-old criminal from the south-west Dublin suburb of Crumlin. He had been involved in crime since the age of eleven when he was convicted for larceny and motor-bike theft. Married with five children, he had been widowed in 1988 when his wife was killed in a crash involving a Hi-ace van he had been driving. Kavanagh had been part of Cahill's gang for at least fifteen years and had been one of the members targeted by the Tango Squad in the 1988 operation. He was considered an effective armed robber and had teamed up with Cahill on several robberies. He had also been training and organising the new generation of young armed robbers sprouting up around south Dublin. Through the years luck was with him and he had accumulated less than a dozen convictions, none of them for serious crime.

With Kavanagh and the man who provided the tip-off about NIB, Cahill set about putting together a plan. From the outset, it was decided that the only way to get at the money in the bank was to kidnap a senior executive. After preliminary surveillance it was decided that the target should be Jim Lacey, the chief executive. Married with four children, Lacey lived in upmarket Blackrock. He was easy to stalk. He left home each weekday morning between 7.30 and 7.45 to make the half-hour journey to his office at Wilton Terrace in city-centre Dublin. 'He's the man that has the key to make the money,' declared Cahill.

The surveillance on Lacey and two other executives at the bank – Eugene Keenan, manager of the College Green branch, and Dermot Bonner, manager in charge of the retail bank – was kept up for four months and the gang built up detailed information on the movements and private lives of the three men. Cahill's plan was basic. The gang would abduct Jim Lacey, his wife Joan and their four children late at night from their home and take them to a hiding place to be decided on later. The gang would be accompanied by a man posing as another kidnap victim. His job was to convince Lacey that his own children had also been kidnapped and that he had been ordered to collect the bank money for the gang. Lacey would be left under no illusion about the fact that if he did not co-operate his family would be shot.

Kavanagh offered to be the stooge for the job. Cahill picked three of his trusted Rottweilers and two others along with Kavanagh and the gang met regularly in Kavanagh's house, off the South Circular Road. Normally a heavy drinker, Kavanagh gave up the booze and went into training to get fit for the job. Three of the gang maintained regular surveillance at Lacey's house and an underworld source would later describe how Kavanagh would return home with mud and leaves on his shoes. Kavanagh also tried out the security measures at the Lacey home and the frequency of Garda patrols in the area.

On a Saturday night before the August Bank Holiday weekend, Joan Lacey was awakened by a loud noise outside at about 4 am. When she looked out, she saw a man, dressed in black, moving furtively through the garden from the direction of the garage. Later she recalled that the man seemed to be familiar with the lock of the gate which was difficult to operate. The man saw her looking down at him and ran across the road and through a neighbour's garden. A few minutes later, a car pulled out of the nearby *cul de sac*. On the night of Saturday, 16 October, the intruder alarm was activated at the Lacey home about 2 am. The alarm company notified the Gardaí but next day Lacey could find no sign of a break-in attempt.

The General decided that the kidnap would go ahead on the night of 1 November. It was no coincidence that he picked the first day of winter for the job. He loved the long dark nights and most of his crimes were carried out under cover of darkness. Cahill often described himself as a bat and many of his underworld associates believed he could actually see in the dark.

One of the gang had found a disused stables not far from where he lived and it was decided to hold the Lacey mother and children there. Two second-hand vans were bought for cash in city garages and Cahill purchased two-piece overall suits, balaclavas, knitted gloves and white runner boots for each of his gang. All of these were to be disposed of immediately after the kidnapping. He also arranged that each gang member would be allocated a number from one to seven, which would be sewn on to the tunic of his overalls and the gang practised calling each other by number only.

There was still a preliminary job to be done. On Sunday morning,

5 September, three armed and masked men burst in to the Crumlin home of Kavanagh's mother-in-law, Esther Bolger, with whom two of his children, Tony, eleven, and Jodie, thirteen, were now living. When the grandmother confronted them, one of the men put a gun to her head and warned: 'This is serious. Open your mouth and you're dead. I mean what I say. Don't make a sound.' He then pushed her against a table.

The men asked the woman if there were drugs or guns in the house. 'What would two children be doing with guns or drugs?' she replied. By now she recognised two of the men as Cahill and Kavanagh. The courageous widow told them that she knew who they were and that masks were no good to them. The raiders huddled together for a moment whispering. Then Esther Bolger took out a gold sovereign she had been wearing on a chain round her neck. Pointing it at Cahill, she said: 'You know who gave this to my dead daughter, Cahill? It was your own wife, Frances.'

Cahill did not reply. Instead he took a Polaroid camera from his jacket and photographed Kavanagh's two bewildered children and their grandmother. He then turned to Esther Bolger and warned her: 'If you get in touch with the police, the next time we come we won't be so friendly.' Then he turned to the kids. 'Don't mention to any of your mates that we have been here. You heard what we told your nan.' The three masked men left the house and vanished into a local park. Another part of the plan had been completed. Now Kavanagh had to be 'abducted'.

The most public place for this operation would be the health centre in Crumlin where Kavanagh trained and swam every day. On the evening of 15 October a man wearing a baseball hat called to the club and asked for Kavanagh. He was directed to the dressingrooms. The man spoke to Kavanagh and told him that one of his children had been in a serious accident. The messenger, who was also a member of Kavanagh's gang, stood in the reception area as if waiting for Kavanagh to get dressed. He made a point of telling the receptionist that Kavanagh's child had been hit by a car. Kavanagh then walked out with the man, deliberately leaving his kit bag at reception so that the incident would be remembered. He jumped into a van outside, leaving his bike behind. The final piece of preparatory work had been done.

Jim Lacey began Monday morning, 1 November, the same as he did most weekday mornings. He rose before 7 am and got ready for work. His children were off school for the day as it was a church holiday. He went to 7.30 am Mass in Booterstown Church and was at his office shortly after 8 am.

He had a busy day ahead. In the morning and early afternoon he had a number of scheduled meetings. Around 3 pm he planned to travel to Clonmel, County Tipperary, with his wife to attend the official opening of a new branch of the National Irish Bank. He knew it was going to be a long night – but he could not have known that it would become the longest and most terrifying night of his life.

At 2 pm Tanya Waters, a twenty-one-year-old neighbour, arrived at the Lacey home to look after the children while their parents were away. Shortly after this a bank employee picked up Joan Lacey and brought her to her husband's office from where they both drove to the Clonmel ceremony, which was performed by the then Fianna Fáil Environment Minister, Michael Smith. In the meantime, Cahill and his gang got ready for the operation. At all times Cahill monitored the movements of his targets and knew the Laceys would be returning from Clonmel late.

Sometime around 11 pm the gang got into their positions around the house. The Lacey children had all been in bed by 9.30 pm. Tanya Waters, who was not staying overnight, sat up watching TV in the living-room. Between 12.30 and 1 am she heard a noise outside the house. She looked out through the front window but saw nothing.

Jim and Joan Lacey left Clonmel to arrive at the gates of their home around 1.25 am on 2 November. They both noticed that the right-hand gate was partially closed. This was unusual because it had been fully open when they left. Joan Lacey felt nervous as her husband got out to open the gate. She drove the car up to the front door as Jim closed the gates. There were lights on in the house.

It was a bitter night and Joan Lacey's hands were so cold that she was unable to select the front door key. Her husband, who had taken some things out of the boot of the car, took the keys and opened the door for her. Just as he was doing so, Joan heard shuffling coming from behind. She looked around and saw two men running out of the garden. They were dressed in black with white boots and hoods. She screamed to her husband who was now stepping into the hallway.

As the banker spun around, he saw two men lunging towards them out of the darkness. He pulled his wife towards him just as one of them reached her. Joan Lacey kept screaming and put up a ferocious fight as her husband tried to fend off their attackers and close the front door. Joan tried to claw at the face of one of the kidnappers and pull his balaclava off. She even grabbed one of the masked men by the testicles and squeezed them hard in her bid to save her family. By now there were at least four men on top of the Laceys. Jim Lacey began shouting at the attackers. One of them hit him hard across the head with a pistol, making a large gash in his forehead, and leaving him dazed. In a split second the Laceys were overpowered and together with some of the hooded men were lying in a crumpled heap of bodies on the hall floor.

Tanya Waters ran to the living-room door the moment she heard Joan Lacey's scream. She saw Mrs Lacey struggling with the intruders and Jim Lacey being pistol-whipped. One of the gang members spotted her and pointed a pistol in her face. She was ordered to lie down on the floor of the living-room.

Jim Lacey was now lying halfway into the sitting-room with his legs in the hallway. Blood oozed from his head wound. He could see Joan was sitting on the floor beside him while being restrained from behind by one of the intruders. Another intruder held a pistol fitted with a long silencer in his face. A third man covered the sitting-room door, pointing a pistol at Tanya Waters while a fourth ran upstairs and a fifth stormed into the kitchen. A sixth man was giving orders to check the rear of the house.

Ten-year-old Louise Lacey, awakened by the violent commotion, stood on the stairs and screamed in terror when she saw the hooded figures charging around the house. One of them grabbed her by the arm and put her beside Tanya Waters in the sitting-room where a gunman continued to cover both of them. The child was extremely distressed and sobbing. Cahill's men were unnerved by Joan Lacey's screams and warned her that everyone in the house would be shot if she didn't stop.

The terrified victims began to notice the fact that their abductors were all dressed identically in new-looking two-piece navy overalls. Each one had a single white number sewn onto the left breast pocket and the hooded figures only addressed each other with the numbers one to seven. All had strong working-class Dublin accents. Each man was wearing black knitted gloves and white-laced canvas boots. Their knitted hoods had neat slits for the eyes and mouth and were extended down over their upper bodies. Each of the attackers was carrying a handgun and at least two of the guns were fitted with long silencers, one was a powerful machine-pistol.

At this stage Joan Lacey was very concerned for her husband who was obviously hurt and looked 'like a corpse'. One of the gang held a gun pointed into his face. She tried to shove the gun away and told the man holding it that her husband had a bad heart. She insisted that the gunman point it at her instead and warned him that she was fiercely protective of her husband and would do anything to protect him. One of the gunmen kept telling her to calm down and that the gang were only after the car. She ordered Cahill's men to take the family car and leave their home. Another gang member patted her on the shoulder and told her to calm down. Joan Lacey prayed for her husband and her children.

By now Jim Lacey realised that his family was in grave danger. The family car was the last thing the men wanted. He asked the attackers several times: 'What's all this about?' Each time he was told to shut up and stay put. The man holding the gun in his face told him not to do anything stupid like activating any hidden panic alarms. There was a lot of activity throughout the house. Lights were turned off. The abductors appeared to be agitated and whispered nervously among themselves. Joan Lacey pleaded with Cahill's gang not to go near her sleeping children or wake them. She warned them not to touch Tanya Waters as she was only a neighbour's daughter babysitting for the family. When Joan tried to talk to Tanya she was threatened and abused and had a gun shoved in her face.

It was now about half-an-hour since the gang had rushed the front door. Jim and Joan Lacey were brought into the living-room and ordered to lie down beside Tanya and Louise. The couple were horrified to see that one of the children had already been awakened by the gang and was obviously terrified by what was going on. One of the gang began searching Jim Lacey for what he referred to as 'buttons', which Lacey took to mean a personal panic alarm. The gang member told him that if he did manage to activate a hidden alarm he would hear it on a scanner he was holding which was tuned into the Garda communications frequencies. The banker was also aware that the gang was using its own walkie-talkie system. He could hear a woman's voice communicating with the gang members.

By now the captives were able to discern that what they later described as 'a broad, plump man about five feet five to six inches in height' was the gang leader. He wore the figure '4' on his jacket and issued all the orders. After another fifteen minutes in the living-room Cahill announced that the gang was going to wake the other three children. Joan Lacey became hysterical and pleaded with them to leave her children alone. She got to her feet but was shoved violently to the ground and threatened by three of the masked men. Cahill repeatedly told her that she could get everybody killed. If anyone was hurt it would be her fault. He kept pointing a gun at her. But Joan Lacey, now deeply distressed for the safety of her family, ignored the threats and pleaded with the gang to allow her wake the children herself to lessen the trauma for them. Eventually Cahill allowed Tanya Waters to go upstairs instead.

Before doing so Cahill called Tanya out into the dining-room. In a low voice and shaking his finger he told the babysitter he thought she was the most sensible of the group and asked her if her parents were expecting her home. When she confirmed that her parents would not be waiting up for her, he allowed her to go upstairs for the children, accompanied by a member of the gang.

Upstairs the first of the sleeping children to be woken was twelve-year-old Robert. He immediately noticed the masked man standing beside Tanya with a pistol in his hand. The raider told the startled youngster: 'Happy Halloween, come on downstairs and help the party'. Robert was brought into the living-room and put lying beside his parents and sister Louise. The men went back up for fourteen-year-old Suzanne and six-year-old Sarah Jane. Tanya gently lifted Sarah Jane out of bed while the child slept and brought the two girls downstairs where the rest of the General's terrified victims were huddled together on the floor. The gang threw duvets over them to keep them warm. The house was in darkness except for the light in the hall and the upstairs landing.

Sometime around 3 am Cahill ordered that the children be dressed in warm clothes because they were going to be taken away. At this, both Jim Lacey and his wife began to panic. Cahill ordered Robert to be dressed first. Joan Lacey became hysterical and pleaded that she should be taken away instead of any of her children. Cahill explained that all of the group would be dressed one by one, but would give no other indication of what was to happen to his victims. This was typical of each of Cahill's meticulously devious plans. The victims of this crime would later tell detectives what other victims had told them in the past. None of the gang informed their terrified victims what they intended to do with them. They carried out their crime with military precision, each man knowing exactly what he had to do and the plump guy in the balaclava with the soft Dublin brogue giving the orders.

Tanya brought each child upstairs to be dressed, accompanied by at least two members of the gang. While she was dressing the children Cahill walked into the room behind her and began playing his game. 'Only seven men are allowed in this house and the gardens. They are all wearing white boots like these,' he said, lifting one of his feet off the ground and pointing to his footwear. 'Now remember that.' Joan Lacey would later recall that Cahill repeated this information like a chant during the next few hours of the hostage drama. It was the equivalent of the irritating mantra which he chanted non-stop when in Garda custody. The General felt most secure when he was repeating himself.

When the children were dressed and back in the living-room, Tanya was ordered to get warm clothes for Joan Lacey, which she put on. About an hour later, around 4 am, Cahill ordered Tanya to bring the children out to the dining-room one by one, which she did. The children would not see their father again during their agonising ordeal. From here on the Gardaí would be given frustratingly blatant clues as to the identity of the perpetrator of the Lacey kidnapping – but not a shred of evidence would be left to put Tango One behind bars.

In the dining-room Cahill put socks over each of the children's hands, tying them tightly and causing them considerable pain. They were each put sitting on a chair with their backs to the wall and facing the door. Tanya was then tied up in a similar fashion as was Joan Lacey who was the last to be removed to the dining-room. As she was leaving the room a gang member put handcuffs onto her husband's wrists. They had also thrown him a shirt with which to wipe away the blood from his head wound. It was now obvious that the gang intended separating Jim Lacey from the rest of his family. Joan begged the gang to keep them all together and asked why her husband had been left in the other room. The gang responded by threatening to kill her and pointed weapons in her face.

Then Cahill produced a Polaroid camera, the same camera he and Kavanagh had used to photograph Kavanagh's sons less than two months earlier. Each of the children and Tanya and Joan were ordered to shut their eyes while the pictures were taken. He put the pictures on a chair and suddenly seemed to go mad, viciously trying to smash the camera, first putting it in a pillowcase and crushing it with his hands before throwing it on the ground and dancing on it. This scared the children. 'See the camera, it's smashed, it's smashed,' he chanted at them with his broad mischievous grin protruding from his mask. A clicking noise from the camera came as the General handed it to the tallest of the gang members, who smashed it a bit more before placing it in a rucksack.

When everyone settled down again, Cahill pointed his finger

menacingly at each member of his captive audience facing him in the dining-room. He threatened them, emphasising that it was 'very, very, very important that youse listen very carefully'. And then came the mantra. 'There are seven of us and only seven, no more than seven.' He repeated this line several times before introducing a new line.

'We are all dressed identically, same suits, same boots, same gloves. We are all wearing the exact same shoes. Nobody is to be allowed into the house or the grounds other than these seven.' Cahill added that 'any other man' who came into the house had nothing to do with the gang. At this point the General, to emphasise his point about the uniformity of his gang's image, ordered Tanya Waters to initial each gang member's shoe with the letters 'TW'. When Tanya asked why she had to do this, Cahill replied: 'You'll see,' adding that he would have a note for her later.

About ten minutes later the General did something even more bizarre. He arrived back into the dining-room and again ordered Tanya Waters to get up. He had a box of Milk Tray chocolates in his hand and a sheet of paper. He told her to write a note saying 'All because the lady loves Milk Tray'. He told Tanya to tear off the cellophane cover of the box which he took and put in his pocket. Then he placed the note under the lid of the chocolate box and put it in the pocket of her jacket. Again Cahill made a very clear point of emphasising that he was taking the cellophane wrapping with him. As the morning wore on Tanya Waters asked one of the gang members what was the name of their gang, to which he replied: 'I'm sure the media will have a name for us tomorrow. We've been doing this for years.'

It was now around 5 am and Cahill was about to put the second part of his complex plan into operation. He again burst into the dining-room, grabbed a chair and sat down next to Robert. Pointing at the Laceys' only son, he said to Joan Lacey: 'He is going to be shot in the hand.'

Joan Lacey screamed in terror. 'If anyone is to be in any kind of danger it should be me,' she shouted at him. A gang member shoved her back into her chair.

Cahill continued with his evil plot. 'No, he's not goin' to get shot, but you're goin' to tell yer husband that he has been shot.' And to get the point across, Cahill's henchmen, who were now standing over the terrified schoolboy, began checking the magazines on their automatics as if getting ready to carry out their General's order.

Cahill then told Joan Lacey that she would have to convince her husband in the next room that their son had been shot through the hand and that she had bandaged the wound which was not serious. If she did not, then the child would be shot for real. Cahill also said that another man was going to be brought to the Laceys' home and kept with Jim while Joan, the babysitter and the children were brought away. The mystery man's family, Cahill claimed, would also be hostages.

Cahill was spending the rest of his time working on Jim Lacey in the living-room. Again he told the banker the 'seven men and only seven men' story. He showed Jim Lacey his boot with Tanya Waters's initials on it to prove his point. He also emphasised that each man had a number emblazoned on his overalls and made a point of showing that he had the figure '4' on his. At this stage the General went back to the dining-room.

Preparations were being made by the gang to move the hostages out of the house to the disused stables on Blackhorse Avenue on the north side of the city. Jim Lacey asked two of the gunmen how his children were. 'You do what we say and they'll be safe.'

Cahill returned to the room and knelt down beside Lacey who was lying on his back on the floor with his hands cuffed in front of him. His threatening voice made it clear that he meant business. 'Now listen carefully. I am not going to be repeating meself. We know who you are. You are Lacey. If you do what yer told you and your wife and kids will be safe. All we are interested in is the bank and the money. We know all about the bank and where the money is. The manager is Mr Keenan. His wife is Betty.' Cahill went on to give precise details about where the manager lived, about his daughter and his friends. He also referred to knowing all about the 'big room, the secret room and all the rooms' in the main bank building. This was the first time the gang revealed that they knew the identity of their hostages.

Cahill got up abruptly to leave the room again. Jim Lacey asked how his family was. Cahill told him: 'Listen to everything that you're told and they will be OK.' After fifteen minutes the General was back again kneeling down and dictating into the bank executive's ear. The General was determined to terrify his helpless victim into total compliance with his demands.

'We will be bringing a man here. He has his instructions. You will go with him to College Green in the morning in a van. He is to stay with you all the time and you are to stay with him. You are to take him in to Mr Keenan and get the van into the bank. You are to instruct Mr Keenan and to organise with him and whoever else you need to empty the place and fill that van with cash and I don't want any bollix about time locks. We know all about this place and the amount of cash there, which is millions. We don't want any small stuff. We want fifties and twenties. You're to make sure the place is totally emptied – the big room, the secret room, all the rooms, right? Because if it's not we'll kill your children. We've already shot your son in the hand just so that you know this is serious.'

Jim Lacey, who was already injured, disorientated and helpless, was now terrified for the safety of his wife and children. He had no idea they were still sitting in the next room. Throughout his ordeal the NIB chief executive believed that his wife, children and himself could be shot at any moment. Lacey tried to explain to the impatient General that he did not operate at the cash-holding centre and he asked what would happen if Mr Keenan was not on duty the next morning.

Again Cahill's intelligence gathering convinced Jim Lacey that his abductor meant business. In the event that the manager was not there, Cahill named the next man who would be able to open the cash vaults and release the money for Jim Lacey. Cahill repeated several times that if the instructions were not carried out to the letter then Lacey's children would be killed. He also warned him that 'very few people are to know'. When the bank executive explained that it would be difficult for him to get one of the gang members upstairs in the bank, Cahill said that they would be 'dressing up' the man who was to travel with him.

Cahill left the room. Outside Jo-Jo Kavanagh was ready for his part in this chilling show. He had changed out of his numbered overalls and initialled shoes and mask. The others had tied up his legs and put a hood on his head. He was dragged into the Lacey sitting-room and dumped in front of the bank executive. His hood was taken off. Jim Lacey could see that the man was heavily built with broad shoulders and a beard.

Cahill told Kavanagh: 'This is Mr Lacey. This is the man who will accompany you to the bank and you know what you have to do. Mr Lacey has been told what he has to do.' Cahill then asked the banker his shoe size and jacket size. The gang members then took Kavanagh upstairs to have a shower and shave. It was now around 5.50 am and everything was going according to the General's plan. At this stage Joan Lacey was told that her husband had a 'little message' to do for the gang. Together with Tanya and the other children they were allowed to go to the toilet before leaving the house. All of the hostages had pillow cases placed over their heads and they were made to pull on balaclavas.

The General was back in the living-room again with Jim Lacey. He knelt down beside the banker and showed him the Polaroid picture of his family and babysitter. 'If you do exactly as you're told you will see your family again.' Cahill told his hostage to close his eyes in order to concentrate on what he was telling him. He said that he had shot Jim Lacey's son in the hand and that he was to stay with the other 'hostage' as instructed. He was not to discuss any of the instructions he had been given with the other man (Kavanagh) after the gang had left the house.

'You know what you've to do. All we want is all the money that's in there. We know what's in there. You get the place empty. You shouldn't worry about the money. That's a matter for insurance and the bank. If you do everything I've told you and if the man with you comes out of the bank with the van full of money and if the police haven't been informed, you will get a phone call at 6 pm from a priest or doctor to tell you what road your family are on. If the police are informed anytime before that, your family will be killed. When you are told where your family are, then you should call the police and tell them everything that has happened here.'

At this stage Joan Lacey, a pillow case over her head, was brought in to say goodbye to him. She bent down beside her husband and told him that she loved him. He told her not to worry, that everything was going to be all right and that he had been told what to do. One of the gang pulled her roughly from the room and stuffed a balaclava down over the pillow case on her head. She was then dragged out the front door, down the steps and into the back of a waiting van. She could tell that it was an old van. She began to smother when several duvets and blankets were thrown on top of her. The gang members cursed her when she cried out to have them lifted off. The four children and their babysitter were then brought out and put into the van one by one. The voices in the van grew impatient and angry. 'Where the fuck is she?' one of them whispered in reference to the female accomplice on the other end of the walkie-talkie link. After about half an hour the van began to move off. It was noisy and in bad condition. Fumes leaked into the back from the labouring engine as the occupants were bumped around in the dark. The journey to the stables on Blackhorse Avenue took over half an hour. The hostages were quickly shuffled along by four or five members of the gang into the stables and up a ladder into the loft where they were allowed to take their pillow cases off. Everyone was told to sit down. The waiting game began.

As the van left the Lacey home around 6.30 am, Kavanagh, now clean-shaven and wearing one of Jim Lacey's suits, was put sitting on a chair behind the banker in the living-room. And just in case Lacey did not recognise him, Cahill's men made sure he knew it was the same man who had been brought in earlier. Cahill took the handcuffs off the banker. He tied his hands and feet with rubber restraints. He left the room momentarily and returned to hand Kavanagh a pair of glasses. He told him to wear the specs at all times and to take them off if things were not going according to plan. He said to Kavanagh: 'You know where the van is. When you arrive at the bank you park first outside the Andrews Street Post Office. Don't park it stupidly where it sticks out. It'll look like a Post Office van.'

Cahill then turned to Jim Lacey and gave him his final instructions. 'This man will release you between 8 and 8.15 am and you can get cleaned up and get that blood off yer head. You leave here between 10 and 10.15 am in your own car. You are to arrive at the bank before 11 and he [Kavanagh] will leave it before 1 pm. We'll be monitoring every move you make. We'll be watching this place and if anything happens that is not according to plan, you will not see your family again.'

At that Cahill and two other gang members went out of the room, leaving Jim Lacey and Kavanagh alone together. There was a lot of movement through the house as Cahill checked that nothing had been left which could give the Gardaí the kind of clues he disapproved of most – the ones which ended up with him standing before a judge. Leaving clues which served to annoy and frustrate them was just as important to the underworld joker. At 6.50 am Jim Lacey heard the front door closing. There were no more noises in the house. The gang had gone. The banker was still tied up lying on the floor and Kavanagh was on the chair. It was almost an hour before Jim Lacey broke the eerie silence.

'Where did you come from?' he asked Kavanagh who replied with the story that he had been kidnapped himself. To be more convincing Kavanagh asked the genuine victim what date it was. November the second. 'I have been held for at least two weeks.' Kavanagh then produced the pictures of his children which he and Cahill had taken back in September. Lacey, who had no idea that the man next to him was one of the gang, then showed Kavanagh the photographs which had been taken of his family. He said he was worried about the safety of his kids. The plan was working. Jim Lacey was tired, sore, confused, terrified, vulnerable. The photographs established a bond between the criminal and his unwitting victim. Kavanagh offered to cut the binds restraining Jim Lacey before 8 am, but the banker thought it best to wait until after that time. He did not want to do anything that might jeopardise his family.

Kavanagh went to the kitchen and brought back a knife to cut the binds. The two men left the living-room and went back to the kitchen where Jim Lacey put on the kettle. The two men talked. The General's co-conspirator then spun the story about being kidnapped outside the swimming pool in Crumlin, having a gun put to his back and being held in a dark room in a sleeping-bag since then. The bank executive became curious as to why his abduction had not been the subject of a Garda search. Kavanagh asked Lacey if he had seen his picture in the paper. He said that following the recent death of his brother he had been depressed. It was not unusual for him to go on a drink binge for anything up to ten days.

The criminal began working on Jim Lacey's genuine fears. Kavanagh showed him the pictures of his children again and told how the abductors had given them to him and told him the children would be killed if he did not do as he was told. Then he told Lacey that the gang claimed they had shot Kavanagh's son through the hand. Kavanagh kept looking at the photographs of his children and mother-in-law Esther Bolger and saying, almost in desperation, 'They have my kids'. Kavanagh said he believed the gang were holding his kids hostage just like the Lacey children.

Kavanagh still refused to tell Jim Lacey anything about himself even though he was trying to pretend that he and the banker were in the same boat. Of his identity he would only reveal that his first name was Joe. When the bank executive asked Joe how they were supposed to get to the van which was to transport the money from the bank, Kavanagh said that he could not divulge this information either. 'I will do exactly what I have to do to safeguard my children because these people are deadly serious.' At this stage Kavanagh told Lacey that the van to be used for moving the money was parked at Merrion Church in south Dublin opposite St Vincent's Hospital. Kavanagh appeared to become agitated and nervous.

Jim Lacey changed his clothes, washed, shaved and dressed his head wound. He rang his office at Wilton Terrace and said that because of the late night at the NIB branch opening he would not be in until lunchtime. A neighbour called looking for Joan. Jim told her his wife had gone to the city centre shopping with the children. At 10 am Jim Lacey and Kavanagh left the house and drove to Merrion

Road. When he arrived at the church car park the banker could not see the van they were supposed to pick up. Kavanagh however 'spotted' it immediately, even though it was parked practically out of view in a corner. Jim Lacey parked his car next to the van, a green Toyota Hi-ace. It was an old battered-looking model. Within seconds Kavanagh was behind the wheel of the van and had the engine running. He reversed it out of the car park and drove onto the road without hesitation or difficulty, despite telling Jim Lacey that he was not a good driver and was nervous about how he would handle the van. Jim Lacey would later recall that Kavanagh was in fact quite a skilled driver. They drove along Merrion Road through Ballsbridge into Baggot Street, Pembroke Street, onto Leeson Street and St Stephen's Green, down Dawson Street, Nassau Street and onto Andrews Street where he parked the van between the National Irish Bank building and the Post Office. It was now 10. 40 am.

Members of the gang continued to keep the van's progress under surveillance from a distance. They were constantly monitoring the Garda airwaves for any hint that the game was up. In the meantime Martin Cahill had an alibi to sort out. He strolled into Rathmines Garda station to present his driver's licence and insurance documents. It would not take long for the police to find out why the General was so anxious to show off his driving documentation even though he had not been required to do so.

Meanwhile Jim Lacey and Kavanagh had walked into the NIB building. A porter led the chief executive and his companion up to the office of the manager, Eugene Keenan. Keenan was on the phone but Jim Lacey walked in with Kavanagh and sat at his desk indicating to him that he should end the call immediately. Time was ticking away. As he closed the office door, Lacey introduced Kavanagh and then blurted out what had happened. He appeared to the manager to be extremely distressed.

'Something dreadful has happened, the kids are all gone,' Jim told his manager. He produced the photographs of his family as well as Kavanagh's. In a short time he had explained the harrowing details of the previous ten hours. He told Eugene Keenan that they had parked outside the bank and had been instructed to fill the van with cash. Kavanagh began to get excited and told the manager that the gang knew about the secret room and how much money was in the bank. But he was also able to tell Eugene Keenan the name of his wife and daughter and the type of car he drove. The apparent 'victim' was even able to tell the manager that the gang knew he was close to his daughter who was his only child. He added details of Keenan's friendship with Dermot Bonner, the manager of the retail bank, and the fact that their two families had been on holiday together. He knew that Keenan lived near Bonner in west Dublin.

Keenan asked Jim Lacey how much he thought they would have to give the gang. Kavanagh again interrupted and informed him that the gang wanted the place emptied of cash. He emphasised again that the gang knew how much money was in the bank. Kavanagh was obviously excited that he was at last almost inside the door of Alladin's Cave and the biggest robbery ever to take place in Ireland.

At this Jim Lacey, although terrified for the safety of his family, began to think on his feet. He was not yet suspicious of Kavanagh but suggested to his manager that there was probably a few hundred thousand pounds in the vaults. The actual figure on that morning was over £7 million. Lacey hoped that Keenan could make it appear to Kavanagh that they had emptied all the rooms in the vault by handing over a figure in the region of £150,000 in used £50 and £20 notes.

Keenan then rang Frank Brennan, the general manager of administration at the NIB's HQ at Wilton Terrace. Both he and Jim Lacey quickly explained the situation and relayed the strict instructions of the gang that the police were not to be informed or everyone would be murdered. Brennan then called the manager of the NIB cash centre and authorised Eugene Keenan to withdraw a total of £233,000 in £50, £20, £10 and £5 bundles so that it would look bulky and give the impression that there was a lot more money.

When he had done that Frank Brennan alerted the company secretary and had the crisis management plan consulted. He then rang the NIB's next executive up the line at the London HQ of the bank's parent company, National Australia Bank Group, where he informed the managing director, John Dawson, of the unfolding drama. The London executive agreed that the priority was the safe return of the Lacey family. Eugene Keenan left his office and went down to the cash centre. He signed a note for the money and put it in a brown nylon bag and returned to the conference room upstairs where Jim Lacey was waiting with Kavanagh.

While they were alone Kavanagh again emphasised that the van had to be filled with cash or he would not leave the bank. 'If that happens then me and my kids will be OK and your family will be killed,' Kavanagh warned. Eugene Keenan arrived back in the room and threw a sack of money onto the table saying that that was all the cash there was. Kavanagh, who had been playing the terrified victim, was now beginning to get angry.

Without looking at the bag he said that there was no way that was all the cash. He said he was told to leave the bank with millions. Both the chief executive and his manager explained that there was a quarter of a million pounds in the bag. But Kavanagh refused to accept the story. He turned to Lacey. 'You better give them everything here because they'll kill your family if you don't. They have been getting information from someone in this place and they know exactly how much is here.' In a dramatic gesture, he took off the glasses Cahill had given him and stuck them into his breast pocket and sat down. Eugene Keenan got on the phone to call Frank Brennan who arrived in the bank about fifteen minutes later. It was now just after twelve noon with less than an hour to go to Cahill's 1 pm deadline.

Brennan talked for a short while with Jim Lacey who was agitated and distressed. He showed Brennan the pictures of Joan and his children and Tanya Waters. The bank chief executive was particularly upset about his son, Robert, who had supposedly been shot. Lacey had no idea how his son was. 'We are dealing with professionals who act like military,' he explained to his colleague. When Brennan asked Kavanagh where he lived and where he had been told to go he again gave the reply that his instructions were to say nothing but to fill up the van with money, all the money. He was beginning to sound like his underworld pal, Martin Cahill, with his monotonous tendency to repeat himself over and over again.

Frank Brennan suggested that he and Eugene Keenan should go back to the cash centre and double check if there was any more cash. They withdrew another £15,000 in £5 and £10 notes. They bundled the money into a plastic bag and brought it back upstairs and said that that was all the money they could get. Again Kavanagh began his diatribe about the gang's instructions. Frank Brennan convinced him that he had all the money available. The only other cash was that in the tellers' tills and that could not be touched without raising the alarm.

The bank officials loaded the money into three black refuse sacks, cutting the bands on the bundles of notes to make them look much bulkier. While this was going on, Kavanagh kept telling Lacey that if anything went wrong it would be on his head. He sought reassurances that he would not be followed when he left the bank. Jim Lacey reminded him to put the spectacles back on. Eugene Keenan had arranged with the head of security to ensure that Kavanagh was properly video-taped while loading the van so that the Gardaí could identify him later. Kavanagh was led out of the office and down to the van at 12.35 pm. A short while later Eugene Keenan returned. 'He's gone.'

Frank Brennan and Jim Lacey had a long discussion about whether to call in the Gardaí. Jim Lacey, having experienced at first hand just how organised and well-informed Cahill's gang had been, was afraid to alert the police before the appointed time of 6 pm. Eventually, however, he agreed but would not make the call from the College Green building because the General had convinced him he knew what was going on in there and might have had someone on the inside.

Lacey and Brennan drove back to Wilton Terrace where the company secretary, using a special number and codeword, called the Crime and Security section of Garda HQ in the Phoenix Park. Within five minutes Detective Superintendent Tom Butler and Detective Inspector Willie Ryan from the Serious Crime Squad at Harcourt Square arrived to talk with Jim Lacey. Shortly after this, a major citywide search began for the Lacey family although the investigation had to be discreet because the gang were using scanners.

Joan Lacey, her four children and Tanya Waters spent twelve cold and uncomfortable hours sitting bound, gagged and blindfolded in the loft of the disused stables. They were guarded at all times by at least one member of the gang who carried three guns and a scanner. They .were not given any food or water. The hostages had no knowledge of what was happening or what the gang intended to do with them. They were terrified. Joan Lacey asked their guard what would happen to them if the money wasn't paid. 'We'll have to shoot each of you in the leg at least so we'll be taken seriously the next time.'

Sometime around 3 pm, the gunman told Joan Lacey that every-thing had gone according to plan and that Jim had done everything he was supposed to. The gang had got more money than 'you could dream about'. The gang members left the stables sometime around 5 pm. Louise Lacey managed to break herself free and then untied the rest of the hostages. They called for help through a hole in the roof. At 6.45 pm Gardaí from Cabra station arrived and whisked the shattered Lacey family and their dedicated babysitter across the city in a convoy of squad cars to Harcourt Square. Jim Lacey was at last reunited with his family as was Tanya Waters with hers. It would take Cahill's latest victims a long time to overcome the trauma they had suffered and they would not return to their home in Blackrock for several weeks. Tanya Waters remembered the box of chocolates she had been given by the gang boss. She retrieved it from her pocket. The box was crushed and the chocolates melted but the note was still intact. The experienced detectives who were gathering for the inves-tigation that was about to start had no doubt now who their chief suspect was. The General was playing his sinister games again.

Jo-Jo Kavanagh and Martin Cahill had planned the van's getaway route well. Cahill and one of his close confidants, one of the so-called Rottweilers, watched the bank from Cahill's van across the road. Kavanagh drove the van on a route which did not have any traffic or security video camera systems from Andrews Street, up Camden Street and into Rathmines. It took only seconds to transfer the money from the van to another car near Maxwell Road in Rathmines. At the same time Kavanagh jumped out and began walking back towards the city centre where he paid an unscheduled visit to the office of his solicitor Garrett Sheehan. The van was then taken into a lane off Maxwell Road by two other members of the General's gang and burned. Here again Cahill was playing his game. He wanted the Gardaí to know of his involvement in the kidnapping and what better place to burn out the van than around the corner from his home.

The investigation HQ was in Blackrock, the nearest Garda station to the Lacey's home. At the first conference the following morning, 3 November, the team of detectives were all in agreement about the identity of their prime suspect. Intelligence was being gathered on all known associates not currently behind bars whom Cahill could trust in such an enormous operation. Detailed statements from all the victims were vital while the terrifying ordeal was still fresh in their minds.

The meticulous militaristic planning for the crime and the bizarre repetitions of the gang leader had all the hallmarks of Cahill. And the description of the gang leader fitted him. There were also similarities to the O'Connors' jewellery heist in that the gang had detailed knowledge, in this case, of the movements and personal lives of all the top executives at the National Irish Bank. The main priority was to identify and locate the mystery 'Joe' character whom the Gardaí correctly suspected had to be one of Cahill's men. During the night of 2 November, when detectives went to examine security video footage at the College Green building, they discovered that for some reason the camera had not managed to film him.

In the meantime Cahill would wait patiently for the Gardaí to arrest him and for the dust to settle to divide out the loot which had been buried. The Gardaí were well aware that if they took him into custody he would simply chant his mantra and they would be forced to release him after forty-eight hours. They decided to wait for several weeks in the hope of getting some evidence or a statement from a gang member. In the days following the kidnapping the Gardaí made sure that the media had the story of how the General lost out on the jackpot of a lifetime – almost £8 million in cash. Cahill sat back and laughed in front of his pals. At least, he said, we made the police look stupid again. But secretly Cahill was furious that he had been duped. So he decided to get back at the system by planning several more kidnappings.

On the morning of 3 November, the Gardaí at Harcourt Square received a phone call from Garrett Sheehan, who informed them that the man known as 'Joe' was in his office and wished to make a statement. The call was handed over to Detective Inspector Felix McKenna, one of the hard-nosed policemen who had been investigating organised crime for several years in Dublin. McKenna, who was now based in the Blackrock district, was ideal for the job because of his extensive knowledge of Martin Cahill and his network. He had also been one of the officers in charge of the Tango Squad in the late 1980s and was attached to several investigations. He was part of the squad that had recovered the Murnaghan paintings in 1989.

McKenna arranged to meet Kavanagh and his solicitor in Terenure Garda station at 11.45 that same morning. He needed no introduction to Jo-Jo Kavanagh. Kavanagh had featured in several investigations he had been involved in and he was also one of the targets of the Tango Squad. Kavanagh said that he wished to make a statement about his own 'kidnapping' but would only dictate this statement to the detective in the company of his solicitor and not answer any questions.

Kavanagh ran through the story he and Cahill had rehearsed about his abduction, incarceration and eventual involvement in the actual Lacey kidnapping. When the statement was over Kavanagh handed over the photographs of his children and mother-in-law. He also handed over the glasses Cahill had given him on the morning of the kidnapping. When he had done this Kavanagh said that he did not wish to say anything else or make any other statements.

The following day Detective Inspector McKenna and another Garda went to Garrett Sheehan's office by appointment. Kavanagh had agreed to meet them there in the presence of his solicitor, and he handed over to the Gardaí a plastic bag containing the suit he had taken from Jim Lacey's home as well as a pair of shoes. An examination would later show that the suit had been dry-cleaned to destroy any forensic evidence. McKenna asked to see his wrists as Kavanagh had claimed he had been handcuffed throughout his two week abduction. There were no marks on them. McKenna also wanted to know the names of anyone who could corroborate his story that he had been missing since 15 October. Kavanagh would answer no more questions.

By now the investigation team, which was under the overall control on the ground of Detective Superintendent Cormac Gordon, was examining the statements of the victims. From the outset Cahill's sidekick was a very obvious suspect and the man most likely to be charged in relation to the crime. There were several glaring contradictions between his recollection of events and Jim Lacey's which would provide compelling circumstantial evidence against him.

Kavanagh had also made it clear that he had no intention of assisting the Gardaí in their investigation, which was at best strange behaviour for the victim of such heinous crimes as kidnapping and intimidation. There was also the suspicious fact that Kavanagh, despite his alleged fears for the safety of his children, made no attempt to find how they were for several hours after he delivered the money.

On 18 November, Detective Superintendent Tom Butler and Detective Inspector Michael Cannavan travelled to meet a friend of Kavanagh's who had been living in the US since September. In a number of taped interviews over two days she described how Kavanagh, Cahill and a third man had planned the kidnapping. She also revealed that Kavanagh had done most of the surveillance on the Laceys and that he was expecting to make millions from the kidnapping. The woman gave the officers a fairly frank description of their suspect: 'He is a very intelligent bastard. He has no time for his kids; he is a selfish fucker who only thinks of himself all the time.' The witness also provided the detectives with the vital information which would fill the gaps in the team's investigation.

Back in Dublin detectives also discovered that Kavanagh had himself collected his Lone Parent's weekly allowance of £133 during the two weeks he claimed he was being held captive. It was a remarkable mistake. On 8 December Det. Insp. McKenna and a team of armed detectives arrested Jo-Jo Kavanagh under the Offences Against the State Act. He was held for forty-eight hours and quizzed about his role in the crime. He refused to say anything and was let go.

But as the investigation progressed, Kavanagh, totally dissatisfied with the haul from the kidnapping, was worried that he was now likely to be the only member of the gang to face charges. He was aware that he had made several mistakes which could have him facing at least a conspiracy rap. He talked to Cahill about the problem. If he was found guilty, he would face twenty years behind bars for a measly £25,000 – a poor return for someone who offered himself as the front man. In return for getting his credibility back in the underworld, he would be basking in the glory in his cell in Portlaoise maximum security prison.

But the General had a rather outlandish solution to the problem. He suggested that he stage another 'crime' on Kavanagh. This time he and his men would burst into Kavanagh's house and shoot him in the legs. They would make it look as if the gang was exacting revenge on him for not getting all the money. Cahill told Kavanagh that when he was shot he should call all the newspapers and give them the story about him being an innocent victim of the Lacey kidnap gang. He could also claim that he was now being victimised by the Gardaí just because of his criminal past. Cahill told him to say that the cunning bastard behind the stroke had more than likely picked him out because the Gardaí would assume he was in on it. The diabetes was beginning to take a toll on the General's grasp of criminal logic.

Kavanagh reluctantly agreed to the plan in the absence of any other alternatives. Cahill and two of the other gang members involved in the Lacey kidnapping called to Kavanagh's house one evening shortly afterwards. They broke up the furniture to make it look as if a struggle had taken place and then carefully shot Kavanagh in the left leg on the inside of the calf muscle. The wound was not serious. 'Now that should do it,' Cahill remarked, as he wiped sweat from his blotchy forehead and slipped off into the night.

When the Gardaí arrived they found Kavanagh standing at the door with his hands and legs tied. He said that the men questioned him about the kidnap and why he had not taken all the money. The 'gang' had told him that he was going to be shot in the leg because he hadn't carried out their orders. He also claimed his 'attackers' said they would shoot him in the head and also kill his son. The following morning the news desks of the *Evening Herald*, *Evening Press* and *Sunday World* got anonymous calls stating that Kavanagh had a story to tell. When journalists visited him in his hospital bed in St James's Hospital he posed for pictures and told them his tale of woe. The journalists, like the police, were sceptical and treated the story warily.

Just over a week later, the investigation team arrested Martin Cahill. Over the next forty-eight hours Cahill held his hand over his face and chanted his mantra whenever he was asked about the kidnapping. But detectives were surprised that he readily engaged in small talk about crime in general whenever they did not concentrate on the actual kidnapping. One detective who had known him for a long time expressed concern to Cahill that he did not seem very well. He was an ill man. The cop even advised him to go and see a doctor. While he was being held the General's thugs were doing their bit in the war – they slashed the tyres of twenty-two cars in the Belgrave Square area of Rathmines.

By March the investigation had wound down. The Gardaí sent a file to the DPP to consider charging Kavanagh with the kidnapping. The investigation team had identified most of the members of the gang but had no evidence to charge any of them, apart from Kavanagh. A total of twenty suspects were arrested, including Cahill and Kavanagh, and questioned under the Offences Against the State Act. In July 1994, Jo-Jo Kavanagh, who was already in custody for another criminal offence, was formally charged before the Special Criminal Court in Dublin. There were four charges – false imprisonment, intent to commit false imprisonment, possession of firearms and demanding cash with menaces.

The case against Kavanagh would not come before the courts for over three years after the murder of Martin Cahill. On 29 October 1997, the court found him guilty of three of the charges. But

Kavanagh was relatively lucky in that a loophole was discovered in the 1997 Non-Fatal Offences Against the Person Act. Counsel argued the legal intricacies but the judges ruled that they were obliged to find him not guilty on the false imprisonment charge which would have resulted in a life sentence.

Instead the court could impose only a twelve-year sentence. Mr. Justice Barr said that the court did not believe Kavanagh's story about the kidnapping. His claim that he was shot in the leg as punishment for not delivering the money to the gang was also 'wholly unbelievable'.

Within days the Dáil rushed to close the embarrassing loophole in the legislation to ensure this would never happen again. Despite his self-satisfied grin as he was being led from the court, Kavanagh is due to be in jail until after 2005. The Lacey kidnap was the last major crime masterminded by Martin Cahill and there was a tinge of irony in the fact that, even three years after his death, the Mickey Mouse villain was still winning victories over the law.

CHAPTER 17

On the Edge

In 1993 Martin Cahill threw a party to celebrate his twenty-fifth wedding anniversary – and a quarter century in crime. It was the underworld bash of the year. The joker booked a hotel which was close to Garda headquarters in the Phoenix Park where many attempts to ensure he never had such a party were mooted. Cahill sat proudly at the head table surrounded by his family, criminal associates and friends from the pigeon club of which he was a member. One of his hoods presented him with a silver-plated jemmy bar with the laconic inscription, 'Where it all began'. There was laughter and clapping as the grinning General took possession of this memento of a life of crime. Another loyal lieutenant presented him with a coin-operated gas-meter in memory of the infamous job in the seventies when he stole £10,000 worth of tenpenny pieces from a gas company van.

There was a nervous silence when a policewoman walked into the packed function room and marched boldly up to the top table where Cahill sat. Instead of slapping handcuffs on the gangster she began peeling off the uniform that he had despised all his life. He rolled his head back and laughed loudly as the strippogram, another present from his henchmen, gyrated on the table in front of him. The pigeon club also made their own presentation to their friend of thirteen years. Cahill had a ball and spent the night dancing with his women in a disco he had hired specially for the occasion.

The members of the Rialto Club of pigeon fanciers were one of the few groups of people not involved in crime with whom Cahill associated. He was extremely well-liked and was generous in donating cash to the charities the club backed. Members of the club say that he left his criminal activities outside when he went to race meetings and social nights at the club. He was quiet and kept to himself. As one pigeon fancier revealed: 'He was idolised by people. He wasn't aggressive or intimidating. In fact he was the last man you would suspect of being a major criminal.' He had great affection for the pigeon fanciers and relaxed in their company. When one pigeon fancier died suddenly leaving a young family behind, Cahill, in a typically low-key way, paid the funeral costs. A friend who had travelled regularly with him to shows died of cancer. The General ensured that the dead man's family was looked after financially. On another occasion when thieves stole valuable birds belonging to a member of the pigeon fraternity Cahill retrieved them. No more pigeons were stolen.

Cahill regularly travelled to England by ferry (he had a phobia about flying) for race meetings. Every January he went with other members of the club to Blackpool for the annual pigeon show there. He would check into a Bed & Breakfast and at night went to strip-shows with his friends. He was considered to be one of the top pigeon racers in Ireland and was well-known in pigeon clubs in France, Belgium and Britain. In 1987 he paid an English loft £55,000 cash for twenty racing and long-distance birds, including top breeds like Busshard and Janarden. He also built elaborate lofts at the rear of Cowper Downs where the Tango Squad sat on the wall and watched him during the surveillance operation.

At one stage Cahill was wrongly accused of using the pigeons to fly heroin into Ireland – an absurd rumour. However his birds did once get involved in a criminal act of sorts when they ate all the seed in a freshly-laid lawn at the back of former Taoiseach Garret FitzGerald's house on nearby Palmerston Road. The General laughed about that for days.

Outside pigeon circles however, Cahill's criminal reputation had made him a legend in the underworld. Like a mafia Don, people respected and feared him. When he was in his homes in either Cowper Downs or Swan Grove there was a constant stream of callers looking for favours. If someone's relative was getting a hard time from other prisoners in Mountjoy Prison, Cahill, who controlled the landings, sent word and the hassle stopped. Contrary to the widespread rumour that he was mean, Cahill was known in the underworld for his generosity. He helped individuals get into legitimate business, giving them the cash to start up. But those who used his name to intimidate or bully people often found themselves being hauled in front of the General's kangaroo court. One offender was even taken up to the mountains where he was ordered to dig his own grave because he had used the General's name to intimidate a former business partner. Cahill's men let him go when he 'saw the error of his ways'. The General relished his image as a big-time gang boss.

Behind the smiles and the fun at his quarter-century celebration, Martin Cahill was not a healthy man. His diabetes had deteriorated and he was prone to fatigue and bouts of bad temper. In his later years Cahill was often forced to stay inside for several days at a time. He did not like doctors and refused to seek treatment for the condition. Instead he took the tablets prescribed for his mother-in-law who suffered from the same ailment. He put on more weight and, despite his illness, continued to eat sweet things. Associates recall how he doggedly refused to acknowledge that he was suffering from ill-health and took out his frustrations on anyone who crossed him. Even a policeman who took him in for questioning six months before his death advised him to go and see a doctor. His worsening temper, his arrogance and the fact that luck eventually runs out, were to put the General on a one-way trip to disaster.

One day, when he was passing a garage in Rathmines, he saw a second-hand Mercedes 500 for sale and decided to buy it. However, the next morning, when he sent an associate down to do the deal, the garage had already sold the car. When the associate reported back, the General flew into an uncontrollable rage. He got on a bicycle and pedalled down to the offending garage. In his paranoia he believed that the police had found out that he was going to buy the car and had told the garage to sell it. In reality there was nothing more sinister afoot than the garage salesmen doing his job – selling cars. He arrived at the forecourt of the garage, threw down his bike and asked for the man who sold the Mercedes. Cahill grabbed the stunned salesman by the throat and snarled: 'Do you know who I am? I am the General.

Now buy that fuckin' car back and give it to me or I'll burn the place down.' The outburst was totally out of character for the once reserved criminal. Eventually his associate managed to calm him down and he was persuaded to buy another Mercedes.

In April 1993, around the time of his twenty-fifth anniversary celebrations, a neighbour called one of Tina's children names and referred to their mother's relationship with their 'Uncle Martin'. Cahill was inside watching a video when one of the kids came in and told him. He got up without speaking, grabbed a sledgehammer, and burst through the front door of his neighbour's house. Inside he and another relative smashed every piece of glass in the house, including the front windows and mirrors. He smashed three TV sets, the microwave and a glass table. When he was finished Cahill smiled and left without saying a word.

Shortly afterwards he was brought into Rathmines Station for questioning. While he was being detained, the son of the woman whose home he had wrecked came in. The son, a petty criminal who worked for the General, told the police that Cahill had nothing to do with the incident at his house. He said it was a domestic row and that it was none of the policeman's business. The General left the station grinning to himself.

In his dealings with the Gardaí, Cahill's skills as a game-player were diminishing. Previously, whenever the cops annoyed him, Cahill would smile and walk away. But he was losing his cool. On Christmas Eve in 1991 Cahill walked into Rathmines Garda Station following a confrontation with the crew of a squad car and asked for the desk sergeant. He pointed his finger at the policeman but refused to look him in the eye. 'I suppose youse culchies think ye'r goin' to have a quiet Christmas? Well, ye'r wrong, 'cause I'm goin' to make sure ye'r kept good and busy and don't have time to be enjoyin' yerselves.' Christmas 1991 was busy in the Garda P district and bad for motorists who parked their cars in the streets of Rathmines. It was also a lucrative one for the garages that had to replace hundreds of slashed tyres.

The Beit robbery jinx continued to dog the General's life as he attempted to turn the stolen paintings into cash. After the botched sale to the UVF Cahill agreed to sell eight of the paintings for over £1 million to a businessman. The businessman, fronting for a number of other investors, paid Cahill £500,000 cash as a deposit for the eight paintings. This left three of the eleven paintings stolen from the collection at large: one had vanished with the Dutch criminal, Van Scoaik, after the Kilakee operation in 1987; one was buried and may never be found because the General couldn't remember where he put it; the last is still missing.

The deal between Cahill and the businessman was to be completed when the works of art were sold and he received the balance of the monies due. The General lent the businessman back £150,000 which he was going to invest in a cannabis deal with an English gang. From the proceeds of the sale of the cannabis deal, the Englishman would be able to repay the money in a short time. Cahill agreed.

Of the remaining £350,000 of the deposit, Cahill split £100,000 among those of his gang involved in the Beit robbery. The rest of the cash was also redistributed. But the bad luck followed the gang wherever they went. In April 1992 London police recovered the £2 million Gainsborough masterpiece, 'Madame Bacelli', when they opened a container in a left luggage office in Euston train station. A receipt for the luggage led police to a block of flats where an Irishman had lived.

Then in March 1993 a burglar made an astonishing discovery when he broke into a house in the St John's Wood area of north London which was being used to hide some of the Beit collection. He made off into the night with two works worth over £4 million – the Palamedesz and the Rubens. The burglar had never before tried to fence anything quite so large and Scotland Yard soon got wind of it. The burglar was arrested after the paintings were found behind a couch in the thief's house in London.

In the meantime the businessman and his associates did the £150,000 cannabis deal with the English gang but the General never saw a penny of it. Cahill began making enquiries of the businessman who assured him the money would be paid.

At the same time, another of Cahill's associates made discreet overtures for the return of the Beit paintings. The deal involved a senior member of the Gardaí with the co-operation of the Beit Foundation and the National Gallery. Gardaí would simply 'recover' the stolen paintings and restore them to their rightful place.

In order to establish that the paintings were still intact, the associate contacted the businessman, who had since moved the remaining four works in his possession to Holland. The businessman handed over photographs of the paintings. One of the photos included a tea-pot standing in front of Vermeer's 'Lady Writing a Letter'. The tentative negotiations dragged on for six months but eventually fell through.

By this time a major international operation, including the Gardaí, Scotland Yard and the Belgian police, had been mounted. During a series of meetings in Norway two buyers – one was a civilian working for the Belgian police, the other an undercover cop from Scotland Yard – negotiated to buy the four paintings. In September, the Belgian police swooped on a car in Antwerp Airport and recovered the four paintings – the £20 million Vermeer along with the works by Goya, Metsu and Vestier.

Back in Dublin Martin Cahill was furious. He began putting pressure on the businessman for his money. In July 1994 Cahill and his henchmen cornered the businessman on a city street. He was told that if he didn't come up with the money he would be shot dead. Cahill did not live to carry out his threat.

A month after the Lacey kidnap an historic event occurred which was to have a major influence on the General's fate. On the steps of No 10, Downing Street, Irish and British premiers, Albert Reynolds and John Major, introduced an ambitious plan for peace in Northern Ireland. The Downing Street Declaration was the forerunner to intensive behind-the-scenes negotiations between the two governments and the various paramilitary and political groups in the North which would lead, nine months later, to the end of twenty-five years of bloodshed on the streets of Northern Ireland. In Dublin senior members of the IRA held secret talks with representatives of the Irish government.

As the tentative negotiations continued in the build-up to the ceasefire there was a dramatic escalation in sectarian violence in the North with the Loyalist terrorist organisations responsible for some of the worst atrocities in the entire conflict. One of the most active 'death squads' was operated by the Ulster Volunteer Force (UVF) in Northern Ireland and led by one of Martin Cahill's business associates.

On 21 May, 1994, a UVF team travelled to Dublin. On the same night, Saturday, Sinn Féin were holding a fund-raising function in the Widow Scallans pub on Pearse Street. The pub was a regular venue for Republican functions. The manager was James Dunne, one of the four men involved in the attempted kidnap in 1984 of Martin Foley which ended with a shoot-out in the Phoenix Park. At 10.50 pm two members of the UVF arrived at the door of the upstairs function room which was packed with over three hundred people. One of the gang carried a handgun, the other a hold-all with an 18lb bomb inside.

IRA man Martin Doherty, a thirty-five year-old father of two from Ballymun, who was on the door, stopped the two men getting in. In an ensuing scuffle Doherty was shot several times and died instantly. A second man, Paddy Burke, who had no association with Sinn Féin, was seriously injured when he was shot through a locked door leading to the function room. Failing to throw the bomb into the packed room, the terrorists left it in the doorway and ran to a waiting getaway car which was abandoned ten minutes later on the North Strand near a pub which had the reputation of being frequented by IRA members. The bomb failed to go off. If it had, hundreds would have been killed or seriously injured.

In the immediate aftermath of the Widow Scallans attack the UVF threatened that it would strike again at Republican targets in the south. There was intense speculation that members of the Dublin underworld had assisted the murder gang. Martin Cahill's name was high on the list of suspects as the IRA launched its own investigation into the atrocity. There was panic among the criminal fraternity as its members feared a backlash from the Provos.

But Cahill was not worried. He had not been involved and told associates that he was not afraid of his old adversaries. It later transpired that no members of the Dublin underworld had helped the UVF group which came from Belfast, not Portadown. Nevertheless, the Provo commanders took an intense interest in the General because of his business dealings with the Portadown gang. The last straw came for the Provos when Cahill refused to attend a meeting to discuss his activities with them. He had never answered questions and he was not about to start. He had done nothing and, as far as he was concerned, that was the end of it. Senior members of the IRA in Dublin detested Cahill's arrogance and open disrespect. Time was running out for Cahill.

The Widow Scallans however, was not the only matter occupying the General's mind. In February a property developer began building three mews house at Mountpleasant Avenue overlooking the back gardens of the houses on Swan Grove, including Cahill's. The General was determined that the houses would not be built. He believed that one of them directly overlooking his garden would be rented by the police to watch him. In March a watchman on the site was approached and told to give up his job to a local man. The man refused. Twenty minutes later, a gunman appeared and fired a shot over his head. The terrified watchman resigned.

At midnight on 13 May Cahill and five of his gang walked into the storeroom where another watchman was sitting talking to two friends. The gangmen were wearing balaclavas and boiler suits and three of them carried guns. As his men took petrol and other flammable objects from the storeroom the watchman and his friends were ordered to lie on the floor. Cahill told them that the builder would be shot if he tried to continue building the houses. Then the gang set fire to the three houses before fleeing. The blaze seriously damaged the roofs of the new buildings.

Following the attack Gardaí moved in to guard the site. A few nights later a car was burnt out around the corner. Cahill also sanctioned attacks in which the tyres of scores of cars were slashed. The number of people bearing a grudge against the General was growing.

In July two renegade members of the INLA assassinated John

Bolger, a former associate of Cahill who had fallen out with him in recent years. Bolger, a thirty-one year-old father of two, was murdered over a row about the proceeds of a 'fund-raising' racket. Afterwards there was speculation that Cahill had some involvement in the killing because of this disagreement. The two hitmen went on the run from their own organisation. Following the Bolger killing, Cahill again found himself in trouble with the INLA in a dispute over a flat which he subsequently burned. During the row the General crossed swords with a senior figure within the organisation.

The INLA decided that it was time to sort the General out. They began planning his demise. The IRA had arrived at the same conclusion and two gunmen were already assigned to despatch the General. They were experienced hitmen and both had been in prison for terrorist crimes. As far as some of the organisation's older hands were concerned, Cahill had it coming. They had wanted him dead ten years earlier. Now with the ceasefire a likely prospect, there was some personal business which needed to be finished. Martin Cahill was living on borrowed time.

CHAPTER 18

The Sisters

·Martin Cahill's love life was like every other aspect of his character – bizarre, complex, different. The overweight, balding man did not look like an ardent lover any more than he did a swaggering gangster. But appearances in Martin Cahill's case were, much to his satisfaction, deceptive. Just as in his criminal activities, in romance Cahill was profuse and totally unorthodox.

Frances Lawless was Cahill's girl next door. As a girl, dark-haired and attractive, she had lived with her large family of brothers and sisters in another cramped flat a few doors away in Hollyfield Buildings. The Lawless and Cahill kids played together in the bleak concrete courtyard in front of the flats. From an early age some of the boys went out together stealing and causing mayhem for the shopkeepers and police in Rathmines. Martin had been quiet and introverted from the time he was a child. Unlike other boys who also mitched from school and were visited constantly by the local police, he was not boisterous or a bully. Frances Lawless saw a gentle, affectionate streak in the sixteen-year-old that attracted her. Even though she was three years younger, Frances interested young Martin too. She was a lively girl who could give as good as she got when the other boys poked fun at her. Soon they became friends and later started going out. They both fell deeply in love and married on 16 March, 1968.

To those who knew him intimately, Martin Cahill was not the conniving, dangerous criminal the rest of the world saw. He had a warm, caring side and he adored Frances. She was his best friend and the one person in the world he could trust above anyone else. Martin was also close to the rest of his wife's family – especially her sisters. He was very well-liked by his in-laws. Less than a year into the marriage, Frances became pregnant with their first child, a daughter they also called Frances. A year later they had a second child, Martin junior. But Martin senior was unable to stick around to help with the dirty nappies for long. On the couple's second wedding anniversary, in 1970, he was jailed for four years.

After he was released in 1973, they had their third child, Christopher. While the General had been in prison, Frances's younger sister, Tina, had moved into her flat to give a hand with the children. The Lawless family flat was overcrowded and her mother was glad of the extra space. When Martin came out, Tina continued to live with them in the one-bedroom flat. Cahill grew very fond of Tina. The three developed a close friendship which was to last for the rest of his life.

Early one morning detectives investigating an armed robbery burst into Cahill's flat to search it. When they walked into the bedroom they found Martin in bed with Frances and Tina. The cops joked with each other about the naughty criminal in bed with the wife and his teenage sister-in-law. At that stage, however, the sleeping arrangements were no more than purely practical. The king-size bed, which took up nearly all of the single bedroom, was the only one in the poky flat and Tina was forced to sleep at the bottom.

Eventually, however, Cahill found himself falling in love with his wife's sister and this led to a deeper relationship between them. Frances accepted the situation. She had anticipated that it would happen and the two sisters had even discussed their feelings for the gangster. Martin had told her how much he loved her and the children, but he also loved and wanted Tina. Even for a *ménage à trois* it was unusual. Not only was Cahill living with two sisters, but the women loved their man so much they were prepared to share him. Far from the situation creating difficulties between them, the sisters remained close friends. In the world of Martin Cahill the moral norms of society did not apply. There was nothing sordid or wrong about his unique relationship. He loved both women and shared everything he had with them. In turn, they devoted themselves to the man who showed them more love and kindness than anyone else in their unprivileged lives. He gave the sisters money to buy nice clothes and go out socialising together.

The love triangle was again interrupted by the people Cahill hated most – the police. Martin was sent down for four years in 1977 for stealing a car. When he got out in 1980 the relationship continued. In the same year, both women became pregnant, Frances with their fourth child and Tina with her first. They bore the General two daughters.

During his protracted war of wits with Dublin Corporation over the demolition of Hollyfield, the growing family moved to the flats across the road from Kevin Street Garda Station – the last place Martin wanted to pitch his tent. Tina also moved in with them.

Two years later, Tina had another son. The two sisters helped each other with the children and Frances brought clothes for the new arrival. Although he was having a relationship with both women, Cahill might not have tolerated the women flirting with other men. And such was their devotion to him that the issue never arose.

The *ménage à trois* became known to the police who kept tabs on the up-and-coming General after Tina had her second child. Members of the underworld also became aware of the situation but it was considered a taboo subject. If anyone in his circle pried too deeply into his secret life Cahill could turn nasty. 'You didn't talk about it much in case Martin heard about it and you certainly didn't mention it to him,' recalled one gangster. Martin and his two women were intensely private and protective of their offspring and their living arrangements.

In late 1983 Cahill, the sisters and their six children moved to a new three-storey red-bricked Corporation house in Swan Grove in Rathmines. Getting the house was one of the conditions under which Cahill eventually vacated the demolished site in his beloved Hollyfield Buildings. Now Cahill decided that his two families needed still more space and he bought extra property. At the time he was awaiting trial for armed robbery and the prospect of a long stretch was a distinct possibility. While he was away he wanted his women to have space and comfort to raise the children.

In 1984 an attractive four-bedroom detached house was bought at nearby Cowper Downs for £80,000 in Tina's name. The private estate was also close to the site of Hollyfield Buildings. He chose the house because it was in the heart of the area he grew up in – he knew every inch of it. The area was criss-crossed by a network of little routes he could utilise in his criminal endeavours.

The arrangement was characteristically complex. Although the new house was in Tina's name, it was Frances and her children who moved into Cowper Downs. Tina moved into Swan Grove, which was in Cahill's name. In later years the house at Cowper Downs was placed in a son's name. Cahill also bought Swan Grove from the Corporation and put it in Tina's name. He continued dividing his time between the two sisters. At night he slept in Swan Grove with Tina and in the mornings he went back to Cowper Downs and Frances. Shortly before the Tango Squad surveillance began in 1987, Frances gave birth to her fifth child, her husband's seventh. The highly publicised Tango operation was to drag the hitherto anonymous Cahill into the limelight. It also shed some unwanted light on his domestic arrangements. The General's routine between the two homes was soon picked up by a media, by now hungry for information about Cahill. When one of his close associates mentioned the fact that his love life was the subject of gossip among baffled journalists and Gardaí, Cahill was happy to use it as another psychological tool against the enemy. 'The thing is that it has fucked up the Guards' heads and they don't know what's what or who's who,' he grinned. In the days after Cahill's death details of his unconventional love life again filled the newspapers. The public was fascinated by it. But the sisters refused to talk to anyone. In 1989 Tina gave birth to Martin's eighth child.

Martin Cahill treated women with respect. In dealing with the wives of his gang members he was scrupulous in ensuring that it didn't appear that he was making advances towards them. In fact, he never visited a gang member's spouse on his own but always brought Frances or Tina with him. He also ensured that the wives of men in prison were not left without money to care for their children.

In the late eighties Cahill suspected that a member of his organisation had ripped off some of the proceeds of a pub they had sold. He went looking for the man to exact punishment with a gun. The criminal left the country and was later jailed in England for a serious crime. But Cahill bore no grudge against the man's wife. Each Christmas he would arrive with Frances or Tina and give the struggling housewife £1,000 to buy the children gifts and generally cheer up their festive season. When the criminal came home Cahill realised that the man had not conned him. They became friends again.

In 1991 he also came to the aid of Joanna Farrelly, another sister of Frances. She had been living in England and returned to live with her husband in a flat in Dublin. The marriage eventually broke up. Later she had a problem with an acquaintance who, she claimed, had robbed a nest egg from her flat. She told Tina and Frances about what had happened and they asked the General to have a few words with him.

Cahill invited the offender for a chat to a laundry which he part-owned. He told him that he needed to 'iron out some pressing problems.' And that is exactly what he did. The man was held down and had his hands pressed with a hot steam iron. Later Cahill often joked about the pressing problem he once had and how he managed to iron it out.

In March 1992 two women acquaintances of the Cahills were in a pub in Rathmines when they met three men. At first all five got on well but a row broke out and the women left. One of them went to Swan Grove and told Cahill that she had been assaulted by the men. Her friend claimed that she too had been assaulted, and she was distraught. Cahill drove to the house of one of the men shortly after three in the morning and confronted him about the allegations the women had made. When the man opened the door of the house Cahill warned him: 'If you lay another hand on them, I swear to God I'll kill you.' A few hours later, when it was still dark, Cahill returned with an automatic pistol and wearing a balaclava. He walked casually into the rooms of the other two men, and shot each of them twice in the legs. Shortly afterwards detectives got a positive identification of Cahill from the two victims. There were other eye witnesses. For a time it looked as if the cops might, at long last, nail their old foe for a serious offence.

A week later detectives arrested the two women under the Offences Against The State Act. They also searched Cahill's homes at Cowper Downs and Swan Grove. As the cops left one of the houses Cahill warned them: 'You know I will carry out my usual protest tonight over this.' While the two women were being questioned in Tallaght and Rathfarnham Garda stations the tyres of over seventy cars nearby were slashed. Eventually the Gardaí decided not to proceed with a charge against Cahill because, it was felt, the essential witnesses might withdraw their testimony.

Shortly before Cahill's death, Tina Lawless gave birth to the General's ninth child, a little boy. The affectionate family man, or public criminal, was chuffed with himself. A few weeks later Frances was spotted walking the baby around Rathmines in the sunshine. She too seemed to be happy for her husband and her sister. Within twenty-four hours the cosy domestic picture would be shattered.

CHAPTER 19

The Hit

The atmosphere in the Dublin underworld had been tense since the attack in May 1994 on the Widow Scallans. Not since the kidnap of Tommy Gaffney in 1984 had the situation on the streets been so volatile. No-one knew who was next or when it would happen. But in the wake of the UVF attack and the Bolger killing it was clear that more blood would be spilt. Martin Cahill reckoned it would not be his.

During his last days, close associates saw a big change in the General. His chronic diabetes was taking a toll. His skin would come out in blotches and he was weak and sweating profusely. At times Cahill was irrational and irritable. He would sit back in his throne-like armchair and rant on about how people were not showing respect. He would say: 'We will have to shoot someone. People are taking advantage and laughing at us. We can't let the fuckers away with it.' Despite the fact that he had built a new close-knit gang around him, Cahill was a vulnerable, lonely character in decline. Most of his closest and most reliable friends were either behind bars, dead or had fallen out with him.

The first person on his list of targets was now the INLA man involved in the fracas over the flat which Cahill had burned. The General also wanted to pull off another audacious crime against the state, in much the same way as a retired boxer wants to win back his old title. One of the planned strokes on his list was the theft of the Book of Kells; another was to steal the Sam Maguire cup. Many Gardaí are GAA footballers and Cahill reckoned the theft of the All-Ireland football trophy would upset them. He even planned to shin up the drainpipe at the rear of Rathmines Station and plant a bugging device in the interrogation room. Cahill had actually asked an associate to buy the eavesdropping device. 'I'll be able to hear who's toutin',' he said. On the domestic front there were other diversions. Tina had just given birth to his ninth child, a baby boy. Cahill loved kids and was very proud of his family. He wanted to spend more time with them.

In July 1994, a senior member of the Republican movement began calling to Cahill's home at Cowper Downs, accompanied by a small-time criminal. The Special Branch men who kept tabs on the Republican member and the surveillance people who watched the General were convinced the visits were connected with the Widow Scallans attack. When the IRA had sent a message to Cahill requesting him to attend a meeting he had told them to 'Fuck off'. Police speculated that the Provos were sending one of their harbingers of death to inform the errant General of his impending death.

In fact, the reality was slightly different. The Republican figure had sought the introduction to Cahill through another well-known criminal figure on the southside. The Republican and his side-kick had a business proposition for Cahill. They were planning the kidnapping of a Dublin businessman for a ransom estimated at over £250,000. There was no mention of patriotism, ceasefires or bombs – it was a crime, pure and simple. And when Cahill listened to the proposal in the front room of Cowper Downs, he was impressed.

The Republican figure is the prime suspect in a £2 million cash robbery in Waterford in 1992. He is also wanted by the British authorities for allegedly providing equipment used in a series of horrific car bombings. When Libya's Colonel Gadaffi was preparing to donate arms and equipment to the Provos, the Republican carried on the liaison on behalf of the IRA. If a hit on Cahill was being planned, say cops and criminals, then he would have known about it. Cahill, now a sick man, was not as cautious as he once was. He accepted the Provo into his company. When he heard there was speculation that he was to be singled out for a hit, he went to the Republican and asked him to confirm this with his IRA pals. The Provo returned to Cahill's home and told him he was in no danger and that there was no valid reason why the Provos would want to 'whack' him. He said he was convinced that Cahill had nothing to do with the Widow Scallans incident. Some of the General's friends have found it hard not to suspect the Republican of blatantly double-crossing him. They don't believe that there was ever a kidnapping organised – but that the Republican was lulling Cahill into a false sense of security. It is something, they say, which will be 'sorted out' in the fullness of time.

In fact, the two experienced gunmen assigned by the IRA already had the General in their sights. Cahill, oblivious to any danger, relaxed and continued his almost monotonous daily routine, travelling between his two families at Cowper Downs and Swan Grove. Had he felt under any kind of threat he would have gone to ground. Every night Cahill slept in Swan Grove. In the early afternoon he got up and drove to Cowper Downs. On the afternoon of Wednesday, 17 August, 1994, the two IRA men watched their target pass them on Oxford Road en route to Cowper Downs from Swan Grove. They left on two motorbikes. Later they made their final preparations. Like professional assassins they checked and tested their equipment and rehearsed their plan. The General had only twenty-four hours to live.

By 3.30 the next afternoon, 18 August, Martin Cahill, the General, was dead. His IRA assassin was professional and cold-blooded as he pumped five bullets into the man who had dominated the Dublin crime world for years. Eye-witnesses reported that the killer smiled as he jumped on to the back of a waiting motorbike and vanished into the busy traffic.

Within minutes every squad car in the city knew that Tango One was down. Five minutes after Cahill pulled up at the Stop sign, a *Sunday World* colleague, Mike McNiffe, and I were actually discussing the General with an underworld source six miles away in the suburb of Clondalkin. A contact on the other end of the mobile phone screamed: 'Cahill's down! Cahill's dead! For fuck sake, they've killed him.' We were stunned, speechless, as we raced to the car. We had covered the Cahill story for many years. We had followed him, we had watched him, we had tried to talk to him – we were fascinated, like so many others, by the legend that was the General.

The police began to arrive on the scene and hurriedly covered the body of their former adversary. It was the ultimate irony. In a bid to prevent photographers taking shots of the bloodied corpse, they spread a tarpaulin over the car. For over twenty bitter years the same police had tried in vain to unmask their adversary to the world. In death the game was finally over and they allowed him to die as he had lived, a faceless man. No doubt the Joker would have had a good laugh at that.

The eerie silence which hung over Oxford Road was shattered as the General's disbelieving family arrived from nearby Swan Grove. There were scuffles as they confronted Gardaí and photographers. Christy, Martin's twenty-one year-old son, arrived on a bicycle. He threw it at a police van, which was blocking the road, screaming: 'Youse fuckers better not have had anything to do with this ... youse fuckers killed him.' Martin junior shouted at the photographers to 'Get to fuck out of here'. Then he lunged forward to his father's side but was restrained by uniformed officers. 'That's me Da. Is he dead? Get yer fuckin' hands off me. Is he dead?' A friendly-faced cop who had been on his father's trail for many years put his hand on Martin's shoulder and told him, 'I'm sorry, Martin. It is your father and he is dead.' Cahill's 'Rottweilers' arrived, looking menacing and melted into the crowd. They were no longer the General's hard men. As the hours slipped by, detectives from every district in the south city arrived to view the last remains of Tango One. Two hundred yards away in Swan Grove the two sisters comforted each other. Frances and Tina sobbed and mourned the man whose love they had shared.

Later a Rolls Royce hearse arrived to take away the crumpled corpse. As the body, wrapped in plastic, was strapped to a stretcher, Cahill's famous hand – the one he used to cover his face – trailed from beneath the covering. Later, when detectives called to Swan Grove to ask a member of the family to identify their dead relative they were told to 'fuck off' and threatened with baseball bats. The family refused to co-operate in any way with the investigation. It was the way Cahill would have wanted it. They were following his wishes.

Before the body had gone cold the paramilitaries, like vultures circling overhead, began claiming responsibility for the General's murder. Within minutes the INLA, who had planned his execution, said they did it. Next the Provos were on the phone-lines to newsrooms across the city saying that they were responsible. The claims and counter-claims made a farce of the incident. Eventually the INLA issued another statement denying that they had carried out the attack and threatening to kill the people who made the first call. Cahill would have found it all very amusing. Then, amid the growing confusion, the Provos issued an extraordinary confession detailing every minute aspect of the assassination as proof that they had carried it out.

'We won't kidnap him. We'll stiff him in the street,' the IRA had warned Cahill's friend, Tommy Gaffney, ten years earlier. In a statement claiming responsibility for his murder, they accused Cahill of being involved in intimidation, robbery and drug dealing. The statement read: 'It was his involvement with, and assistance to, pro-British death squads which forced us to act. Cahill's gang was involved closely with the Portadown UVF gang which, apart from countless sectarian murders in the twenty-six counties, was responsible for the gun and bomb attack on the Widow Scallans pub.' The statement included a chilling message to the rest of the big-league Dublin underworld that would cause several of them to go into hiding. 'The IRA reserve the right to execute those who finance or otherwise assist Loyalist killer gangs. We have compiled a detailed file on the involvement of other Dublin criminals with Loyalist death squads. We call on those people to desist immediately from such activity and to come forward to us within fourteen days to clear their names.'

But the attack on Martin Cahill had little to do with his dealings with the Loyalists or drug dealing. During his life there had not been enough evidence to label him a drug pusher. The Provos had picked their moment carefully. The General was to be their last murder victim before the ceasefire which began less than two weeks later on the morning of 1 September. In the short history of Dublin crime Cahill had been the only gangster prepared to take on the IRA. Blowing him away in such a cold-blooded and typically gangland fashion was likely to set the tone of things to come in the wake of the ceasefire. It was also a publicity coup. They had done the state a favour by getting rid of a major thorn in its side. No-one will ever know the full story.

The large floral wreath in the hearse alongside the polished mahogany casket said it all: '*Que sera sera*, whatever will be will be'. It was one of Cahill's favourite phrases. The removal and funeral had all the hallmarks of a mafia farewell to one of their boys. In Massey's funeral home, where Cahill had been patched up and laid out, associates from all over the country came to pay their respects. They filed past the open coffin where Cahill was laid out in a neat suit and tie. It was the best-fitting suit he ever wore. The hard men threw themselves across their godfather and wept. His brothers, Eddie and John, refused to come out of Portlaoise prison to view their dead brother's remains. They would have had to be accompanied by prison officers and that was unacceptable to them. The warders in the prison were put on full alert in case of confrontation between the IRA prisoners and members of Cahill's gang. Michael Cahill, who was serving a sentence for larceny in Mountjoy, visited the funeral home before the removal ceremony began. He was handcuffed to a prison warder.

On Monday, 22 August, the funeral took place at the Church of Our Lady of Refuge in Rathmines. Criminals and cops eyed each other up as one of three priests who celebrated the funeral mass urged the violence to stop. 'Break the cycle of violence,' pleaded Fr Jim Caffrey. 'The way of violence can only lead to death because it is the way of hatred, fear and revenge. Choose life, not death. Choose light, not darkness. Choose forgiveness, not revenge.' When the mourners were asked to offer each other the handshake which signifies peace, the criminals standing at the back of the church kept their hands in their pockets. Martin junior broke down and sobbed half-way through the readings. A guitarist played one of Cahill's favourite songs, 'Just When I Needed You Most'. A choir sang 'Ave Maria' and 'The Lord's My Shepherd'.

Martin Cahill made his last trip in style. Traffic came to a standstill as the convoy of ten black stretch limousines followed the hearse to his final resting place, a grave beneath the ruins of an old abbey in

Mount Jerome cemetery. Cahill had been to many burials in the huge cemetery over the years – but they were mostly burials of jewellery or other 'liberated' property.

Frances Cahill wore black and looked up at the clouded sky through black sunglasses. She put her arm around Tina Lawless and stroked her sister's hair. They threw single red roses on the coffin in the grave below them as a musician sang 'Every Time You Touch Me I Become A Hero'. He ended with '*Que sera sera*'. The mourners joined in. Some months later, a black marble headstone was erected over the grave. The inscription read: ''Tisn't life that matters, it's the courage you bring to it – Frances.'

Epilogue

In the first edition of this book, published in May 1995, the criminals who would take over from Cahill in the Dublin underworld were described as even more cold-blooded and calculating than he. As one member of the Dunne family, the country's most notorious drug family in the early eighties, predicted: If you thought we were bad, just wait till you see what's coming next.

Between August 1994 when Cahill was murdered and June 1996 there was a total of eleven gangland murders in Dublin. One of the first was that of Paddy Shanahan who originally planned the Beit art robbery with the General.

Later, Shanahan had gone straight and was employed in the building business, but one of his former gangster pals had other ideas about his 'retirement'. In October 1994 he died on a pavement from a single gunshot to the head, fired by a hitman suspected of at least three other such killings in recent years.

All of the other victims were involved at varying levels of the criminal underworld. In June 1995, thirty-one-year-old David Weafer was gunned down at point-blank range in the hallway of his home in Finglas, North Dublin, by a lone gunman carrying a sawn-off shotgun. Weafer had worked for a major cannabis smuggler and was suspected by gang members of stealing a consignment of drugs. The man suspected of ordering the hit has since been jailed for drug-related offences. In the same month, Fran Preston, a thirty-year-old single man from Baldoyle in north county Dublin, was killed by an assassin who casually rode up to him on the street on a push-bike and shot him twice in the head. This time another major drug dealer had ordered Preston's murder because he had fallen out over a woman.

The worst day of the gangland murder spree was 8 December, 1995, which became known in the criminal world as Bloody Friday.

In the early hours of the morning, Eddie McCabe, a thirty-year-old married father of three, and his companion, Catherine Brennan, a twenty-eight-year-old unmarried mother, were shot down in cold blood on a street in the sprawling west Dublin working-class suburb of Tallaght. The suspect for this crime was once a member of the General's gang and is currently on the run. Fourteen hours later, a lone gunman shot and killed small-time fraudster Christy Delaney at his home in Finglas, north Dublin. Delaney, a compulsive gambler had frittered away a large amount of cash he had been supposed to launder for a notorious drug baron who had been in hiding in Holland for six years. The gang boss ordered one of his men in Dublin to give Christy the message. And the killing continued into 1996 with the murder of feared criminals, Gerry Lee, Johnny Reddan and John Kelly. In each case the motive was punishment for infractions of gangland rules.

On Wednesday, 26 June, 1996, the Dunne gangster's warning about worse time to come became a chilling reality. At five minutes to one on that afternoon, a gunman calmly stepped off the back of a motorbike and shot *Sunday Independent* crime reporter Veronica Guerin five times at point-blank range as she sat in her car at traffic lights. The other road-users looked on helplessly as the motorbike tore off at high speed through the traffic at one of the country's busiest motorways, leaving the courageous thirty-six-year-old mother slumped dead in her car.

The people who ordered that brutal murder totally under-estimated the effects of their actions, not just on their own criminal activities but on organised crime in general. After twenty-five years of apparent immunity, the gang responsible for the murder thought they were untouchable. They had seen the way the General had led the Gardaí a merry dance and the force's poor track record in solving gangland murders. They believed that they could execute with impunity anyone who got in their way and that the Guerin murder investigation would be dormant by the end of the summer. How wrong they were.

The Guerin murder was a chilling warning to the politicians, judiciary, Gardaí, media and the ordinary man and woman in the street that organised crime had become so powerful as to threaten the very security of the State.

The Government immediately launched a major overhaul of the criminal justice system. The Gardaí were finally given the support they had sought for many years. Pat Byrne, a talented former Special Branch officer, was appointed Commissioner. A young, action-oriented policeman, he re-invigorated the force and launched one of the most successful crackdowns on organised crime seen anywhere in Europe. A controversial new unit called the Criminal Assets Bureau (CAB), comprising Gardaí, customs and revenue officials, was set up to trace and expropriate the assets of major criminals. By April 1998 the CAB had confiscated cash and property worth almost £15 million.

Byrne also re-organised the Serious Crime and Drug Squads. The newly-formed Garda National Drug Unit cracked practically every major drug network in the country, making scores of arrests and causing at least five of the country's most dangerous drug barons to flee the country. In the first few months of 1996 they had seized almost £40 million worth of heroin, ecstasy, amphetamines and cannabis and since then many multi-million pound seizures have been made. By early 1998 serious crime had dropped dramatically for the first time in twenty years. Gangland assassinations dwindled from an average of one a month to two for the whole of 1997 and up to April 1998 there had been no such slayings in the country. Crime on such a large scale no longer pays for the criminals. If Martin Cahill was still alive it is likely he would be racing pigeons on the Costa del Sol or languishing in a cell in Portlaoise prison. Today there would be no fun left in the game. The cops are doing all the winning.

Glossary

blag – armed robbery
consultant – senior doctor
Corporation – Dublin Corporation
Dáil (Éireann) – the house of parliament in Dublin
digger – bulldozer
estate – housing development
GAA – the Gaelic Athletic Association
Garda/Gardaí – member of the Irish police force
getting one over on – making a fool of
house-breaking – breaking and entering
INLA – Irish National Liberation Army
Loyalist – person loyal to Union with Britain, often meaning an extremist Unionist
mitch – play hookey
Mountjoy – main Dublin prison
petrol – gas
Provo – member of the Provisional IRA
senior counsel – barrister/trial attorney
stroke – robbery
turf – peat
UVF – Ulster Volunteer Force, pro-British Loyalist paramilitary organisation

OTHER BOOKS FROM
O'BRIEN
The No. 1 Publisher

THE MAMMY
Brendan O'Carroll

It's 1967 and in the teeming streets of the Jarro, home of Dublin's dealers and dockers, Agnes Browne struggles to raise seven children, the only legacy of her dead husband 'Redser'. With her pal Marion and an assortment of characters as colourful as the fruit on her Moore Street stall, she copes with propositions, puberty and the problem with Sr. Mary Magdalen.
And when she has time she dances with Cliff Richard.

£5.99pb/ ISBN 0-86278-372-0

SEQUEL TO THE NO.1 BESTSELLER *The Mammy*
THE CHISELLERS
Brendan O'Carroll

It's three years since Redser's death and Agnes Browne soldiers on, being mother, father and referee to her fighting family of seven. Helped out financially by her eldest, and hormonally by the amorous Pierre, Agnes copes with family tragedy, success and the move from the Jarro to the 'wilds of the country' – suburban Finglas.
And when the family's dreams are threatened by an unscrupulous gangster he learns a costly lesson – don't mess with the children of Agnes Browne!

£5.99pb/ ISBN 0-86278-414-X

THE GRANNY
Brendan O'Carroll

Agnes, now forty-seven, a granny and happily widowed for thirteen years, watches over the changing fortunes of her family – marriage, prison, broken relationships, literary success. Then the family begins to fragment and it seems that not even their mother's iron will can bring them together again. But you can never write off Agnes Browne!

£5.99pb/ ISBN 0-86278-489-1

SPARROW'S TRAP
Brendan O'Carroll

From the rowdy backstreets of Dublin, full of earthy humour and spirit, emerges a young boxing hopeful – Sparrow McCabe. Sparrow's dream is the World Lightweight Championship. But when he finally has it in his grasp he can't deliver that finishing punch. Sparrow's life falls apart, and fifteen years later he is a bum, a loser. Then something happens that convinces him there are still things worth fighting for ...

£5.99pb/ ISBN 0-86278-538-3

A SELL-OUT PLAY BY BRENDAN O'CARROLL

THE COURSE
Brendan O'Carroll

A group of no-hopers sign on for a Positive Mental Attitude Course run by a conman. Then the bona fide American supervisor arrives, threatening to shut down the course and sack the tutor unless five of the six participants pass the exam. The students, including an alcoholic, a prostitute, a golf widow and a 'resting actor', rise to the challenge, with unexpected results.

£5.99pb/ ISBN 0-86278-493-X

THE JOY

MOUNTJOY JAIL: THE SHOCKING, TRUE STORY OF LIFE INSIDE
Paul Howard

A riveting account of the reality of living behind the bars as a prisoner in Dublin's Mountjoy Jail, as told to journalist Paul Howard.

£6.99pb/ ISBN 0-86278-491-3

THE LONG WAR

THE IRA & SINN FÉIN: FROM ARMED STRUGGLE TO PEACE TALKS
Brendan O'Brien

The IRA war strategy; the rise of Gerry Adams; the secret peace negotiations; prospects for a lasting peace. An authoritative and objective account from award-winning investigative journalist Brendan O'Brien.

£9.99pb/ ISBN 0-86278-425-5

MARY ROBINSON

THE WOMAN, THE PRESIDENCY, THE POLITICS
John Horgan

Mary Robinson has had a remarkable career – crusading barrister, senator, first woman President of Ireland, and now UN High Commissioner for Human Rights. She has gained an international reputation for her commitment to justice and the rights of the marginalised. John Horgan, a personal friend and political colleague, assesses her achievements and reveals the personality behind the political figure.

£14.99pb/ ISBN 0-86278-540-5

REBELLION!

IRELAND IN 1798

Daniel Gahan

In 1798 three separate rebellions inspired by the ideals of the American revolutionaries and French republicanism swept across Ireland hoping to secure Irish independence for the United Irishmen. This is the account of that important period in the country's history and also the official book of the National 1798 Visitor Centre.

£5.99/ ISBN 0-86278-548-0

Send for our full colour catalogue.

These books are available from your bookseller.

In case of dififculty you may order direct, using this form.

ORDER FORM

Please send me the books as marked

I enclose cheque / postal order for £.......... (+ £1.00 P&P per title)

OR please charge my credit card ☐ Access / Mastercard ☐ Visa

Card number ☐☐☐☐ ☐☐☐☐ ☐☐☐☐ ☐☐☐☐

EXPIRY DATE ☐ ☐ ☐ ☐

Name: .... Tel: ....

Address: ....

....

Please send orders to : THE O'BRIEN PRESS, 20 Victoria Road, Dublin 6.
Tel: +353 1 4923333   Fax: + 353 1 4922777   email: books@obrien.ie
http://www.obrien.ie

In the US and Canada: IRISH AMERICAN BOOK COMPANY, 6309 Monarch Park Place,
Suite 101, Niwot, Colorado 80503. Tel. 800-452-7115 Fax. 800-401-9705